PITTSBURGH THEOLOGICAL MONOGRAPHS

New Series

Dikran Y. Hadidian

General Editor

D1548583

11

PROPHET, PASTOR, PROTESTANT

The Work of Huldrych Zwingli

After Five Hundred Years

Prophet Pastor Protestant

The Work of Huldrych Zwingli
After Five Hundred Years

Edited by

E. J. Furcha and H. Wayne Pipkin

PICKWICK PUBLICATIONS

Allison Park, Pennsylvania

1984

Copyright © 1984 by Pickwick Publications
4137 Timberlane Drive, Allison Park, PA 15101

All rights reserved
Printed in the United States of America

Library of Congress Cataloging in Publication Data
Main entry under title:

Prophet, Pastor, Protestant.

  (Pittsburgh theological monographs ; new ser. 11)
  1. Zwingli, Ulrich, 1484-1531—Addresses, essays,
lectures. I. Furcha, E. J. (Edward J.), 1935-
II. Pipkin, H. Wayne. III. Series
BR345.P76   1984   284'.2'0924   84-14723
ISBN 0-915138-64-6

Printed and Bound by Publishers Choice Book Mfg. Co.
Mars, Pennsylvania 16046

CONTENTS

v

PREFACE

Huldrych Zwingli, 1484-1531, deserves better than the distant third he is generally given in English language accounts of the sixteenth century Reformation in Europe. In his own relatively short life he established a sound reputation as pastor and preacher. Ever since early 1519 when he accepted the call to be people's priest at the Greatminster in Zurich he involved himself creatively in the affairs of the community, promoting truth and justice within the social structures--often against strong opposition from political and ecclesiastical power blocs. Skillfully and with prophetic force he called his contemporaries to address the issues before them in response to the word of God which he sought to interpret faithfully. His sermons and tracts focus on clerical stipends, military service to foreign powers, the just distribution of wealth, education of the young, adequate government, the true worship of God and acceptable theological understanding. There is hardly an issue on which he does not focus the light of the gospel. If one remembers that much of his eucharistic teaching is still acceptable to Protestant believers in the twentieth century, his work as theologian and liturgist is remarkable. In balancing political and socio-economic interests with the ethical demands inherent in the gospel his skills equal those of John Calvin.

Why then has he had few followers outside German speaking Switzerland and fewer still who promoted his thought as genuinely reflecting the essence of the gospel?

The question is difficult to answer. Inaccessibility of his writings outside German-speaking Switzerland certainly goes a long way in explaining the limited press he had when compared to that of Luther and Calvin. His writings in English have never been widely circulated (and Zuerideutsch, after all, is difficult to read).

More prominent an obstacle to Zwingli's popularity may be the fact that his work came to stand in the shadow which his contemporary Martin Luther cast over Western christendom north of Switzerland. As it happened, John Calvin's return to basic evangelical teaching dominated Geneva from the late thirties of the sixteenth century and the Reformers of Strasbourg radiated their influence far beyond the confines of that city. Thus, England, Scotland, the Netherlands, and France, though not unaffected by Zwingli's work, often received it through the agency of others without consciously recognizing the source. Add to that Zwingli's premature death in 1531 and the fact that his successor Heinrich Bullinger, 1504-75, and others integrated their views with his, and we go a long way to explaining why the Reformed Tradition owes Zwingli a debt without generally being conscious of it.

It may well be a deeply ingrained trait of his character to work unobtrusively as member of the body politic. Thus, any ideas and plans for renewal of the social and political life would be introduced as the reform agreement of all, rather than the work of one individual. Though Zwingli was the "antistes" of a significant center of trade and commerce, he rarely, if ever, pushed himself or his position into a place of prominence. Instead, he advanced the teaching of the word of God as it affected everyone and stressed the work of the Holy Spirit rather than the achievements of any given individual.

When on the occasion of the five-hundredth anniversary of his birth an attempt is made in many quarters to redress the balance and give Zwingli a hearing, especially in the English language context, we do so in order to acknowledge his unique contribution to reformation history without wishing to create a Zwingli cult. To provide scholars and interested lay persons and anyone who desires to be informed in the history of Western thought with a guide to Zwingli's world, we invited a number of persons to contribute to this volume of essays. Naturally, we could not ask everyone who is engaged in studying Zwingli and the reform work in Zurich. Some who were asked had to decline for a variety of reasons.

To those who graciously accepted our invitation to contribute to this volume we are most grateful, especially since they submitted so willingly to the imposition of fairly strict deadlines. Because of their promptness we are able to offer this collection of papers to the public, early in the Fall of 1984. May the varied expressions of scholarly opinion contribute to continued appreciation of the Reformed Tradition and stimulate debate on its essential features far beyond the circle of specialists to all who are interested in the almost infinite possibilities of reform to which Zwingli contributed forthrightly in his own day when he broke with ecclesiastical tradition and began preaching from the Gospel of St. Matthew in January 1519.

This volume is intended as a companion to the two-volume set of translations, translated and edited by H. Wayne Pipkin and E. J. Furcha, and published by Pickwick Publications.

H. Wayne Pipkin, Rüschlikon/Zurich

Edward J. Furcha, Montreal

LIST OF ABBREVIATIONS

Bullinger   Heinrich Bullinger, **Reformationsgeschichte,** 3 vols. Edited by J. J. Hottinger and H. H. Vögeli, Frauenfeld, 1838-1840.

Calvin, Inst.   John Calvin, **Institutio Christianae Religionis,** Geneva, 1559.

DTC   **Dictionnaire de Théologie Catholique,** Vols. 1-15, Paris, 1930-1950.

EA   **Amtliche Sammlung der ältern Eidgenössischen Abschiede,** Serie 1245-1798, edited by A. P. von Segesser, Lucerne, Berne, 1874-1886

Furcha/Pipkin   **Huldrych Zwingli Writings.**
Volume One. **The Defense of the Reformed Faith,** tr. by E. J. Furcha; Allison Park, PA, Pickwick Publications, 1984.

Volume Two. **In Search of True Religion: Reformation, Pastoral and Eucharistic Writings,** tr. by H. Wayne Pipkin; Allison Park, PA, Pickwick Publications, 1984.

H   **Zwingli Hauptschriften,** edited by Fritz Blanke, Oskar Farner, Rudolf Pfister, Vols. 1-4, 7, 9-11, Zürich, 1940-1963.

HBWB   **Heinrich Bullinger Werke,** Abteilung 1, Bibliographie, Vol. I, edited by Fritz Busser, prepared by Joachim Staedtke, Zürich, 1972.

IDC   **Reformed Protestantism.** Sources of the 16th and 17th centuries on microfiche. I. Switzerland, A. Heinrich Bullinger and the Zürich Reformation, edited by Fritz Busser, Zug, n.d.

KAKG	Kurt Aland, **Geschichte der Christenheit von der Reformation bis in die Gegenwart,** 2 vols., Gütersloh, 1982.
Latin Works	**The Latin Works of Huldreich Zwingli,** Vol. I, edited by S. M. Jackson, New York, 1912. Vol. II, edited by William J. Hinke. Vol. III, edited by Clarence Heller, Philadelphia, 1922, 1929.
LCC XXIV	**Zwingli and Bullinger.** Vol. XXIV of Library of Christian Classics, edited by G. W. Bromiley, Philadelphia, 1953.
Locher	Gottfried W. Locher, **Die Zwinglische Reformation im Rahmen der europäischen Kirchengeschichte,** Göttingen, Zürich, 1979.
LW	**Luther's Works,** edited by Jaroslav Pelikan and Helmut Lehmann, 55 vols. St. Louis, Philadelphia, 1955ff.
MQR	Mennonite Quarterly Review, Goshen, Indiana, 1927-.
Potter	G. R. Potter, **Zwingli,** Cambridge, 1976.
RE	**Realencyclopädie für protestantische Theologie und Kirche,** Vols. 1-24, 1896-1913.
S	**Huldreich Zwinglis Werke.** Erste vollständige Ausgabe durch M. Schuler u. J. Schulthess, 8 vols. Zürich, 1828-1842.
WA	**D. Martin Luthers Werke.** Kritische Gesamtausgabe, edited by J. K. F. Knaake, G. Kawerau, et al., Weimar, 1883-.
Z	**Huldreich Zwinglis Sämtliche Werke.** Edited by E. Egli, et al. Corpus Reformatorum, 88ff., Berlin, Leipzig, Zürich, 1905-. (in progress)
ZKG	**Zeitschrift für Kirchengeschichte,** Gotha, 1877-
Zwa	**Zwingliana, Beiträge zur Geschichte Zwinglis, der Reformation und des Protestantismus in der Schweiz,** Zürich, 1897.

IN DEFENCE OF ZWINGLI: 1536

(An Essay on the Self-understanding of the Zurich Reformation)

Fritz Büsser
Zurich

The following exposition is based on three premises which have developed from my studies in the history of the Zurich Reformation over the last years.

The first is that the year 1536 is a point in time, in which the self-understanding of the Zurich Reformation, with regard to the understanding of Zwingli in the Zurich Reformation, should be analyzed. This year has not been chosen arbitrarily. Our choice is based on the consideration that, on one hand, in 1536 much is still in flux in the secular dispute which we nowadays call the Reformation while on the other, a hardening of fronts is taking place. Apart from the condemnation of the Reformation by Rome the two large groups within the reformation movement had already committed themselves confessionally: the Lutherans in the Confessio Augustana (= CA), the Reformed in the "Tetrapolitana" or with Zwingli's "Fidei ratio". Yet because of the question of the Lord's Supper, the Protestants had to define and distinguish themselves more sharply against each other precisely in the year 1536: on one hand by the Confessio Helvetica Prior (= CH 1), and on the other hand by the Concord of Wittenberg. [1] This defining and distinguishing took place no less in view of the hope, expectation and call by all the parties for a general council. Actually it was the Council of Trent which was to bring with its anathemas, dogmatic decisions and reform decrees a final separation. And finally, in 1536, Calvin's **Institutes of the Christian Religion** was published in Basel, a book which signals in its own way a situation open in both directions.

The second presupposition from which I proceed consists in the assumption that in 1536 the opinions concerning Zwingli had been made. One clearly comes to this conclusion if one examines the Zwingli biographies both of Protestantism and of Catholicism. Exactly fifty years ago (in 1934!), Kurt Guggisberg inquired into the Protestant conceptions of Zwingli in his **Das Zwinglibild des Protestantismus im Wandel der Zeiten.** In 1968, I myself described the Catholic perspectives in **Das katholische Zwingbild. Von der Reformation bis zur Gegenwart.** [2] On the basis of several sources we attempted to show the picture of Zwingli his contemporaries already had drawn and how they understood his work. Both sides saw him as reformer, yet according to their point of view, the one as a great prophet, theologian and states-man, the other as a heretic who died at Kappel a well-deserved death. Since we sought to give an overview, Guggisberg limited himself for understandable reasons, especially in the 16th century, to relatively few selected sources. I am of the opinion that today the time has come to interpret anew sources already considered, as well as to add important further sources for the contemporary estimation of Zwingli. Interestingly, a closer look suggests precisely the year 1536 as especially fitting and fruitful for this undertaking. In this year no less than four texts originate which, in my opinion, contain extremely interesting information on the self-understanding of the Zurich reformation: an actual apology for Zwingli by Theodor Bibliander, two confessional writings (the already men-tioned CH 1 and Zwingli's "Fidei expositio" published posthumously by Bullinger) and the biography of Zwingli by Oswald Myconius.

Related to this is a third decisive supposition. As far as I see, nobody has yet undertaken the attempt to think through consistently a suggestion given by the great Catholic Zwingli scholar of our time, J. V. Pollet. In 1951 Pollet concluded his excellent description of Zwingli's theology in the "Dictionnaire de Théologie Catholique" with the following remark: Zwingli "est donc . . . un témoin indirect de la verité du catholicisme." [3] Under no circumstances is this sentence to be strained. However, it deserves attention insofar as it points to the state of affairs which proves to be the substance of the self-understanding of the Zurich reformation reflected especially in the above-mentioned sources of the year 1536: that the contemporaries, friends and co-workers of Zwingli considered the reformer and themselves as members of the catholic, i.e., the general, universal Church. In other words: Zwingli unmistakably dissociated himself from the Roman Catholic Church yet this dissociation was not understood at that time in any way as a renunciation of the truly catholic church. [4] With this observation my intention is not, so to speak, to re-catholicize Zwingli, but, on the contrary, to put in its proper place the exclusive claim of representation as Catholicism by the Roman Church, an assertion not at all secured in the 16th century. The twofold realization ought finally to belong to the secured findings of modern, ecumenically-oriented Reforma-tion research that none of the so-called reformers intended a schism from the one church, [5] and that the claim of Rome for catholicity had been held no doubt theoretically since the Middle Ages, but that de iure it is a product of modern times, i.e. of the Roman statements by the Council of Trent and the definitions of the church by the two Vatican Councils. In 1536 all Christians understood themselves to be Catholic!

That Zwingli did not intend to found a new church shall be illustrated first by an apology: Bibliander's introduction to **Joannis Oecolampadii et Huldrichi Zuinglii epistolarum libri quatuor,** Basileae 1536. [6] This collection of letters, which has in addition to the introduction also the biography of Oecolampadius by Grynaeus and Capito, the one of Zwingli by Myconius, a preface by Bucer and several epigrams, has been known to scholars since its publication. It has served as the basis for the critical edition of the letters (and of several works) of the two reformers. Even though an analysis of its contents would be more than revealing, hardly anybody has dealt with it closely. At best one learned from E. Egli that it contains "the letters in exact wording separated into four groups according to content. First come those which deal with important texts of Scripture and difficult questions of the Christian religion; then follow those on baptism and against re-baptism, then those on the Lord's Supper and finally a selection of epistles of practical content, on church government and on the civil community." [7]

Without doubt Bibliander's introduction (or as it understands itself more fittingly as "purgatio") is with its fifty-nine pages prolix and at points tiring to read. Nevertheless, as does the content of the correspondence, so does also the introduction deserve our full attention, not only because of its dedication to Landgrave Philipp of Hesse, Duke Ulrich and Count George of Württemberg, but especially because it provides "proof, that Oecolampadius and Zwingli are truly Catholic teachers" (Egli). In other words: Bibliander wants to show that the writings of "his teachers are being condemned unjustly and especially undeservedly," that, on the contrary, it is precisely the opponents of the two reformers who "conentur evellere doctrinam aeternae veritatis radicibus contra omne falsae ratiocinationis argumentum stabilitam et canonicis scripturis aptatam". (f.a4^r)

What does this attempt of Bibliander look like and how is it to be evaluated? Basically, one is impressed that Bibliander knows very well the original sense and the actual meaning of the term "catholicity". For him catholic is not the Roman Catholic Church, but the universal church, and church encompassing the whole world, the body of Christ, whose sole head is Jesus Christ, the community of the saints which, according to the famous dictum of Vincent of Lerins, "keeps firmly what has been believed in all places, always, and by all". Nothing illustrates that more clearly than the disposition of the "purgatio". Despite its prolixity, a closer look reveals that it is structured in a meaningful way. Bibliander treats three large complexes of issues and problems:

first, the canon ("Biblia" ffa5^r -b1^r), then the faith ("Theologiae Compendium" ffb1^v -b5^r) and finally, the church, or rather, the administration and reform of the church ("De scripturae explicatione"; "Quomodo functionem ecclesiasticam tractarint Zuinglius et Oecolompadius": ffd2^v -e1^r). In addition to this it contains two digressions: following the second part, detailed comments on the question of the Lord's Supper ("De coena": ffb5^r -d2^v), following the third part the real "purgatio", i.e. the purge of the two reformers from the accusation of heresy ("Quibus malis artibus opprimantur Zuinglius et Oecolampadius" ffe1^r -z1^r). If one, however, takes no account of these digressions and sticks to Bibliander's basic division into the three parts, then a striking picture emerges: Bibliander's three main themes correspond with the three classic categories which constitute the catholic church since the second century: canon, rule of faith, and office of Pastor. In Rome these categories coalesced early into a unity still valid today. The reform of the church of the 16th century has relativized them by its stress on the sole authority of scripture, i.e. it elevated Scripture above dogma and teaching office.

What now does Bibliander write in detail about the above mentioned three complexes of issues?

He starts--est nomen omen?--with expositions on the Bible. Seen as a whole they read like a hymn of praise on the Scripture principle and, on the "clarity and certainty of the word of God" (Zwingli). As expression of the will of God, as "organum . . . coelestis philosophiae" and "armarium spiritus sancti" (fa5^v), the Holy Scripture contains everything about the "will of God" and the "attainment of the Highest Good" which is necessary and useful to know for our salvation. However, in spite of all his high esteem for the Bible, Bibliander is far away from understanding it in a fundamentalistic way simply as a book of rules. Thus the description of Scripture as "canonical", which is identical with "orthodox" and "catholic", is for him less a formal or historical criterion than one of content:

> "Hanc igitur scripturam divinitus inspiratam et per eximios homines conscriptam vocarunt Ecclesiastici patres Canonicam, ut ego existimo duabus de causis: et quod ad Canonem principalis legis quadraret, hoc est, ad divinam voluntatem, et quod norma esset omnium cogitationum, dictorum, scriptionum, actionum totius denique vitae martalium." (fa5^v)

Characteristic for the real intention of the "Purgatio" is then, of course, that in this context Bibliander deals with two objections brought forward against the Scripture principle over and over again: first, that the Bible nonetheless does not contain everything which would be necessary for the existence of the church; and secondly, that the Bible contains passages which are obscure or ambiguous. In regard to the first objection Bibliander observes that the Bible is in fact not a perfect and complete book of law. Yet in spite of that it is sufficient, for Christ promised to his disciples the Holy Spirit who would lead them into all truth. Consequently, the Bible does not contain anything, for example, on the Patrimonium Petri, on the Constantinian Donation, on annuals, bulls of indulgence, on mendicant orders, on Arius and the "Homoousion", on Valentinus with his aeons, on Epicurus and especially on Aristoteles. Nonetheless, "the church still always had in its rich storeroom sufficient means to dispel lies of all kinds." (fa5^v). The second objection Bibliander also accepts as valid to a certain degree: there are in fact obscure, ambiguous and contradictory passages. That is why the desire for learned interpreters is understandable (he mentions Jerome, Augustine, Gregory the Great, Bernhard, Thomas, Duns Scotus and Nicolas of Lyra). Seen as a whole, however, Bibliander urges restraint especially in this matter. Concretely, in principle, always to appeal to Christ himself:

> Postremo, si standum videtur vel in assertione dogmatis vel explicatione scripturarum sententiae humanae, et non potius investiganda mens Christi per operam hominis, an non quaerimus alium magistrum vitae quam Iesum Christum, qui unus per sanctum spiritum ecclesiasticae scholae magister est? (fb1^r)

In the second place Bibliander deals with Zwingli's teaching. To prove it to be orthodox is, of course, the ultimate purpose of the "Epistolae" itself. In the "Purgatio" Bibliander refers in the meantime also--"out of many to few"--especially important writings of Zwingli, namely to the 67 Articles ("quas tuendas explicandasque proposuit coram Ecclesia Tigurina, ultro provocatis in harenam, si qui confiderent a se posse alquid ad refellendum offeri") (Z I: 451-465; II: 1-457), to the book de vera et falsa religione (Z III: 590-912), to the anamnesis de providentia divina (Z VI/III: 1-230), as well as to the Fidei ratio (Z VI/II: 753-817) and the Fidei expositio (S 4: 42-78; Latin Works II: 235-293) ("liber nunc primum in lucem prodiens"). However, these are all writings of reformation character in which, taken as a whole, not a polemical but a basically conciliatory tone is dominant--one emphasizing orthodoxy. In the "Purgatio", however, Bibliander hardly sticks to these writings any longer. Without many direct references or quotations (when necessary, of course), with detailed knowledge of the totality of Zwingli's writings, he undertakes the proof of Zwingli's orthodoxy. This proof takes place in three parts.

First, Bibliander formulates Zwingli's teaching in the classical form of the Catechism, i.e. in the three main parts of the Decalogue, the Lord's Prayer and the Creed. These parts belonged, as is well-known, from ancient times to the catechesis of the church. Naturally then they also delivered to the Reformation an entirely self-evident structure and framework of doctrine: for the catechisms of Luther, for Calvin's _Institutes_ (from the first to the last edition) and for Bullinger's _Decades_ and the "Summa christlicher Religion". Also Bibliander himself calls the three parts of this "Theologiae Compendium" which "summatim deduxit totius scripturae textum, ex quo cuncta penderent, quo referrentur et omnia inter se connecterentur", a catechism. (fb1^v). In detail he writes:

> Oratione dominica vitae scopus et vera beatitudo proponitur, ad quam sumus conditi, quorsum eamus, quorsum tendere debeamus in omnibus institutis nostris, quid optemus votis et desideriis nostris, quid postulemus, idque a deo bonorum omnium thesauro.

In the Creed a concise but yet extraordinarily clearly formulated "cognitio de negocio salutis per Christum" is handed down. The Decalogue gives us

> praeceptionum divinarum et iudicandi et agendi, quod vere pietati congruat, specimen . . . eximium, quatuor captitibus perstringens pietatem ad deum praecipue spectantem, sex autem membris omne officium erga homines. (fb2^r)

Characteristic for Bibliander, because it indicates his own theology, is the second point:

> For the true and old--as one extols it today--and certain adoration of God consists in pious devotion of the heart to God and in contemplation of the supreme will of God towards all these who take part in human destiny, insofar as our works can reach it. Without these is nobody pleasing to God, nobody agreeable to him. By them, all were pleasing to God who, since the creation of the world, have shown themselves to be models of holy living and perfect fear of God, and that not only among the people who expressly belong to God, but also among the others. For who will want to expell the pagan out of the bosom of the mercy of God when he realizes God's mercy, justice and patience towards all without respect of person, and the expressions of true adoration of God, just as if he were the only son of the house--them, whom the apostolic word of Peter lets rest deep in the bosom of heavenly grace? (ffb2^{v}f)

This is not the place to define "vera religio" more closely, yet I should like to make a three-fold observation. First, we have here an early evidence of Bibliander's so-called "universalism" (and of others from Zurich?). [9] Secondly, Bibliander does not only take up Zwingli's definition of religion in general as it is found in the "Commentarius" (Z III: 639ff.), he also points specifically to some essential concerns of Zwingli's theology: the stress on the mercy of God, the importance of pneumatology, a broad understanding of election, and related to this, the ethical dimension of faith which aims strongly at sanctification and which might possibly give the impression of being legalistic. [10] Finally, Bibliander anticipates here the thoughts of modern Roman Catholicism, as they are contained for example in the "Declaration on the Relation of the Church to Non-Christian Religions" of Vatican II.

In the third place Bibliander defines the "vera religio" briefly by the three Christian virtues "fides", "spes", and "charitas".

> For in faith the truth is grasped as an absolutely certain conviction (Cf. Hebr. 11:1). In faith God is approached, God is heard, God is understood, God is sought, found, grasped and held on to. By perseverance in the contemplation of the right and the true the highest good found is adhered to in defiance of all the temptations of seductive appearances (contra omnes spectrorum avocantium occursiones). In love the human being unites with God, becomes one spirit with him, one with all those who are united with God; hence he sacrifices himself totally for the increase of the honor or the immortal God and for the sake of the will of God for the service for the well-being of others". (fb3^r)

As the third category which traditionally constitutes and guarantees the catholicity of the church we mentioned the teaching office. Bibliander does not hesitate a moment to defend his teachers also in regard to this point, i.e. to call them legitimate holders of the office of bishops. In order to understand this, however, we have to free ourselves (also here again) from the usual Roman Catholic interpretation of the office of bishop: Bibliander did not understand it in an institutional way in the sense of the Roman hierarchy and of an uninterrupted Apostolic succession but--if I may say so--in a prophetic way, in the sense of a special charisma--the one of interpreting Scripture--and of a succession in regard to the content of faith. (The difference might best be seen in the different interpretation of Mt. 16:18!) What does that mean? Zwingli, and Oecolampadius, were primarily exegetes, preachers of the Gospel, and as such, reformers of cult and church. How careful, reliable, and faithful but also how educated and true his teachers might actually have been in the interpretation of Scripture, Bibliander does not want to comment on himself. For him it is decisive and absolutely undebatable that they fulfilled their ecclesiastical office faithfully as proclaimers of the word of God, that they understood their "ecclesiastical powers" as a commission received from God, concretely as the administration of the keys of the Kingdom of Heaven. Like an Ezekiel or Jeremiah they understood themselves to be called to warn of coming misfortune (Ez. 33f.), "ad evellendum, destruendum, disperendum, dissipandum, sed simul ad aedificandum et plantandum". (Jer. 1:10) (fd3^r). To rebuild again the house of God with living stones, to repair the ruins of the holy city of Jerusalem was their supreme goal. Grounded in this, however, also lies the reason why envy, hatred, clamor, slander, etc. rose up against them. But all these adversities were not able to break the courage and the perseverance of the reformers. They faced disputations. They also defended the cause of the Gospel away from home, naturally through their writings, partly in letters written by hand, partly in printed form. When they put the worship in order they attempted to reestablish the original orders: "Eamque ob rem diligentissime verbo divino externae ceremoniarum formae sancitae sunt et a prophetis dei correctae, atque pientissimis principibus in nativum splendorem semper assertae sunt". (fd4^v) With this some further aspects of the Zurich (and Basel) reformation have been touched, to which Bibliander himself attaches great significance, which I, however, at this point can only mention. To this belongs first the observation, that the political authorities did not only assist Zwingli and his co-workers in the purification of the church, but that they undertook the whole enterprise basically by themselves. They were "author", "originator" and driving force behind the abolishment of the mass and the images.

A second aspect concerns the view of Bibliander that the return to the "primitive church" (which will be dealt with immediately below) took place in great liberty, but especially always in the knowledge that according to Paul (1 Cor. 3) "it is not the gardeners with their planting and watering who count, but God, who makes it grow". Seen as a whole nothing was neglected or left out in this reform of the church. It feels almost like an anticipation of L. Lavater's description "De ritibus et institutis" of 1559 when Bibliander elaborates in detail how carefully the worship services, baptism, Lord's Supper and prayers, the school and also pastoral care were ordered. [11] (ffd5^{r}f) For this, just one example:

> Neither the public nor the private care for the poor has been neglected. The sick were being visited and strengthened by the comfort of the Scripture in their trust in God. They were being anointed by the doctors (sic!) in the face of death. Brethren who have died ("qui extremum diem clauserunt") are being payed the last

honors, in a human way, without much display, without deceit or superstition. (fd5^v)

It is of interest that in this context Bibliander also comes to speak on the possibility and the chances of a council: the reform of the church ought to be the task of the pope and bishops, therefore a regular council would be by all means desirable, yet--as history shows--even councils could err; therefore it would be, according to the example of the prophets of the Old Testament, the task of individual bishops and of the secular authorities to reform the church. (fd5^{v}ff)

A third aspect: as already indicated several times, Bibliander defends Zwingli as reformer in the original sense of the word, i.e. as re-former, as theologian and churchman who wanted to return consciously--as it is, of course, self-evident for a humanist--to the ancient origins of the church. I shall give three examples from the great abundance of corresponding comments. In connection with the canon he says:

> Sic Christi ecclesiam longe meliori fuisse forma in primordiis, cum paucis canonibus ex ore dei sumptis bona fide utebant, quam posteris seculis, quibus immensa volumina decretorum et decretalium et sententiarum et canonistarum et opinatorum molesta curiositas ecclesiae occuparunt subsellia. (fa6^r)

In connection with his expositions on the reformation he remarks:

> Can anything seem to be more worthy, more certain and more true to the confessors of the Christian name than that all institutions of the church are being led back to their original simplicity (ad primitivam simplicitatam), when there were only few ceremonies but an abundance of piety and holiness? The greater the pomp of the church was, the worse was the morality of the people. (fd4^v)

And furthermore,

> As Kingdoms are easily held together by the means from which they originate so is also the state (status) of the church not secured in a better way than when she is referred back to her origins . . . : Certe forma Ecclesiae mihi videtur optime instituta aemulatione simplicitatis primitivae, quam Apostolorum acta et Ecclesiasticorum--qui proximi fuerunt Apostolis, scripta testantur. (fd5^r)

With this it is at least indicated that Bibliander also very understandably uses the fathers (of the church) in order to support his views. Errors excepted, he prefers Augustine (mentioned 19 times), Jerome (14), Tertullian (4), Ambrose, Hesychius, Origen (each one 3 times). He refers also to John Damascene, Cyprian, Gregory, Anastasius, Eusebius and other fathers of the old church as well as the church of the Middle Ages and to articles on the church in the Codices Theodosiani and Justiniani. In this context, by the way, Bibliander confirms explicitly a statement by F. Schmidt-Clausing that Zwingli utilized--contrary to Luther-- the **Corpus Juris Canonici** as a reformation tool. [12], [13]

II

Zwingli as representative of a reformed Catholicism--this theme shall be investigated secondly on the basis of two confessional writings: the **Confessio Helvetica prior** (CH I) and Zwingli's **Fidei expositio.**

Some introductory remarks are necessary. In principle it is to be remarked that due to the nature of our theme the consideration of confessional writings is considered imperative. Confessional writings are "a typical phenomenon of the reformation". [14] The Reformation faith has brought them into being and only in light of the Reformation faith can they be appreciated appropriately. Again, here is not the place to investigate more closely this typical phenomenon of the Reformation: its different relevance within the Lutheran and the Reformed Churches, its content or even its theology. Only the following, after Jacobs, shall be mentioned: the Reformed confessional writings are of no special importance in the sense of the Holy Scripture, they "may not be seen as the principles of doctrine, but as guides of faith". "Their significance lies not in the confessional formula but in the performance of the confession, in the witness." "They deserve and need to be seen in their historical context." Their purpose is to direct attention not primarily to the differences but to the common point of reference of the word of God, to Christ himself, and by this to the unity and the community of the body of Christ, whom they want to serve." [15]

It will be evident that for our undertaking especially the two last mentioned accents are of relevance: the Reformed confessional writings are to be understood in their historical situation as expression of the will to unity! The two confessions of faith which concern us came into existence in the second phase of the Reformation. That means already less dispute than consolidation.

A new horizon opens up: the one of church union. A new theological situation has broken through: the predominance of the one, pugnacious personality has been superseded by the co-operation of a number of heads. Not only that: other traditions are bringing their influence to bear. They are, however, grown on the same soil: humanism. [16]

This is shown in an especially impressive way by the **Confessio Helvetica I:** after the cities of Zurich (1523), Berne (1528, 1532) and Basel (1534) and also Geneva (1536) had given themselves first their own confessions of faith, the First Helvetic confession was

a common confession of the holy, true and ancient christian faith and of our fellow-citizens and fellow christian believers in Zurich, Berne, Basel, Strassburg, Constenz, Santgalln, Schaffhusn, Millhusen, Biel (& zbasell) drawn up, ordered and delivered at Basel February 1, 2, 3 and 4 1536. [17]

In its initial drafting Bullinger from Zurich and Myconius and Grynäus from Basel had participated. Later Jud from Zurich and Megander from Berne joined, finally, though not necessarily to the joy of all of them, also Capito and Bucer from Strassburg. At a closer look, Zwingli's "Fidei expositio" may also be counted in this second phase of the forming of the Reformed confession of faith. With regard to the point of time: Bullinger published the last larger theological writing of the "fidelissimus evangelii praeco et Christianae libertatis assertor constantissimus H. Zuingliuus . . . cygneum" very consciously at the end of February, 1536, i.e. at the time of the decisive negotiations on the CH I. Concerning the content: Zwingli's "Fidei expositio" belongs to a larger frame of reference. Only in connection with his other later confessional writings can it be appreciated appropriately, namely in connection with the sermon on the creed of 1528 held on the occasion of the Berne Disputation and the "Fidei ratio" (incl. "Ad Germaniae Principes [De convitiis Eccii]") written for the attention of the Diet of Augsburg of 1530. These three confessions of faith belong absolutely together as well because of their common, extremely significant structure and because of their common purpose: to give witness for the unity of the church and for the unconditional will of Zwingli to understand himself and the churches reformed by him as parts of the <u>one</u> body of Christ. In their structure they all follow the twelve, or rather, the three articles of the Apostolicum. [18] Their common purpose might become most apparent if we look at the addresses to whom Zwingli directed these three confessions of faith. The "target group" was in 1528 the Swiss Confederation, in 1530 Emperor Charles V, who "was holding the German diet in Augsburg", and in 1531 the "Rex christianus" of Francis I of France. Taken together, these three represent the totality of Christianity. These were expected to judge him according to a formulation of Zwingli in the "Fidei ratio" by Scripture under the guidance of the Holy Spirit. [19]

With this, the main theme of this section has been laid down: on the basis of the two Reformed confessions of faith of 1536 it will be seen that Zwingli and the Zurich church professed clearly their loyalty to the catholic, i.e. universal church. We will show this below by two specifically chosen texts: first by the ecclesiology of the CH I, then by the liturgy of the Lord's Supper in the "Fidei expositio".

1. Even a sketchy analysis of the CH I shows that it is divided into three, or rather two main parts, and that the articles on the church--just as in many other Reformed confessional writings --are especially numerous and detailed. Articles 1-5 treat the basis of the Reformation faith (1. The Holy Scripture; 2. The Interpretation of Scripture; 3. The Early Teachers; 4. The Doctrines of Men; 5. The Purpose of Holy scripture), articles 6-14 the most important teachings of faith which are to be deduced from Scripture (concerning 6. God; 7. Humanity; 8. Original Sin; 9. Free Will; 10. How God has saved Humankind by His Eternal Counsel; 11. Christ the Lord; 12. The Purpose of Evangelical Doctrine; 13. How Christ's Grace and Merit are communicated to us; 14. Faith). [20] The remaining articles 15-28 treat questions on the church (15. The Church; 16. The Ministers of God's Word; 17. The Authority of the Church; 18 The Election of Ministers; 19. Who the Shepherd of the Church is; 20. What the Office of Ministers and of the Church is; 21. The Power and Efficacy of the Sacraments; 22. Baptism; 23. Lord's Supper; 24. Sacred Assemblies; 25. Adiaphora; 26. Those who divide the Church; 27. Temporal Government; 28. Holy Matrimony.)

It is fairly certain that the CH I was not printed and did not receive any official validity. Yet, as an expression of the Reformation faith it has its significance especially in regard to the question of understanding of the church. It is this which is of interest for us at this point. Most impressive is the text of the two central articles: 15 "Concerning the church" and 17 "Concerning the Authority of the Church". [21] Even a sketchy analysis of article 15 "On the church" demonstrates that the usual three forms of the church known from Zwingli (the gathering of the elect; the universal church; the local parish), or rather, the division into visible and invisible church do not stand in the foreground for the composers of the CH I. Instead it is the more important questions of the relationship between the head and the church, of unity and plurality. I am thinking concretely of the description of the church as "sancta sanctorum omnium collectio", and as "Christi sponsa". Here shines through the ancient concept of the "community of the saints" which the church forms from the beginning of the earth until its end, of the church militant and also of the triumphant church, but above all, also the basic relationship of head and body, of Christ as head of the church, of the church as the body of Christ. And with this, the precise understanding of the basic unity which is given because it is a church which Christ "also loved and gave himself up for, to consecrating and cleansing it by water and word, so that he might present the church to himself all glorious, with no stain or wrinkle" (cf. Eph. 5:26f). This unity displays itself, however, in further elements in article 15: in the introductory reference to the importance of faith based on the biblical proof texts of 1 Pet. 2:5, Mt. 16:18, Mt. 16:16, etc., (given not without good reason), as well as in the reference that the church is visible, and indeed that it must be constituted by external signs, customs and orders which were instituted and regulated by Christ himself, and through the word of God, as through a general, public and regulated order. This is to say that the church becomes visible in the sacraments of baptism and the Lord's Supper, in proclamation and in church discipline. According to the words quoted, this unity is not based in these orders themselves, but only in Christ who has instituted them and from whom they are to be administered.

It would be tempting at this place to examine also the other articles on the church of the CH I in more detail. It would then soon become apparent that, as article 15, they all revolve around the same theme of the unity of the body of Christ, that they are determined by Christ as the head of the church. Some examples may suffice. So it is said in regard to the "ministers" that they are "God's co-workers, as St. Paul calls them, through whom He imparts and offers to those who believe in Him the knowledge of Himself and the forgiveness of sins, converts, strengthens and comforts men etc." (Art. 16) "Concerning the Authority of the Church", it is asserted that it consists in the task "to preach God's Word and to tend the flock of the Lord, which properly speaking is the office of the keys . . . ". (Art. 17) In regard to the head of the church: "Christ Himself is the only true and proper Head and Shepherd of His Church. He gives to His Church shepherds and teachers who at His command administer the word and office of the keys in an orderly and regular fashion . . . ". (Art. 19) Finally, in regard to the office of the ministers and of the church: "The highest and chief thing in this office is that the ministers of the Church preach repentance and sorrow for sins, improvement of life, and forgiveness of sins, and all through Christ." (Art. 20) True belief and orthodoxy of the churches re-formed by Zwingli could not be more clearly formulated for the Swiss Confederation. It is unnecessary to mention that practically all statements of the CH I are either expressed directly in form of words of the Bible or at least substantiated by them in detail.

2. We come to the same surprising and convincing result when we now turn to that issue, which has been mentioned once in a while, but which in the year 1536 stood in the center of any defense of Zwingli: the Lord's Supper. This applies to all of the above mentioned publications of the same year: to Biblian-der's edition of the letters of the reformers including the preceed-ing "Purgatio", to Bullinger's introduction to the "opus articulorum Zuinglii", to the CH I and now even much more to Bullinger's edition of Zwingli's **Fidei expositio**. Staying with the two confes-sional writings, we see that in the CH I and the **Fidei expositio** the expositions on the Lord's Supper form even the center of the expositions on the "communio sanctorum", the unity of the body of Christ. To formulate it even more pointedly: according to these two confessional writings the Lord's Supper is the expres-sion of the communio sanctorum, the most visible confession of faith, of the membership in the body of Christ. In order to understand and to appreciate this assertion correctly we need, however, to free ourselves from many old prejudices and false judgements. We need to read these texts as objectively as possible. First, it is once again true for the CH I. Article 22 says, "Concern-ing the Lord's Supper":

> according to the institution of the Lord the bread and wine are highly significant, holy, true signs by which the true communion of His body and blood is administered and offered to believers by the Lord Himself by means of the ministry of the Church--not as perishable food for the belly but the food and nourishment of a spiritual and eternal life . . . With this spiritual, quickening, inward food we are delighted and refreshed by its inexpressible sweetness and are overjoyed to find our life in Christ's death. [22]

This perspective is even more true in the sections of the **Fidei expositio** on the Lord's Supper. In order to understand that, how-ever, we need first to refer to two extremely important facts which modern Zwingli research (J. Schweizer, M. Jenny, F. Schmidt-Clausing and G. W. Locher) has re-discovered, but which has yet hardly been taken notice of by theologians and historians. [23]

First, that "for Zwingli the liturgical treatises are more important than the polemical". What does that mean? As little as there was a debate in the New Testament and until late into the Middle Ages (actually until 1215!) on the substance of bread and wine in the Lord's Supper, so was Zwingli, as a matter of fact, little interested in this question. More important for him was the celebration of the Supper in commemoration of the death of Christ and of the grace resulting from it. That the celebration of the eucharist as a meal of remembrance, thanksgiving, joy and fellowship was of central importance to him is shown already in the headline of his Lord's Supper liturgy: "Action or Use of the Supper" (Z IV:1-24), as it was celebrated after Maundy Thursday, 1525 in Zurich.

Second, that so-called appendix, including the description of the Zurich Lord's Supper liturgy contained therein which was attributed until recently by scholarship to Bullinger, comes also from Zwingli. [24]

These facts have decisive consequences for the understanding of Zwingli based on the Fidei expositio: First, we find in the appendix itself a literal confirmation that the liturgy is more important than the teaching developed in the polemical treatises. Following numerous quotations from the letter to the Hebrews which illustrate the uniqueness of the sacrifice of Christ and a long quotation from Augustine, Zwingli writes to Francis I:

> I want, however, to subjoin the order of service which we use in celebrating the supper, that Your Majesty may see that I do not alter or make void the words of Christ, or distort them into a perverted meaning, and that I preserve entire in the Supper the things that ought to have been preserved in the Mass, namely, prayers, praise, confession of faith, communion of the Church or the believers, and the spiritual and sacramental eating of the body of Christ, while, on the other hand, we omit all those things which are not of Christ's institution, to wit, "We offer efficaciously for the living and the dead": "We offer for the remission of sins", and the other things that the Papists assert not less impiously than ignorantly. (Latin Works II, 286f.)

Of much more importance is now, however, the liturgy of the Lord's supper itself! The "Order of service we use at Zurich, Berne, Basel, and other cities of the Christian Alliance" (287-290) which belongs to the **Fidei expositio** (and which is by the way, commented upon in detail in the "Purgatio") contains the following main parts: Introductory prayer, the lesson from 1 Cor. 11:20-29, Gloria (alternating), Agnus Dei, lesson from Jn. 6:47-63, prayer for forgiveness, Apostolicum (alternating), admonition for self-examination, Lord's Prayer (kneeling), prayer for unity and truthfulness of the church as body of Christ, Words of institution of 1 Cor. 11:23-26, communion while being seated, Ps. 113:1-9 (alternating), dismissal. Zwingli wrote after this, in the **Fidei expositio** itself, a little more detailed yet still summary description of his Lord's Supper liturgy:

> Here you see, most wise King, how nothing is lacking which is required for the proper, apostolic celebration of the Eucharist, as far as the substance of things is

concerned, but that the things which are suspected of having been introduced from greed of gain are omitted". (290f.)

And summarizing it all: "The Mass was so thoroughly deserted that we found it necessary to cast about for a simple and Christian form of celebration." (292)

I can only indicate at this point that this Lord's Supper liturgy of Zwingli as a whole finds itself in the best company: looking back in its relation to the early church and medieval tradition, looking forward in comparison to Calvin's "manière d'administrer les Sacrements". [25] However, I want clearly to underline that precisely in its basic intention it does not intend to stress anything else but the unity of the body of Christ, which we have treated in this section on the confessional writings of 1536.

As J. Schweizer has shown first, at the center of the Eucharist, at the change of the elements, "instead of the transubstantiation of the elements the spiritual change of the church into the body of Christ was placed". [26] Immediately before the recitation of the words of institution and the administration of the Supper the minister prays:

> Lord, God Almighty, who by Thy spirit hast united us into Thy one body in the unity of the faith, and hast commanded Thy body to give praise and thanks unto Thee for that bounty and kindness with which Thou hast delivered Thy only begotten Son, our Lord Jesus Christ unto death for our sins, grant that we may fulfill this Thy command in such faith that we may not by any false pretenses offend or provoke Thee who art the infallible truth." (289)

From these words it is clear that in the center of the eucharist Christ is not sacrificed anew, that bread and wine are not sacrificed either, but that the believers give thanks to God by giving themselves according to the example of Christ as sacrifices pleasing to God. To formulate it once again in a different way: already for Zwingli (and not first with Calvin) the believers ("we") are, in the sense of the priesthood of all believers, the subject of the celebration of the Lord's Supper. [27]

III

"In Defence of Zwingli", the "oldest biography of Zwingli", appeared in the edition of the Reformers' letters, published for the first time in 1536--though already written in 1532: "De Domini Huldrichi Zuinglii fortissimi herois ac theologi doctiss imi vita et obitu, Osvaldo Myconio autore". [28] It is not possible at this point to deal in more detail with the text and interpretation, much less with the further particulars of the biography (writer and addressee, intention and nature, etc.). Yet I would like to complete my previous expositions by the remark that Myconius, as a close friend of Zwingli and as successor of Oecolampadius in Basel, also demonstrated biographically in his description "De vita et obitu" of Zwingli how much people understood Zwingli in 1536 as a "Catholic" reformer, or as "reformed" Catholic. Rüsch states that without doubt the writing was intended to be an apology: "Myconius wanted to draw a picture of a friend, to pay a debt of gratitude", but "not only to glorify" Zwingli. Myconius did this by taking up already in the headline "De vita et obitu", but then also in numerous themes:

> some basic and continuously repeating motifs of the lives of the saints and martyrs and by confirming them in a reformation understanding: the rich talents and blessings given by God, the deep life of faith which radiated his surroundings in a strengthening and beneficial way, the inner life of prayer, the following of Christ in the procla- mation of his word, in the brave struggle against injustice and heresy, standing the test of temptations and the lying in wait for the evil one, the courageous endurance and the blessed end which is surrounded by miraculous events. [29]

What does that mean?

I cite as the only and final quotation the end of the biography on the death of Zwingli:

> Hostibus digressis post diem tertium, accedunt amantes Zuinglii, si quid reliquiarum eius offenderent, et ecce cor (mirabile dictu) se offert e mediis cineribus integrum et illaesum. Stupebant boni viri, miraculum quidem agnos- centes, sed non intelligentes. Quare Deo tribuentes quicquid esset, nonnihil, tanquam certi magis de cordis viri sinceritate facti superne, gaudebant. Venit non multo postea vir mihi notissimus, sed et familiarissumus, rogans an portionem cordis cupoam cidere Zuingliani, quod secum ferat in loculo: quia propter sermonem hunc inopinatum horror quidam totum corpus pervaserat, negaram, alioquin et huius rei possem esse testis oculatus. (72f.)

NOTES

1. "Wie einige Fürsten und Reichsstände, die in betreff des Sakraments der Lehre des Martin Luther abhangen", zu Schmalkalden sich vereinigt hatten (Dezember 1535 was der Schmalkaldische Bund erneuert worden), so schien es "notwendig und gut, wenn die Eidgenossen, die im Glauben gleichförmig sind, sich beförderlich durch ihre Prädikanten und Ratsboten zusammenverfügen und auch in der Folge Angelegenheiten, welche die Religion betreffen, in gemeinsamer Versammlung beratschlagen würden (EA IV Ic, 598)", RE VII 641.

2. Kurt Guggisberg, **Das Zwinglibild des Protestantismus im Wandel der Zeiten,** Leipzig, 1934; Fritz Büsser, **Das katholische Bild. Von der Reformation bis zur Gegenwart,** Zürich/Stuttgart, 1968.

3. J. V. Pollet, DTC XV/2 (1951) 3925.

4. Cf. Hanns Rückert, "Die Einheit der Kirche und der Zwiespalt der Konfessionen," in: **Vorträge und Aufsätze zur historischen Theologie,** Tübingen, 1972, S. 329-340. P. 329: "Es ist der schwerste Vorwurf, dass sie die Einheit der christlichen Kirche zerstört habe"; P. 332: "Der Katholik, er die Dinge so sieht, träge das Bild seiner heutigen Kirche in die Zeit von damals hinein. Heute ist die Lehre der katholischen Kirche so festgelegt, dass man ziemlich an allen Punkten sagen kann, was verbindliches Dogma und Lehre der Kirche ist und was man nicht bestreiten darf, ohne sich von dieser Kirche zu trennen. Im 16. Jh. war das nicht so. Ausser der Lehre von der Dreieinigkeit Gottes und der von den zwei Naturen Christi--denen ja auch Luther niemals widersprochen hat--gab es ganz Weniges, was dogmatisch feststand. Auf weiten Gebieten, z.B. auf dem für die Reformation so entscheidend wichtigen Gebiet der Gnadenlehre, war alles offen und fliessend."

5. Cf. Luther, WA 8, 685; Calvin, Inst. IV 1, 12; Bullinger, **Confessio Helvetica posterior,** Art. XVII ss.

6. Cf. Rückert, l.c., p. 333.

7. I quote in the following partly from the copy of the Central Library of Zurich (ZBZ) with the signature ZB 5. 23, which is also the basis of the edition of Reformed Protestantism. Sources of the 16th and 17th centuries on microfiche. 1. Switzerland, A. Heinrich Bullinger and the Zurich Reformation. Ed.: F. Büsser. IDC: EPBU--392 and which bears valuable marginal remarks by the hand of Rudolf Gwalter. My quotations are noted in the text itself.

8. Emil Egli, **Analecta Reformatoria II. Biographien: Bibliander +
Ceporin + Johannes Bullinger,** Zurich 1901, p. 42f. (now also IDC: EPBU - 449).
To this day Egli has remained as the only church historian who has dealt with
the life and works of Bibliander in detail. Based on the printed and unprinted
works and letters he comes to the conclusion that Theodor Buchmann who was
born in Bischofszell (canton of Thurgau) around 1504/1509 and who died in Zurich
in 1564 was by no means only an inferior imitator of his more famous contemporaries Bullinger (born 1504) and Calvin (born 1509, died 1564) and a student and
defender of his teachers Myconius, Zwingli and Oecolampadius. As successor of
Zwingli in the theological teaching office of the "Prophezei" he was already for
his contemporaries like Pellikan, Bullinger, Gessner, but also for G. Postel "an
incomparable man". He ought to be that even more for posterity when one considers
that to the main works of Zwingli's successor in the theological teaching office
of the "Prophezei" belong numerous commentaries on the Old Testament and on
the Apocalypse, but also the first printed Latin edition of the Koran and a "Commentary concerning the common way and manner of all languages along with
a short explanation of the moral life and the religion of all people", etc.

9. Cf. Egli, op.cit., 86f.

10. Bibliander writes in continuation of the just given quotation: "Neque
vero Dei timor ingenuus obtingere potest, nisi munere divino per sanctum spiritum:
nec quisquam sanctificari, nisi per Christum verbum Dei et sapientiam et potentiam".
(f 3^v)

11. Ludwig Lavater, **De ritibus et institutis ecclesiae Tigurinae opus-
culum,** Zurich 1559 (= IDC: EPBU - 305). Cf. Fritz Büsser, "Les institutions ecclési-
ales à Zurich au XVIeme siècle", in: **Les Églises et leurs Institutiones au XVIeme
siècle.** Actes du Veme Colloque du Centre d'Histoire de la Réforme et du Protestan-
tisme, recueillis par Michel Péronnet, Montpellier (1978), 201-213.

12. Fritz Schmidt-Clausing, "Das Corpus Juris Canonici als reforma-
torisches Mittel Zwinglis", in: ZKG 80, 1969, 14-21.

13. At this point I would like to refer expressly to a parallel of Bibliander's "Purgatio" which likewise deserves to be saved from oblivion: Bullinger's
introduction to the first Latin edition of Zwingli's "Auslegen und Gründe der Schlussreden", edited by Leo Jud and published . in 1535 by Froschauer in Zurich. Cf.
Z II 11. This Latin edition of the first Reformed dogmatics served, of course,
the same purpose as the edition of the Epistolae and, a few years later, the first
complete edition of the Opera Zuinglii by Gwalter and Jud, Zurich 1544-45 (=
IDC: EPBU - 476).

14. Paul Jacobs, **Theologie reformierter Bekenntnisschriften in Grund-
zügen,** Neukirchen, 1959, 9ff.

15. Op.cit. 14ff.

16. Cf. Benno Gassmann, **Ecclesia Reformata. Die Kirche in den reformierten Bekenntnisschriften,** Herder Freiburg/Basel/Wien, 1968, 83.

17. First print of the German text in H. A. Niemeyer, Collectio Confessionum in Ecclesiis reformatis publicatarum, Leipzig, 1840. In the following this essay is based on the German-Latin edition given in Philipp Schaff, **The Creeds of Christendom**, with a history and critical notes, 4th ed. vol. III, New York 1877, 211-231. For details on the materialization, difference between the German and Latin text, ratification, obligation, etc. cf. also RE VII, 641ff. The underlinings in the text are of the present writer who also published the CH I with a commentary, "on the basis of a manuscript which had remained unknown" in: Fritz Büsser, **Beschreibung des Abendmahlsstreites von Johann Strumpf**, Zurich, 1960, 65ff.

18. I refer to the corresponding comments by L. v. Muralt, F. Blanke, G. W. Locher, as well as O. Farner and R. Pfister on the Credo-sermon. They are in Z VI/I: 444f., and HS 2: 19; on "Fidei ratio" in Z VI/II: 756, and HS 11: 254; on the "Fidei expositio" in G. W. Locher, **Die Zwinglische Reformation im Rahmen der europäischen Kirchengeschichte**, Göttingen and Zurich 1979, 340f., and HS 11, 298.

19. Z VI/II: 815: 21-23.

20. From this Article the numbering differs. The German version combines "Christianus et officia eius" and "De fide" to one article, the Latin version lists them separately. Therefore the German version has twenty-seven, the Latin twenty-eight articles. See Niemeyer, 109 and Schaff, 218. I follow the Latin version.

21. The text of the two articles is translated by Cochrane as follows:
"15. Concerning the Church. We hold that from living stones built upon this living rock a holy, universal Church is built and gathered together. It is the fellowship and congregation of all saints which is Christ's bride and spouse which He washes with His blood and finally presents to the Father without blemish or any spot. And although this Church and congregation of Christ is open and known to God's eyes alone, yet it is not only known but also gathered and built up by visible signs, rites and ordinances, which Christ Himself has instituted and appointed by the Word of God as a universal, public and orderly discipline. Without these marks no one is numbered with this Church (speaking generally and without a special permission revealed by God.)"
"17. Concerning the Authority of the Church. The authority to preach God's Word and to tend the flock of the Lord, which properly speaking is the office of the keys, prescribes one pattern of life for all men whether of high or lowly station. Since it is commanded by God, it is a high and sacred trust which should not be violated. This administrative power should not be conferred upon anyone unless he has first been found and acknowledged to be qualified and fit for the office by divine calling and election and by those who after careful deliberation have been appointed and elected as a committee of the Church for that purpose." Arthur C. Cochrane, **Reformed Confessions of the 16th Century**, Philadelphia, 1966, 105-106. Schaff, 218-220 gives in parallel columns a German translation that goes back ultimately to Leo Jud and the binding Latin text.

22. Cf. Locher, 342f.

23. Ibid., 336, n. 455f., where all necessary bibliographical references are given.

24. G. W. Locher, "Zu Zwinglis Professio fidei. Beobachtungen und Erwägungen zur Pariser Reinschrift der sogenannten Fidei Expositio", in: Zwa VII. 689ff., especially 695. That the mentioned "Appendix on the Eucharist and Mass" was attributed to Bullinger, was held following Schuler-Schulthess (S IV 68ff.) respectively by W. Köhler (**Zwingli und Luther** II, 431f.), Preble-Baillie (in: Latin Works II, 276), and Pfister (HS 1, 299). The re-publication of the "Fidei expositio" which is being prepared by the present writer for Z VI/IV takes, of course, account of this new finding; he has already presented this view in: **Huldrych Zwingli. Reformation als prophetischer Auftrag. Persönlichkeit und Geschichte** 74/75, Göttingen, 1973, especially 65ff. I am quoting in the following the "Fidei expositio" according to the above mentioned English edition by Preble-Baillie.

25. J. Calvin, Opera Selecta II, 39.

26. Julius Schweizer, **Reformierte Abendmahlsgestaltung in der Schau Zwinglis**, Basel, n.d., (1954), 104.

27. Cf. Léopold Schummer, "La Cène eucharistique à la lumière du sacerdoce universel". In: **Communautés et Liturgies** 4-5/1982, 357ff.

28. Epistolae, without pagination. Cf. Ernst Gerhard Rüsch, **Vom Leben und Sterben Huldrych Zwinglis.** Das älteste Lebensbild Zwinglis. Lateinischer Text mit Uebersetzung, Einführung und Kommentar, St. Gall, 1979; idem, "Bemerkungen zur Zwingli-Vita von Oswald Myconius", in: Zwa XV, Heft 3/4, 1981/1 and 2, 238-258. The credit goes to Ernst Gerhard Rüsch for not only having re-published this well-known text in a critical edition but also for having reinterpreted it. I quote, of course, according to the modern edition of Rüsch.

29. Zwa VI, 241. Rüsch refers in this context also to the big difference of the appraisal of Zwingli by Bullinger, which he wrote in the closing part of "De prophetae officio" in January 1532. Cf. F. Büsser, "De prophetae officio. Eine Gedenkrede Bullingers auf Zwingli", in: **Festgabe Leonhard von Muralt**, Zurich, 1970, 245-257.

ERASMUS AND ZWINGLI'S
ON THE TRUE AND FALSE RELIGION

Dorothy Clark

Zwingli to Vadian, 28 May 1525.

> When Erasmus of Rotterdam received my Commentary
> (**On the True and False Religion**) he exclaimed, as a friend
> of his reports: "My good Zwingli, what do you write
> that I have not first written?" [1]

The statement attributed to Erasmus can only be described as
startling, because the judgment of the humanist that the Reformer
Zwingli's **On the True and False Religion** echoed his own Christian
writings contradicts the common belief that by 1525, a year
after the debate with Luther on free will, Erasmus had taken
a definite stand against the Reformation. Though it cannot be
proved that Erasmus actually said what Zwingli reported, the
question here is whether such a comment might plausibly have
come from Erasmus.

Zwingli's Commentary attempted to be a comprehensive
description of "true" religion and necessarily covered a broad
range of theological topics. Erasmus was never so systematic
in expounding his Christian belief. However, Erasmus's views
on many of the topics covered by Zwingli in the Commentary
can be gleaned from a variety of his works such as **Enchiridion
Militis Christiani** and **De Libero Arbitrio**. Before comparing the
two men's writings in detail, their shared intellectual pursuits
and religious outlook, as illustrated by **On the True and False
Religion** and Erasmus's writings before 1525, should be examined
to provide a general context for the comment Zwingli attributed
to Erasmus.

Erasmus was regarded as the leading humanist of Europe
in the early sixteenth century. Zwingli was his disciple from 1515/
1516 on, occasionally receiving a letter from the great humanist,
until their relationship soured in 1523 when Zwingli befriended

Ulrich von Hutten, a man Erasmus detested. Their relationship was based on similar scholarly interests: classical scholarship led both men to the development of linguistic skills in ancient Latin, Greek and, in Zwingli's case, Hebrew, and literary skills in textual criticism and exegesis. Erasmus used his knowledge of ancient Greek and Latin to revise the Vulgate and Zwingli demonstrated the same application of humanist learning to Scriptures throughout his Commentary. He compares Hebrew, Greek and Latin texts and often has harsh words for the Vulgate: "the Latin translator (of the Vulgate), however, is everywhere so bold and I often wonder whether his learning or his boldness was the greater." [2] Both Erasmus and Zwingli used ancient philosophical categories to describe God. Erasmus called him "the supreme Good", Mind and the "Idea of highest beauty, highest pleasure, highest good." [3] Zwingli tells us God is Being, Wisdom, Foresight, Good, "called by the philosophers . . . the perfect, efficient, and consummating power." [4] Ironically, before this description in the Commentary Zwingli writes "we can in no way attain of our own effort to a knowledge of what God is . . . All, therefore, is sham and false religion that the theologians have adduced from philosophy as to what God is." [5] The theologians criticized here are scholastics, whose teaching authority both Zwingli and Erasmus essentially rejected. Throughout the **Praise of Folly** Erasmus criticizes the "wise" theologians of his day for their "subtle subtleties" and calls them play actors making a "disgraceful pretence to piety". [6] In the Adage **Dulce bellum inexpertis** he deplores the incursion of Aristotelian philosophy into theology and goes on to say:

> All the doctrine of Christ is so defiled with the learning of logicians, sophisters, astronomers, orators, poets, philosophers, lawyers and gentiles, that a man . . . must come to Scriptures infected with so many worldly opinions, that either he must be offended with Christ's doctrines, or else he must apply them to the mind of them that he hath learnt before. [7]

Both Erasmus and Zwingli profess a common distaste for scholasticism while defining God in ancient philosophic terms.

Not only did Erasmus and Zwingli share a wide humanist knowledge of and respect for ancient literature but also they had read widely in patristic literature. Both men quote frequently from Ambrose, Augustine, Chrysostom, Jerome and Origen. [8] The two men justify their use of the Fathers in different ways. For Erasmus they lend a necessary weight and authority to his argument since he does not want his readers to feel that they must "trust instead the private judgement of this or that individual." [9] For Zwingli, the individual can have possession of the truth directly from the word of God: if the Fathers happen to agree, quoting them only aids in the task of persuading readers that this is the truth.

> I have quoted these things from the weightiest of the
> Fathers, not because I wish to support by human authority
> a thing plain in itself and confirmed by the word of God,
> but that it might become manifest to the feebler brethren
> that I am not the first to put forth this view, and that
> it does not lack very strong support. [10]

The different justifications for using the Fathers reflect the contrast between Erasmus's belief that Scriptures supplemented by the Fathers, within the Roman Church, are the content of Christian tradition, and Zwingli's Reformation belief in sola scriptura with no other sources of religious authority. This difference leaves the two men divided by the Reformation. However, the fact remains that Erasmus and Zwingli are steeped in the study of the same Church Fathers. The importance of their quoting the same patristic sources lies as much in the similar content of their thought as in the common scholarly background it reveals.

The major shared characteristic of Erasmus and Zwingli is their spiritual interpretation of religion, which for both men is the primary inspiration of their advocacy of religious reform. Their common concern with internal attitudes rather than with correct religious observances, with getting behind the letter and form to the spiritual content, makes their use of the same Church Fathers important; the spirituality in the writings of Ambrose, Augustine, Chrysostom, Jerome and Origen--although on predestination Zwingli uses Augustine differently from Erasmus--explains why they are quoted frequently by both men. The writings of Erasmus and Zwingli abound in examples of their spiritualism; only a few can be quoted here. Erasmus makes it quite clear what he considers to be the only approach to God at the start of his **Precatio Dominica in Septem Portiones Distributa:** "Oh, Father of spirits, give ear to your spiritual children, who pray to you in spirit." [11] The importance of the spiritual for Erasmus leads him to recommend "that you follow the Platonists among the philosophers, because in most of their ideas and in their very manner of speaking they come nearest to the beauty of the prophets and the gospels." [12] His Platonism is reflected in his description of visible objects as copies of realities. [13] Man must "advance from things visible which are for the most part imperfect or of neutral status, to things invisible." [14] This implies that "whatever is sensorily experienced in the body should be understood of the soul." [15] "God is Spirit, and those who worship Him must worship in spirit and truth." [16] The importance of this Platonic spiritualism for Erasmus is demonstrated by the fact that his section on the Fifth Rule in the **Enchiridion,** entitled by one translator, Himelick, "From the Visible to the Invisible;

The Way to a Pure and Spiritual Life," is by far the longest in the book.

Zwingli shares this approach to religion, stressing the importance of the internal life of the Christian rather than trusting external practices for piety. "They, then, who trust in any created thing whatsoever are not truly pious." [17] "The Law is spiritual, while we are carnal. Unless, therefore, the Spirit enter into us, we shall remain carnal forever." [18] In his paraphrase of Christ's saying "The bread which I will give is my flesh, for the life of the world" (John 6:51), Zwingli explains that Christ wants his followers to progress and ascend from the external to the internal. "Why rise ye not, therefore, at last to higher things? . . . I purposely go from these external and crude things to the internal and spiritual . . . I am occupied with the way in which I may put into the mouth of your souls food that is spiritual." [19]

Their common spiritual view of religion is the source of various similarities in the writings of Erasmus and Zwingli. Both have a belief in a gradation among believers, like that of Origen. Zwingli advocates caution in enforcing observance of what he calls the true religion because "as long as your brother is weak and not contumacious, you must spare him." [20] He also uses the term "children" for persons who will not discard creaturely worship and human rules for God's word. "Why do we ever remain children, when we see that God takes delight in other things than those with which we have hitherto wearied Him?" [21] Erasmus implies that same gradation when he says a reliance on ceremonies causes "perpetual infancy in Christ." [22] Creaturely worship should be used as a Platonic ladder: "flesh has its value in that, by a kind of gradual process, it draws our weakness towards spirituality." [23] Erasmus, more than Zwingli, talks in terms of Platonic Augustinianism: "(Holy Wisdom) offers her milk to those who are little babes in Christ . . . She stoops to your incompetence; but you, conversely, should mount upward toward Her sublimity." [24] The difference between Erasmus and Zwingli on this issue is that Zwingli has a definite goal in sight; his true religion will soon be introduced fully and then there will be no more creaturely worship. The caution shown the weak and the children during the introduction of the truly reformed faith is a temporary measure only. For Erasmus, ceremonies and ritualistic observances must always be tolerated for the sake of the "babes in Christ." His criticism is directed, therefore, not to all the weak but specifically to those who rely too heavily on outward observances when they could be moving forward to a more spiritual, inward faith. "I do not so much censure those who do these things out of a kind of ingenuous superstition as I do those who . . . parade certain observances . . . as if they represented the highest and purest devotion." [25]

The arguments of both Erasmus and Zwingli for a spiritual approach to religion rest heavily on John 6:63. Erasmus quotes it frequently [26] and, as a humanist, applies it to learning as well as to piety. "If in Christ's teachings spirit is so important that it alone gives us life, we must strive to reach the point where in all our studies and in all our deeds we are mindful of the spirit rather than the flesh." [27] Zwingli uses this verse of John repeatedly, especially in his section on the eucharist where there are at least twenty references to it. [28] In this section Zwingli enunciates clearly the importance of the verse for him: "I saw no more effective armor for this conflict than the sixth chapter of John. There that indestructible adamant, 'The flesh profiteth nothing,' is so firmly imbedded in its form and substance that it stands uninjured, however you beat upon it." [29]

The spiritualism of Erasmus and Zwingli, with its roots for both in the classics, gives the two men a similar anthropology, although, as will be seen, they do not have the same views on original sin. Erasmus wrote in the **Enchiridion** "in regard to soul . . . we have that capacity for the divine which enables us to surpass even the nature of angels and be made one with God. If you had not been given a body, you would be part of Godhead; if you had not been endowed with this mind of yours, you would be a beast." [30] Here Erasmus is drawing on Plato's view of the human being as a dichotomy, with spiritual and physical parts participating respectively in the invisible and visible worlds. [31] He also describes the person as a trichotomy in the **Enchiridion**, using Plato's categories of reason or immortal soul, mortal soul and sensual appetite [32] and Origen's division of the person into spirit, soul and flesh, with soul as a morally neutral intermediary between spirit and flesh: "the soul makes us men: spirit makes us good men, flesh makes us vile men, but the soul in itself makes us neither good nor bad." [33] Zwingli usually describes the person as a dichotomy: "I have made of one man two, the inward who obeys the Spirit and the old who never varies from his own law, that is, from self-love and self-esteem." [34] "The soul strives to fashion itself upon the pattern of Him towards whom it is hastening . . . The body resists, because by its nature . . . it yearns for the things of earth . . . Hence that constant battle between the flesh and the spirit." [35] These classical interpretations of human nature, which also concern the dynamics of an individual's relationship with good and evil, leave a strong mark on Erasmus's views of original sin: "Nature, or rather God, hath shaped this creature, not to war but to friendship, not to destruction, but to health, not to wrong, but to kindness and benevolence . . . Nature not yet content with all this, she hath given unto man alone the commodity of speech and reasoning . . . Finally she hath endowed man with a spark of a godly mind." [36] The anthropological assumptions shared by Erasmus and Zwingli might seem to imply a "humanist" emphasis on the dignity of man, but in fact elsewhere both Erasmus and Zwingli contradict this optimism, although to different degrees.

In the **Enchiridion** Erasmus wrote "sin has evilly corrupted what was happily created," [37] which compares with Zwingli's comment on the Fall, following a passage on man being made in the image of God: "God here gives man up as degenerate, because he has become wholly flesh." [38] For Erasmus the person is left with "three evils which are the residue of original sin . . . Blindness affects our judgement, the flesh corrupts our will, and frailty undermines our constancy." [39] Erasmus has a concept of original sin not unlike that of the late scholastic Gabriel Biel. It leaves the descendants of Adam with a tendency, but not a compulsion, to sin, in contrast to the mainstream Reformation belief in man's total corruption by sin. Erasmus even approaches Biel's formula facere quod in se est: "if the weakness and frailty of our nature make it impossible for us to attain that spiritual state, nevertheless we must not slack off one bit in our effort to come as near to it as possible." [40] In **De Libero Arbitrio** Erasmus defines his view of the limited effects of original sin: "as the sin of our progenitors has passed into their descendants, so the tendency to sin has passed to all, though grace by abolishing sin so far mitigates it that it may be overcome, but not rooted out." [41] This view must be accepted as Erasmus's basic one, not only because it corresponds with his belief that grace operates at baptism to reduce the legacy of original sin, but also because he criticizes Reformers for magnifying original sin: "they immeasurably exaggerate original sin, by which they would have even the most excellent powers of human nature to be so corrupt that they can do nothing of themselves except to be ignorant of God and to hate him." [42] Of course this criticism of the Reformers includes Zwingli, who believed that original sin is inherited so completely that it makes everyone sinful in nature as well as in deeds: "that sin that is transgression is born of the sin that is disease." [43] "The mind of man and the heart of man are, therefore, evil, from his early years, because he is flesh, because he is a lover of self." [44]

These conflicting views on original sin are reflected in the two men's differences on the issues of grace and free will. Erasmus is convinced of the importance of retaining some measure of free will, however small, in order to defend human responsibility, which he feels is necessary to promote all effort for improvement in individuals and in society. Erasmus still sees religious life in terms of effort and reward. "By free choice in this place we mean a power of the human will by which a man can apply himself to the things which lead to eternal salvation, or turn away from them." [45] If the person applies himself--studies the gospels and prays to God for an increase of faith--"I will be surprised if you are able to be wicked very long." [46] However, the new, virtuous life is not to be attributed to the human effort: "a man owes all his salvation to divine grace, since the power of free choice is exceedingly trivial." [47] Erasmus takes care to preserve a movement, however small, of the person towards God which begins a relationship dominated by God's grace. Because of Erasmus's frame of reference centered on effort and reward, the human part is essential even though God dominates the relationship: "God crowns his gifts in us." [48]

For Zwingli, the frame of reference is completely different and totally dominated by God. "The acquired faith about which you talk so much is a fiction . . . Faith is not of him that willeth, nor of him that runneth, but of God that hath mercy." [49] An act of choice or free will has no place here, for God's grace when it comes, is irresistible: "he whom He calls is forced to respond whether he will or not." [50] Belief in the arbitrary election of God leads from predestination to ideas of all-controlling divine providence. "God is in the universe what reason is in man . . . All things are so done and disposed by the providence of God that nothing takes place without His will or command." [51] "We know that the potter has the power to make of the same clay one vessel unto honour and another unto dishonour." [52] Erasmus, defending free choice, cannot allow that God has this control: "We are to submit to God as a vessel to the hands of the potter. Yet in truth this is not to take away free choice wholly, nor does it exclude our will from co-operating with the divine will in order to attain eternal salvation." [53]

The conflicting views of Erasmus and Zwingli on original sin and free will produce their differences over predestination and providence, and also influence the writings of both men on the Christian life. Both Erasmus and Zwingli emphasize the importance of a pure life for a Christian. Erasmus writes in the **Enchiridion**: "now, our example is Christ, who alone embodies every principle of living happily; Him we may emulate without qualification." [54] For Zwingli "the Christian religion is nothing else than a firm hope in God through Christ Jesus and a blameless life wrought after the pattern of Christ." [55] The difference between the two men is that for Erasmus the pure Christian life is the product of effort as well as grace, while for Zwingli "if we are successful here (in faith), the most excellent fruit will be put forth spontaneously by the good tree." [56] Zwingli avoids all connotations of merit and reward in religion because "Christ is of no use to us if righteousness comes from our works," [57] and "those who rely upon works repudiate grace." [58] Erasmus still retains a belief in divine reward and punishment on the grounds of merit: "Christ will scorn all [merely ceremonial merits] and will require the fulfillment of His own precept, namely charity." [59] This Augustinian stress on the grace behind human merits does not dilute the contrast here between theologies with different frames of reference.

Thus far we have compared the scholarly interests and religious attitudes of Erasmus and Zwingli: Erasmus's pre-1525 works and Zwingli's **On the True and False Religion.** As humanists both men had studied Scriptures, the Church Fathers and the ancients in detail, honing their linguistic and exegetical skills by this study. Their immersion in the pagan and Christian classics led to their shared familiarity with ancient, Platonic philosophy. Both the humanist and the Reformer emphasized the spiritual rather than the external in religion. This became a reforming impulse for both. They advocated the development of each believer from a reliance on external observances to an increased awareness of the importance of internal piety. However, on sin, free will and grace their views diverged. Erasmus saw religion in terms of effort and reward while for Zwingli a person's relationship with God was dependent entirely on grace. Before judging the appropriateness of Erasmus's comment reported by Zwingli, "My good Zwingli, what do you write that I have not first written?", a more detailed comparison of the two men's views on the specific topics covered in Zwingli's Commentary is necessary.

Both Erasmus and Zwingli agree that the law produces a knowledge of sin. Erasmus wrote in **De Libero Arbitrio** that law "doubles sin and engenders death, not that it is evil, but because it commands actions which we cannot perform without grace." [60] Zwingli's analysis of the law is similar: "we should not know what sin was unless God had manifested in his Word what should be done and what not done." [61] Zwingli goes on to say "we have not been made free from the Law in the sense of not being bound to do what the Law bids; for the Law is the unchangeable will of God . . . Love is the completion of the Law." [62] This agrees with Erasmus's evaluation of the law; he warns against a fleshly concern with outward form in approaching the law by saying "Christ is the ultimate mark of the Law, and . . . Christ is, moreover, spirit and love." [63] Despite the two men's different interpretations of grace, their spiritualism leads them to similar interpretations of the law. A Christian life must be (by effort, Erasmus) or will be (spontaneously, Zwingli) lived under the law, not by sticking to the letter but by Christ's grace and spiritual example.

Both Zwingli and Erasmus use the same terminology to describe the church. In **Dulce bellum inexpertis** Erasmus argued the absurdity of Christians fighting each other by talking of the unity of the church as a body with Christ as its head, his message being that the members of one body should not fight. [64] Zwingli echoes this description when discussing the eucharist: "all who assemble there for the purpose of proclaiming the Lord's death and eating the symbolic bread certainly show that they are the body of Christ, that is, members of His church." [65] This similarity between the two men is a reflection of their common, humanist concern for the unity of the church which was an important and constant assumption behind their reforming ideals. Erasmus demonstrates this concern in his writings against war and in his eventual stand against the Reformation simply because it broke apart the Western church: "of what use are the terms of discord where unity is everything." [66] Zwingli has no less a desire for unity, despite being what Erasmus would call a schismatic; he believed he was rediscovering the true Catholic faith, not breaking from it. "I shall not cease from aiming to restore the ancient unity of the church, and I will prove that I am neither a leader of faction nor a heretic." [67] In this context, he retained the humanist concern for unity: "whenever there is true faith, there also the Heavenly Spirit is recognised as present; and wherever the Heavenly Spirit is, there everybody knows is zeal for unity and peace." [68] However, despite the fact that a similarity can be detected between the two men on this point, Erasmus would not have admitted it. Since he saw Zwingli as a schismatic, he did not recognize Zwingli's concern for unity as identifiable with his own.

There is a partial, but not absolute, divergence between the views of Erasmus and Zwingli on the sacraments. Zwingli writes "I am brought to see that a sacrament is nothing else than an initiatory ceremony or a pledging . . . A sacrament, therefore, . . . cannot have any power to free the conscience. That can be freed by God alone." [69] And so on baptism he says "this was an initiatory rite with which he initiated all the repentant, not a cleansing." [70] This conflicts directly with Erasmus who writes of God that He "with one baptism purges and cleanses . . . nourishes with the common sacraments of the church." [71] The operation of grace at baptism is vital for Erasmus's limitation of the strength of original sin. This explains his divergence from Zwingli on baptism but does not imply a rejection of all of Zwingli's writings on the sacraments. Although Erasmus believes that all "common sacraments" nourish with grace, he does not focus on the operation of grace through the eucharist. When discussing this sacrament he concentrates on the message "whatever is sensorily experienced in the body should be understood of the soul." [72] an instruction which would sound very familiar to Zwingli. Erasmus and Zwingli interpret the sacrament of the eucharist spiritually. Erasmus wrote that Christ "has even scorned the eating of His flesh and the drinking of His blood unless they are taken in a spiritual sense." [73] Zwingli has the same dualistic, spiritual analysis: "the thing of which I am speaking is a spiritual thing, and has nothing to do with bodily things." [74] Erasmus's orthodox belief in the efficacy of grace in the sacraments is a muted theme in his comments on the eucharist because the humanist has a reformist purpose. He wants to raise people above "the fleshly stage of the sacrament." [75] "If your whole mind smacks of nothing but the world, you are a Christian only in the eyes of the world, but in reality more heathenish than the heathen. Why? Because you grasp at the body of the sacrament but are empty of the spirit." [76]

The common reforming aims of Erasmus and Zwingli affect their attitudes to ceremonies, images and monasteries. Both stress the spiritual inner state of mind behind externals, although again Zwingli is more radical than Erasmus in the extent of his criticism. On ceremonies Erasmus writes "observing . . . rituals . . . is all very well, but relying upon them is perilous . . . They will be conducive to piety only if you employ them for that purpose; if you begin to revel in them, they immediately extinguish all that piety." [77] Zwingli is more critical: "it is false religion or piety when trust is put in any other than God. They, then, who trust in any created thing whatsoever are not truly pious." [78] "Ceremonies are no proof that we love God, but the fact that we obey His will." [79] The similarity of these criticisms is qualified only by Erasmus's caution; he condemns exploitation of, and unnecessary emphasis on, ceremonies but would not abolish them since they can be useful for babes in Christ. [80]

The same attitudes--a shared spiritual interpretation, with individual divergences due to Erasmus's caution and Zwingli's radicalism--are to be found in the discussions of the two men on the veneration of saints. Adolph in the colloquy "The Shipwreck" says that when all around him were praying for rescue to saints he "went straight to the Father himself . . . No saint hears sooner than He or more willingly grants what is asked," [81] which is what Zwingli writes on the veneration of saints: "since you say, 'I know that all my hope rests on God,' why do you not in all adversities flee to Him?" [82] Again, Erasmus did not feel so strongly as to advocate iconoclasm. He dismissed Reformed hostility to the veneration of the saints with gentle irony in "A Pilgrimage for Religion's Sake", a colloquy written in 1526. Here he used the device of a letter from the Virgin Mary to Glaucoplutus (Greek for "Huldrych"). [83]

Both men are critical of monasteries, though again Zwingli is the more outspoken. However, Erasmus was prepared to be extreme on this issue, in his own way, because of his monastic experiences. In 1584 the following passage from the **Enchiridion** was put on the Index in Madrid: "monasticism is not piety but a way of living, either useful or useless in proportion to one's moral and physical disposition." [84] Erasmus was scathing towards monks, condemning them for relying on ceremonies [85] and describing them as filthy, ignorant, coarse and impudent. [86] Both

Erasmus and Zwingli warn that states should not let idle monasteries proliferate within their borders. [87] Zwingli suggests that monastic wealth should be given to the poor and that monks should not take vows of poverty, obedience and chastity since they prove so difficult to keep. [88] Again, concern for true piety is behind the criticisms of both men; they disdain externals which prove to be so open to abuse.

The same reforming stress upon the internal over the external lies behind the two men's common criticisms of the mercenary abuses of works righteousness in the Catholic Church. Erasmus criticized the financial preoccupations of the papal Curia: "popes, however diligent in harvesting money, delegate their excessively apostolic labours . . . " [89] Zwingli said openly that such pecuniary concerns were irreligious: "let them flatter and by their adulation squeeze out as much money as possible, but let them not mix up Christ with these practices." [90] Because of his belief that he was restoring pure religion which had previously been corrupted by human notions inculcated from Rome, Zwingli is much more hostile to the hierarchy than Erasmus, who was for reform from within. Zwingli blamed the pope for corrupting, defiling and perverting everything "in order to satisfy his own greed," [91] and also called the pope the Antichrist. [92] The criticisms of the two writers are based on the same concern for inner piety; the difference lies in the severity of their attacks, which are premised upon different concepts of church unity.

By now it is clear that Erasmus had some basis for agreement with Zwingli on the majority of religious issues raised in the Commentary. This concord rested on the two men's spiritualism, which produced a desire for sincere, inner piety and criticism of the Roman Church for over-dependence on external observances. There were three areas of major disagreement between the humanist and the Reformer. First came the matter of free will and original sin. Erasmus judged this issue "hidden", [93] not revealed incontrovertibly by God, so his quoted opinion on the Commentary is still plausible. The same applies to a second area of disagreement --righteousness based upon meritorious works, a frame of reference foreign to Zwingli and used by Erasmus. Erasmus could have judged this issue in terms of the weight he assigned to the grace of God. Both Zwingli and he stressed the importance of grace heavily, and this similarity must have been sufficient for him. It would be incongruous if a man who described free will as a "hidden" issue, which therefore should not divide Christians, had then considered disputes over the merit to be assigned to works as an insurmountable barrier dividing Christians.

The third and most important area of disagreement concerns Zwingli's belief in the truth and purity of his religion, as opposed to the false religion of Rome. What was behind this disagreement is the fundamental conflict between Erasmus's belief in a traditional consensus and Zwingli's confident belief that God has revealed his Word through him. Erasmus would not encourage contentiousness or promote schism over free will, original sin and the merits of works. His own opinions on these issues were informed by what he believed was the consensus of Christian tradition, but he did not categorize his opinions as incontrovertible truths necessary to salvation. In contrast, the root of Zwingli's disagreement with Erasmus on the above issues is that he felt himself to be in possession of truth and would avoid insisting on religious issues only temporarily, for the sake of order in society during the introduction of the true religion.

The clearest expression of Erasmus's belief in consensus, and his commitment to the existing church, is in his **De Libero Arbitrio** where he wrote:

> so far am I from delighting in "assertions" that I would readily take refuge in the opinions of the Skeptics, wherever this is allowed by the inviolable authority of the Holy Scriptures and by the decrees of the church, to which I everywhere willingly submit my personal feelings, whether I grasp what it prescribes or not. [94]

> I would ask that the reader will also consider whether it is reasonable to condemn the opinion of so many doctors of the church, which the consensus of so many centuries and peoples has approved and to accept in their stead certain paradoxes on account of which the Christian world is now in an uproar. [95]

This concern of Erasmus leads him to urge caution with respect to reform: "it is better not to enforce contentions which may the sooner harm Christian concord than advance true religion" and "there are some errors that it would cause less damage to conceal than to uproot." [96] Erasmus would never ask a reader to accept a single individual's point of view on religion, thus his stress upon citing authorities. [97]

Zwingli, on the other hand, demands that his individual ideas be accepted because they come straight from God: "it is . . . perfectly easy for me . . . to render an account as it were, of my faith, since I have drunk it in not from the stagnant pools of human wisdom, but from the living water of the divine Spirit, which is the word of God." [98] Erasmus might have retorted to Zwingli, as he did to Luther: "I confess that it is right that the sole authority of Holy Scripture should outweigh all the votes of all mortal men. But the authority of the Scripture is not here in dispute . . . Our battle is about the meaning of Scripture." [99]

This conflict between Zwingli's confident certainty and Erasmus's cautious uncertainty explains why the two men ended up on opposite sides during the Reformation despite their many similarities. Erasmus judged all of his differences with Zwingli to be inessential except for the final one over conceptions of Christian truth. This last he recognized by not joining the Reformation. Zwingli did not treat his disagreements with Erasmus as inessentials because they were the very issues which characterized his different concept of Christian truth. Zwingli's break with medieval and patristic tradition over free will, which produced his stress on original sin and rejection of merit theology, arose from his acceptance of sola scriptura and consequent rejection of extra-scriptural authority. In this manner he was carried into the Reformation away from his humanist mentor.

Assuming that it is authentic, Erasmus's verdict on the Commentary--"My good Zwingli, what do you write that I have not first written?"--would have to rest on the two men's shared spiritualism. Their spiritual approach to religion provided a strong bond between them. It led not only to similar definitions of the law and the church but it also informed their programmes of reform. Both Erasmus and Zwingli wished to improve Christian faith and worship by shifting emphasis from external observances to inner piety. Their attitudes to the sacraments, ceremonies, images and mercenary works righteousness were the same because of these shared reforming ideals; Zwingli was simply more radical than Erasmus because of his rejection of all extra-scriptural tradition.

I would argue that the statement attributed to Erasmus becomes completely credible when one realizes that the two men's spiritualism was the product of a more general bond between them, overriding the differences that placed them on different sides during the Reformation. That bond was humanism.

Such a statement obviously demands an explanation of what is meant by humanism. Paul Oskar Kristeller's definition of humanism as a cultural, literary movement based upon a rhetorical education still stands. [100] The primary interests of humanists concerned linguistic skills and literary elegance and eloquence. The movement grew out of classical scholarship in which the aim was to reach a full understanding of each text by total immersion not only in its language, grammar and style but also in the culture, including science and philosophy, of the society which produced the text. The humanists believed that the spirit of a past age was accessible to them through the corpus of its literature. They contrasted the ancient world with their world not just from the internal evidence and content of texts, but from the words themselves, because of the knowledge that language develops and can be corrupted over time. Humanists were Christians as

well as classicists and thus some of them applied their skills
to Scriptures and the Church Fathers; here their literary methodology had theological implications.

The Vulgate version of the Bible was written in Latin
that had been corrupted from its ancient form and therefore
attracted humanist textual criticism. Valla had pointed out corrupted passages in his **Annotations on the New Testament** before
Erasmus produced his edition based on comparisons between early
Greek and Latin texts and the Vulgate. The theological implications
of such textual criticism arise from the humanist approach to
literature. If the spirit of the classical age could be gleaned from
pagan texts, then Christian texts contain the spirit and revelation
of God. If the language of this revelation had been corrupted
then the spiritual message had also been corrupted. Here lies
the link between humanist literary renewal and humanist religious
reforms. The nature of the reforming ideals grew out of the relation
between humanist hermeneutic and theology. [101]

God chose to communicate with human beings in the
medium of language. Not only must we use all linguistic skills
to reach the original expression of this revelation, but we must
also use all literary skills to get behind the words themselves
to the divine mysteries in the text. The tools of poetic analysis--
metaphor, allegory, parable, transposition--are the key to understanding Scriptures. Moving from the letter to the spirit becomes
the organizing principle of humanist biblical exegesis. There is
no more systematic aim than to understand as much as possible
with a humble faith. God reveals what is sufficient for salvation,
not what makes a rational theological system. The guiding principle
for biblical exegesis becomes the criterion for the Christian life.
Faith must grow from the letter to the spirit, from dependence
on fleshly external observances to a pure internal relationship
with Christ. It is the impulse to move from the letter to the
spirit that Erasmus and Zwingli share. Their common humanist
approach to biblical texts and religious life overrides their differences on consensus and Christian tradition. The constancy of
the letter-to-spirit hermeneutic leads Zwingli to date his Reformation beginnings in 1515-1516, when he began his humanist study
of Scriptures. It is the spiritualism of their exegesis which divides
humanists and the Reformed with humanist training from Luther
and his radical linking of the Spirit and the Word in the world.

The importance of this understanding of humanism for
an explanation of Erasmus's verdict on Zwingli's Commentary
is that it concerns methodology, not specific beliefs. Zwingli
took his exegesis further than Erasmus, insisting on more and
different revealed truths. But Erasmus was not recognizing only
specific similarities between himself and Zwingli, and counting
the differences as inessentials, in the credible comment, "My

good Zwingli, what do you write that I have not first written?"
He was recognizing a kindred "spirit", a man with a similar outlook
on and approach to the Christian religion. The fact that the two
men differed on the nature of Christian consensus and that this
left them divided by the Reformation did not lead Erasmus to
forget their common humanist bond. Instead, the comment relayed
to Zwingli seems to have contained an ironic recognition of how
much they still had in common. [102]

NOTES

1. The primary source references are to the standard editions: **Hul-
dreich Zwinglis Sämtliche Werke.** E. Egli, G. Finsler, etc. (eds.), Leipzig & Berlin,
1905ff. [abbreviated "Z"]; wherever possible **Omnia Opera Desiderii Erasmi.** Cornelis
Reedijk, etc. (eds.), Amsterdam, 1969ff. [abbreviated "ASD"]; otherwise **Desiderii
Erasmi Roterodami Opera Omnia.** Jean LeClerc (ed.), Leyden, 1703-1706 [abbreviated
"LB"].

Translations of Zwingli texts come from the standard English edition:
The Latin Works of Huldreich Zwingli. Samuel M. Jackson, etc. (eds.), New York,
London, Philadelphia, 1912-1929, in this case vol. 3, Clarence N. Heller (ed.).

Since the **Collected Works of Erasmus,** Toronto, 1974ff. does not yet
contain any of the works cited here, it has been necessary to use English translations of single works: **The Enchiridion of Erasmus.** R. Himelick (trans.), Bloomington,
1963 ["Enchiridion"]; **Luther and Erasmus: Free Will and Salvation.** E. G. Rupp
and P. S. Watson (eds.), Philadelphia, 1969 ["Free Will"]; Desiderius Erasmus, **The
Praise of Folly.** C. H. Miller (trans.), New Haven and London, 1979 ["Praise of
Folly"]; **The Colloquies of Erasmus.** C. R. Thompson (trans.), Chicago and London,
1965 ["Colloquies"]; Desiderius Erasmus, **The Education of a Christian Prince,** L.
K. Born (trans.), New York, 1964 ["Education"]; **Erasmus Against War.** J. W. Mackail
(ed.), Boston, 1907 ["Against War"]; **Erasmus of Rotterdam: A Quincentennial
Symposium,** R. L. De Molen (ed.), New York, 1971 ["Erasmus Symposium"]. The
last two works contain Tudor translations of the **Dulce bellum inexpertis** and the
Precatio dominica, respectively. The language of the latter has been modernized
for editorial consistency in this essay.

The initial citation is from Z VIII, 333, as translated in Samuel M.
Jackson, **Huldreich Zwingli** (New York, 1900), 220.

2. Z III, 682; **Latin Works** III, 107-108.

3. LB V, 25B-C, 37D, 55E; **Enchiridion,** 95, 126, 174.

4. Z III, 645; **Latin Works** III, 65.

5. Z III, 643; **Latin Works** III, 61-62.

6. ASD IV-3, 148, 168; **Praise of Folly,** 90, 106.

7. LB II, 961C; **Against War,** 40.

8. LB V, 8D; **Enchiridion,** 53; Z III, 809-815, 860-861; **Latin Works** III, 239-247, 287.

9. LB IX, 1219A; **Free Will,** 43.

10. Z III, 816; **Latin Works** III, 247-248.

11. LB V, 1219D; **Erasmus Symposium,** 105.

12. LB V, 7F; **Enchiridion,** 51.

13. LB V, 28B; **Enchiridion,** 102: "Compared to things unseen the objects of the visible world present to the eyes nothing more than insubstantial copies of those realities."

14. LB V, 27D; **Enchiridion,** 101.

15. LB V, 28C; **Enchiridion,** 103.

16. LB V, 30E; **Enchiridion,** 109.

17. Z III, 674; **Latin Works** III, 97-98.

18. Z III, 661; **Latin Works** III, 82.

19. Z III, 698; **Latin Works** III, 126-127.

20. Z III, 892; **Latin Works,** 323.

21. Z III, 911; **Latin Works** III, 342.

22. LB V, 35B; **Enchiridion,** 120.

23. LB V, 30C; **Enchiridion,** 108.

24. LB V, 8F; **Enchiridion,** 54.

25. LB V, 27B; **Enchiridion,** 100.

26. E.g., LB V, 9A, 30B-C, F; **Enchiridion,** 54, 108, 109.

27. LB V, 30C; **Enchiridion,** 108.

28. Z III, 773-820; **Latin Works** III, 198-253.

29. Z III, 816; **Latin Works** III, 248.

30. LB V, 11F, 12F; **Enchiridion**, 63.

31. LB V, 16E-F; **Enchiridion**, 73.

32. LB V, 13E-14C; **Enchiridion**, 66-67.

33. LB V, 19A-E; **Enchiridion**, 78-80.

34. Z III, 714; **Latin Works** III, 146.

35. Z III, 909; **Latin Works** III, 340-341.

36. LB II, 952A-F; **Against War**, 6-9.

37. . LB V, 13B; **Enchiridion**, 64.

38. Z III, 658; **Latin Works** III, 79.

39. LB V, 21B-C; **Enchiridion,** 84.

40. LB V, 51B; **Enchiridion**, 161.

41. LB IX, 1221F; **Free Will**, 49.

42. LB IX, 1246B, **Free Will**, 93-94.

43. Z III, 709; **Latin Works** III, 140.

44. Z III, 659; **Latin Works** III, 80.

45. LB IX, 1220F-1221A; **Free Will**, 47.

46. LB V, 22A; **Enchiridion**, 86.

47. LB IX, 1244C; **Free Will**, 90.

48. LB IX, 1242E; **Free Will**, 88.

49. Z III, 667; **Latin Works** III, 89.

50. Z III, 668; **Latin Works** III, 91.

51. Z III, 842; **Latin Works** III, 272.

52. Z III, 844; **Latin Works** III, 274.

53. LB IX, 1233C-D; **Free Will**, 71.

54. LB V, 40C; **Enchiridion**, 133.

55. Z III, 705; **Latin Works** III, 135.

56. Z III, 844; **Latin Works** III 274.

57. Z III, 706; **Latin Works** III, 137.

58. Z III, 847; **Latin Works** III, 390.

59. ASD IV-3, 162; **Praise of Folly**, 100.

60. LB IX, 1222B; **Free Will**, 50.

61. Z III, 707; **Latin Works** III, 137.

62. Z III, 710; **Latin Works** III, 140-141.

63. LB V, 38E; **Enchiridion**, 129.

64. LB II, 960B-C; **Against War**, 36.

65. Z III, 802; **Latin Works** III, 232.

66. LB V, 45D; **Enchiridion**, 146.

67. G. R. Potter, **Zwingli** (Cambridge: Cambridge University Press, 1976) 83.

68. Z III, 752; **Latin Works** III, 377.

69. Z III, 759; **Latin Works** III, 181.

70. Z III, 693; **Latin Works** III, 121.

71. LB V, 1225F; **Erasmus Symposium**, 119.

72. LB V, 28C; **Enchiridion**, 103.

73. LB V, 30F; **Enchiridion**, 109, preceding a quotation of John 6:63.

74. Z III, 782; **Latin Works** III, 208.

75. LB V, 30F; **Enchiridion**, 109.

76. LB V, 31C; **Enchiridion**, 110.

77. LB V, 36B-C; **Enchiridion**, 123.

78. Z III, 674; **Latin Works** III, 97-98.

79. Z III, 850; **Latin Works** III, 278.

80. ASD I-3, 255; **Colloquies,** 68; LB V, 32E-F; **Enchiridion,** 114.

81. ASD I-3, 329; **Colloquies,** 142.

82. Z III, 836; **Latin Works** III, 385.

83. ASD I-3, 472-474; **Colloquies,** 289-291.

84. LB V, 65C; **Enchiridion,** 198-199.

85. LB V, 35A-B; **Enchiridion,** 120.

86. ASD IV-3, 160; **Praise of Folly,** 99.

87. ASD IV-1, 198; **Education,** 226; Z III, 632; **Latin Works** III, 48.

88. Z III, 826-828; **Latin Works** III, 260-262.

89. ASD IV-3, 176; **Praise of Folly,** 115.

90. Z III, 742; **Latin Works** III, 177-178.

91. Z III, 907; **Latin Works** III, 337.

92. Z III, 894; **Latin Works** III, 325.

93. LB IX, 1216E; **Free Will,** 39.

94. LB IX, 1215D; **Free Will,** 37.

95. LB IX, 1248C; **Free Will,** 97.

96. LB IX, 1216C, 1217D; **Free Will,** 38, 40.

97. LB V, 6F; **Enchiridion,** 49; LB IX, 1219A-B; **Free Will,** 43.

98. Z III, 639; **Latin Works** III, 56.

99. LB IX, 1219B; **Free Will,** 43.

100. Cf. Paul O. Kristeller, **Renaissance Thought: The Classic, Scholastic and Humanist Strains** (New York: Harper and Row, 1955); Hanna H. Gray, "Renaissance Humanism: The Pursuit of Eloquence," Journal of the History of Ideas XXIV (1963); George M. Logan, "Substance and Form in Renaissance Humanism," Journal of Medieval and Renaissance Studies VII (1977).

101. The following draws on the recent literature on Erasmus's hermeneutics, a field of study with important implications for a further understanding of Christian humanism. Cf. C. A. L. Jarrott, "Erasmus' In principio erat sermo: A Controversial Translation," in Studies in Philology LXI-1 (Jan. 1964). Three articles

followed in J. Coppens, ed., **Scrinium Erasmianum**, vol. II (Leyden: Brill, 1969): G. Chantraine, "L'Apologia ad Latomum," J. K. McConica, "Erasmus and the Grammar of Consent," and J. B. Payne, "Toward the Hermeneutica of Erasmus." Jarrott's focus was taken up in Marjorie O'Rourke Boyle, **Erasmus on Language and Method in Theology** (Toronto: University of Toronto Press, 1977).

102. Another treatment of this theme has been published since the composition of my article: Richard Stauffer, "L'influence et la critique de l'humanisme dans le De vera et falsa religione de Zwingli," in Richard Stauffer (ed.), **Interprètes de la Bible** (Paris, 1980), 87–102 (German trans., "Einfluss und Kritik des Humanismus in Zwinglis 'Commentarius de vera et falsa religione'," **Zwingliana** XVI (1982/1983), 97–110). Stauffer stresses the critique of Christian humanism in Zwingli's **Commentarius** and speculates that Erasmus may not have read beyond the preface, in which the polemic against scholastic theology would have pleased him; otherwise he could not have taken pleasure in Zwingli's work. Obviously I cannot accept this conclusion; but, because of differences of approach, Stauffer's article and mine are rather complementary than opposed. Stauffer has a sharp eye for Zwingli's specific criticisms of the Christian humanists who did not join in the break with the papacy (and these rebukes are a definite element in Zwingli's **Commentarius**), but he tends to ignore the common ground between Zwingli and Erasmus in spiritualism and humanist theological method. While valuing Stauffers's insights, I think I have the more plausible interpretation of the comment attributed to Erasmus.

IN DEFENCE OF THE SPIRIT
ZWINGLI AUTHENTICATES HIS REFORMS
[IN SIXTEENTH CENTURY ZURICH]

E. J. Furcha

> Darumb ist zyt das du min
> stryt fuerist fuerhin.
> (**Das Pestlied** <u>Z</u> I, 68.24-26)

Zwingli's hermeneutic has not been subjected to detailed analysis in recent studies of his work. [1] Though his entire ministry in Zurich centered on the right understanding of the gospel and begins with the momentous decision of the Leutpriester at the Grossminster to break with tradition by preaching seriatim from the Gospel according to St. Matthew, analyses of Zwingli's work tended to focus on Zurich politics, on relations between Zwingli and the papacy, on the role of the magistrates, etc. rather than on principles of interpretation which governed the Reformer's work. This omission strikes one as all the more surprising when one examines some of the writings of the 1522-25 period in which Zwingli discusses his hermeneutic. [2] One finds emerging there a forceful defence of the evangelical faith which asserts freedom from papal decisions and ecclesiastical control, purports to be under the influence of the Holy Spirit and clearly in line with Scripture.

We know that Zwingli considered Scripture to be "theopneuston". We know that he learned a great deal of respect for an ancient text from Erasmus whose work he admired even when their personal relations had cooled. [3] Indeed, if we accept the well-argued thesis by J. W. Aldridge on the nature of the Erasmian hermeneutic and compare Zwingli's method of interpretation with that of Erasmus, significant points of contact become apparent. [4] Erasmus urges a return to the sources (ad fontes) as the important first step in any attempt to understand the word.

The so-called "philosophia Christiana" is a second hermeneutical principle in Erasmus--an almost simplistic love ethic
which he develops in his **Enchiridion** as a desideratum of Christian
life and scholarship. This "philosophia Christiana" is not an abstract
principle, but of the very essence of every rational coming to
terms with the relevant Biblical records and with the living Christ
of the universal church.

Closely related is a third principle which Aldridge calls
the principle of erudition. It is a learned, grammatical, objective,
scientific investigation of the sources. [5] U. Gaebler has emphasized a strong Augustinian influence on Zwingli in a recent assessment. [6]

Kuenzli carefully examined the so-called "mystical sense"
in the reformer's work, but limited his study to Zwingli's use
of the Old Testament. This limitation is much to be regretted
since in our assessment of Zwingli's use of the Bible the New
Testament plays a much more prominent role.

It is our concern in this paper to measure the work of
Zwingli by the hermeneutical yardstick he himself sought to apply.
For this purpose we will draw on his writings during the period
1522-27, giving special attention to his **Von Klarheit Und Gwuesse
Oder Krafft Des Worts Gottes**, the pamphlet Von Goettlicher
Und Menschlicher Gerechtigkeit and the major treatise **Auslegen
Und Gruende Der Schlussreden.**

As guardian of the word, the reformer of Zurich considered
it one of his God-given tasks to assure that no violence be done
to Scripture. [7]

Zwingli urged regular and diligent reading of the Old
Testament and New Testament as one sure means of getting
to know and learning to understand the word of God. [8] Zwingli
is sure of his position, not because of any definite support from
the theologians of the Church--he warns, after all, that one should
not trust anyone except the Lord since all persons are liars [9] --
but because he had drunk,

> not from the stagnant pools of human wisdom, but from
> the living water of the divine Spirit which is the word
> of God. [10]

We must note in passing, however, that there are areas
in a Christian's life which Zwingli acknowledges not to have been
covered by Holy Writ. In such instances he willingly concedes
that,

There are many things in human society which God did not think of instituting in his word. [11]

What then is the key to his hermeneutical methodology? One important dimension is order--the regulating of human affairs, private and public. Proper calling or the office of ministry is a second principle. In case of the communicator or interpreter of the word, linguistic skill in the classic languages is a third aspect. How else is the teacher enabled to discern the spirits? [12]

Apparent inconsistencies in his position can be dealt with by recourse to above principles. In the case of Faber, Zwingli can argue that "anything not based on God's word is invalid", while over against the Anabaptists he can maintain that "a great deal is not found in God's word, yet valid". [13]

We must now turn to the edited and enlarged version published late in 1522 of a sermon Zwingli had preached during that summer to the Dominican nuns at Oetenbach. [14] We have it on good authority that the brothers of the Predigerkloster who had previously held the position of spiritual counsellors to the sisters were opposed to Zwingli's reform stance and resented not a little his interference at the sister house. Zwingli, nonetheless, preached the word of God at the Oetenbach cloister and eventually managed to have Leo Jud assigned to the task of spiritual counsel to the sisters.

In **Von Klarheit** the reformer expounds the position that any Christian person may come to a clear grasp of God's word by giving diligent attention to the truth which is revealed in Scripture. No external aid is needed in this process, since Scripture is its own interpreter and--more important still--has its own clarity. [15]

According to the views advanced in this sermon, the transmission of divine truth to the human heart is achieved through the soul which is God-like and has an inherent attraction to God who thus reveals himself to a person through his Holy Spirit. Since God's word is more venerable than any of its interpreters, neither Christian traditions nor contemporary insights can aid in any significant way. If there is misunderstanding of Scripture-- which Zwingli would not deny--it comes from the stubborn insistence of the readers (and hearers) of Scripture to bring to it their own understanding. After all, he would concede, human nature is made up of a spiritual and animal nature with only the former being capable of subjecting itself to God's Spirit. Discerning Christians must be able to set aside private opinion (spirit-filled interpretation obviously is not license to think and do as one pleases), and to bring their own opinion in line with Scripture. Zwingli seems to have had no doubt that human judgments would thus be corrected by God's Spirit, the sole guide to truth.

Parables, riddles and such like, which may be found in Scripture, are not perceived as hindrance, but rather an enticements to us to experience the riches of God's word. If they are given room to unfold their meaning, God through them gives clarity to his obedient children, without any human intervention. Zwingli, incidentally, quotes freely from both the Old and New Testaments, to show the ways by which such clarity is achieved. Beyond that, as the writer of 1 John 2:27 has it, "You need no one to teach you".

Zwingli, of course, is also a careful pastor. He leaves the good Sisters at Oetenbach with a critical apparatus, simple enough so that even an unschooled person might test whether the preaching of the priest is in line with the word of God. The twelve checkpoints he gives them evolve essentially around the diminishment in a person of the "old nature", a growing sense of God's greatness and a firming up within one's conscious experience of the gracious work of renewal of the inner being by which the mighty are humbled and the persons of low estate are elevated, with the result that whoever is thus affected, learns to disregard human teaching and becomes confident of God's grace and of eternal salvation. [16]

Zwingli has come to the heart of the matter. He challenges the "regale sacerdotium" by which authority is vested in an established magisterium whose knowledge and understanding in his day was largely nurtured on Scholastic theology. In its place he sets the priesthood of all believers which is grounded in Jesus Christ. This new seat of authority eliminates intermediaries and enables each true Christian to discern the intention of the Spirit in all matters pertaining to life and faith. "God himself is the school master and the tool he employs, Scripture, is theopneuston." [17]

To bind God to human institutions would be to curtail his freedom. Hence, no human agent can determine what defines God's word. God speaks and verifies his word; we merely ask for illumination.

Nonetheless, Zwingli tends to equate the law of God and the gospel and suggests that an "advocate" or interpreter of the law is needed who can make known the meaning of the law to the uninitiated. [18] How else are simple Christians to distinguish between their Scriptures and divine Scripture? Ever so subtly, Zwingli seems to have moved to a rather elitist position which assumes--no less forcefully than the authorities he had rejected--that truth is not with the masses, but with the few who are in Christ.

The apparent impasse notwithstanding, Zwingli restates in the first article of his **Auslegen** that the gospel does not need ecclesiastical sanction. Since it is God's word it does not depend on human prattle for authentication (Calvin was to agree with him on this point. In his **Comm. Ep. Gal.** he asserted in a similar vein that the gospel is learned by revelation and cannot be understood or confirmed except by God's grace alone).

In our assessment thus far a few significant points may be noted. [19] There is the suggestion, first of all, that Old and New Testament are not to be distinguished. Both are Scripture and both are word of God. Whether or not Zwingli learned this from Erasmus as early as 1514/15, as Davies maintains, cannot concern us here. [20] It should be noted, however, that the Reformer's actual use of Scripture shows far greater reliance on the New Testament than his official position would lead one to believe. New Testament quotations outnumber those from the Old by two to four times. [21]

The faith which has been given by God motivates the internal being and is the correct expositor of Scripture. Councils and popes, on the other hand, are not called to be arbiters of Scripture.

More than Luther's approach to the word of God, Zwingli's appears to be intellectual. He obviously saw the prophet of the Christian community (in Zurich it was he himself), to be the instrument of faith, the spiritual guide of the people and of the magistrate. However, unwittingly he might have conceded more control to the magistrate than he initially intended, in order to preserve harmony and maintain unity.

Those who assessed Zwingli's position have interpreted him differently. W. Thomas in his 1902 doctoral dissertation, at the University of Leipzig stated that Zwingli only appears to be following Biblical authority. [22] He noted a marked trace of rationalism in Zwingli's approach to Scripture and argued convincingly--if not conclusively--that his exposition of Scripture was somewhat arbitrary since he allowed personal "conviction" to be a gauge of truth.

P. Barth, writing in 1931, concluded more favorably that Zwingli was thoroughly grounded in faith in the living God who is attested to in Scripture.

R. E. Davies, some fifteen years later (1946) concurred

and went on to state that for Zwingli, word of God and Scripture were identical.

When E. Kuenzli examined Zwingli's attitude to Scripture he reached the conclusion that the reformer modified his erstwhile position on account of the Anabaptists. According to this scholar, Zwingli, prior to 1525, seems to have viewed the Old Testament as shadow of the New which set aside the law, but that after 1525 he came to stress the unity of the two testaments. He saw both of them as having their origin in God and as containing the gospel. Kuenzli consolidated this position in a follow-up article in 1950 in which he noted the prominence in Zwingli's hermeneutic of the sensus mysticus and its significance for his understanding of and approach to the word of God. [23]

Zwingli's mature position on the matter is undoubtedly well stated here. One must, however, use caution in ascribing the reason for the change to Zwingli's trouble with the Anabaptists. It seems to us that the Reformer's chief concern is to find a valid authority principle by which to contain those other "authorized" agents in the church whose work caused dissention in the Zurich Church rather than upbuilding it. This struggle--if Bullinger is to be trusted--was supported by a mandate of the Zurich Council, dating back to 1520, long before the Anabaptists gave Zwingli any trouble (unfortunately, documentation of this action is no longer extant). Zwingli seems to have banked on such official support when he proceeded against the order of preachers in Zurich and delineated his position in **Von Klarheit.**

In would seem that the Reformer had no doubts about the legitimacy of his "call" to reform the church. He had to oppose any counter claim, not by taking recourse to drastic measures, but by falling back onto the highest possible authority. Even then, Zwingli preferred to temper zeal with considerations of expediency, or, to say it more positively, with a genuine pastoral concern to have his flock with him on matters that affected their worship and work. In insisting on the self-authentication of Scripture he had gently removed from his adversaries any temptation to boast of their own prowess or authority.

When after 1523 he found similarities to his own views among the Anabaptists, he was forced to sharpen his own position further. Their reluctance to work within established structures-- which his conservative and orderly mind affirmed as God-given, though corrupted by human wilfulness--he could not tolerate. As a result he would compromise his own earlier stance by conceding powers to the magistrate rather than allow antinomian tendencies to destroy the work of reform in Zurich.

As had been the case with Luther in his confrontation

with the enthusiasts (among whom, as we know, he included Zwingli) the reformer of the Church in Zurich accepts <u>some</u> duly ordered human agents as the lesser of two evils when other human agents threaten to undermine efforts toward unity and to abort the harmonious course of reform. In such instances, the "prophet who is known" and the Christian magistrate, are the final arbiters.

Zwingli's reform platform and his hermeneutical principles were to receive a major test in 1523. His **Auslegen und Begruenden der Schlussreden,** a major work by any standard, best reflects the issues. While at first glance it may seem surprising to find Zwingli engaged in defence of a position which earlier in the year had been affirmed by the Zurich City Council, a closer look suggests that there were formidable opponents who had not yet been won over by the argument advanced in the 67 Articles and in their oral defence in January, 1523. Was there perchance some internal opposition still, despite the official support of Zwingli? One might be permitted to wonder whether the reformer himself felt somewhat uncomfortable with the speed and/or direction of the reforms, hoping that a major book expounding the issues might gain him some "converts". Perhaps he needed to firm up in his own mind the principles that undergirded such reform.

There were clearly two fronts during the mid-summer of 1523. The strongest opposition came from the ecclesiastical hierarchy of the day, represented at the First Zurich Disputation (in January of 1523) by the episcopal emissary John Faber, no mean theologian and a staunch defender of the established order.

Equally strong opposition came from within the ranks in the form of challenges to speed up reforms, undertake some drastic changes in liturgy and ecclesiastical structures and to carry to their radical conclusion some of the principles which Zwingli had espoused in sermons, and pamphlets since at least 1519.

The "Schriftprinzip" Zwingli adopts in the **Auslegen** seems to follow the line of Scripture interpretation delineated in **Von Klarheit.** It is a refined position which takes into account the conflicting interest groups which were present in Zurich during the summer of 1523. As we suggested earlier, Zwingli had to dispel any doubts that what he offered was a rather simplistic Biblicism. He had to establish on the soundest possible basis that his evangelical preaching was of the highest order. He had to convince the "reactionaries" that his reform programme would in no way violate whatever was sound in the Tradition. In other words, change in things essential could come about without serious offence to the weaker members of the body politic.

A fourth possible reason for the rather hasty production and publication of the **Auslegen** and its attempt to "flesh out" the skeleton of reform may be found in Zwingli's self understanding. He undoubtedly saw himself as the "Luther of the South", a midwife able to assist during the birth processes of a new evangelical faith. This booklet would then serve as the white paper, as it were, which would detail how a truly reformed church must look, think, and function. The centrality of the word of God as the gauge of depth and authenticity and as the life-giving source could not be questioned.

Zwingli assumes the office of the prophet to whom the word of the Lord comes as he tackles the structures that need changing. The authority with which he speaks and acts is not his own, but the Lord's. The words he speaks are not merely human prattle, but word of God, grounded and affirmed in Jesus Christ and revealed by God's spirit to every believing rational person.

One cannot stress enough in an assessment of Zwingli's work his commitment to the transmitted faith and the conviction that he was called to proclaim the word of God as a true and obedient prophet. His ministry in Zurich cannot be fully appreciated if it is seen exclusively as a political act, an intellectual venture or the judicious purging of dubious practices in the church. Nor must he be seen merely as standing between Luther in the North and--at a later stage, of course--Calvin in Geneva.

To a point he might have been conscious of his dilemma. Repeatedly he affirms that his insights had not been gained by following Luther, but in the independent pursuit of truth, in constant interaction with Holy Writ and under the guidance of the Holy Spirit. It is this claim, of course, which bears testing.

Of some significance in understanding Zwingli's mature hermeneutical stance are Articles 2 and 3 of his **Auslegen**. Here he relates the work of Christ as sole mediator to the process of understanding by which the meaning of God's word is made known to the believer. Since Christ, the true Son of God, has revealed God's will, he is the only way to salvation. Christ then is the pivotal point in the God-human relationship. Rather sweepingly Zwingli dismisses the understanding of Pope and Council as false (when their understanding is different from his), possibly on the assumption that their respective Christologies are faulty, possibly because he cannot conceive of them possessing the spirit of God who acts as master interpreter, as long as they end up with a different "truth" from his. To block one of the possible points of departure, he rejects dependence on the Fathers as a key to the right interpretation of the word of God, reiterating again and again that Scripture must be its own interpreter (cf. Article 8).

Zwingli's hermeneutic may strike us as rather subjective and it is not without serious flaws. Major among these is the reformer's tendency to attach a moral judgment to the right understanding of the faith. Not only does he allege false motivation in the case of theological opponents, but he demands visible fruits in the form of moral action by all who truly know and live the gospel (a fair degree of theological mud-slinging was obviously in order to help maintain one's own position in an agreeable light).

On the positive side of the ledger it must be noted, however, that Zwingli has succeeded perhaps in overcoming or at least diminishing the dichotomy between law and gospel. He does not deny the law, but proffers a transformation--elevation perhaps-- by which in Christ the law becomes gospel. Frequently throughout the **Exposition** he stresses that the gospel is God's will, made known to humankind, complete in itself and without need of additions or fetters.

When applied by some of his radical contemporaries, Zwingli's position tends to lead to antinomian expressions of internalized rather than individualistic churchmanship. Zwingli himself, however, retains a sharp tension since he is able to combine the gospel of Christian freedom with a high doctrine of the church as the community of believers who are held together in their common faith and are made responsible citizens who seek to bring all things under the dominion of Christ.

This is not to say that Zwingli's hermeneutical position did not come across as a precarious one. Its libertine dimensions frightened Luther who undoubtedly suspected Zwingli of theological (or psychological?) naiveté and feared an uncontrollable spiritualism of the kind he had encountered with the "Schwaermer" in his own camp.

Did Luther see beyond the affirmation of the Spirit-led interpretation of God's word the consequences that would lead by some such route to the fragmentation of Protestantism in later generations?

One wonders, of course, whether Zwingli's insistence on the work of the Spirit in authenticating the word--laudable as that might sound--is workable in a hermeneutical system. In enabled him, no doubt, to invalidate other authority principles because he judged them to be outside the influence of the Spirit of God, hence untrue. But does such insistence on the activity of the Spirit in the process of "opening the sense of Scripture" not invite idiosyncracies, willful bending of ancient texts and arbitrary interpretations of injunctions, precepts, law or gospel?

More to the point still, can one ever take recourse to the work of the Spirit (who blows where he wills, without our knowing his comings and goings), and then proceed at once to lay down rules by which the spirits are to be discerned?

Any consistent adherence to the spirit principle in hermeneutical processes would leave the exegete open to the charge of subjectivity. One would still have to explain divergent understandings of one and the same text by different interpreters, all of whom claim their respective positions to be authoritative, though they may prove to be diametrically opposed.

Dare one suggest that a hermeneutic which places heavy emphasis on a Spirit-led understanding of the word, as advanced in **Auslegen**, allows Zwingli to reform the Church with a good conscience, without laying to rest altogether the problem of authenticating the truth; especially when one observes that Zwingli, when pushed into a corner, does not shy away from manipulating the Spirit. The total freedom of a Christian person--essential in a reformed church which is to be forever reforming under the Spirit--was after all curtailed in Zurich as much as in Wittenberg, Rome or Geneva by the demand to reform the church decently and in order. But then, does a reformer have much of a choice in the matter if he desires to be heard, heeded and respected by his peers as well as by the "commoners" in the faith who look to him for guidelines and direction that they might stay clear of the pitfalls of excessive orthodoxy without, on the other hand, losing firm ground in the quagmire of change.

Zwingli's reasoned harnessing of the Spirit may therefore still prove to be the shortest path to truth, since its ultimate criterion is our doing of God's will.

NOTES

1 One of the earliest attempts to treat Zwingli's hermeneutic in our century is the doctoral dissertation by W. Thomas, Das Erkenntnis-prinzip bei Zwingli, University of Leipzig, 1920. Among other works, the following are noteworthy: Peter Barth, "Zwinglis Beitrag zum Verstaendnis der biblischen Botschaft" in Reformierte Kirchenzeitung, 81, 1931; R. E. Davies, The Problem of Authority in the Continental Reformers, 1946; E. Kuenzli, "Zwinglis theologische Wertung des Alten Testaments" in Der Kirchenfreund, 83, 1949; Ibid, "Quellenproblem und mystischer Schriftsinn in Zwinglis Genesis und Exoduskommentar" in ZWA 9, H. 4 and H. 5 (1950/2 and 1951/1 respectively); Ibid, Zwingli als Ausleger von Genesis und Exodus. Dissertation, Zurich, 1951. Since this article was written,

Christine Christ published a very helpful essay on, "Das Schriftverstaendnis von Zwingli und Erasmus im Jahre 1522" in ZWA XVI/2 (1983), 111-125.

2. Among the writings in which Zwingli speaks of his exegetical principles are the **Apologeticus Archeteles** (August 1522), Z I, 249-327; **Von Klarheit und Gewissheit des Wortes Gottes** (September 1522), Z I, 328-384; **Auslegen und Gruende der Schlussreden** (1523), Z II, 1-457; **Von Goettlicher und Menschlicher Gerechtigkeit** (1523), Z II, 458-525; **De Vera et Falsa Religione** (1525), Z III, 590-912; **Wie sich die Moenche zu Rueti mit Lesen und Hoeren der heiligen Schrift verhalten sollen** (1525), Z IV, 520-529; **Von dem Predigtamt** (1525), Z IV, 369-433.

3. Cf. J. M. Usteri, "Initia Zwinglii", **Theologische Studien und Kritiken,** 1885, 1886.

4. Cf. J. W. Aldridge, **The Hermeneutic of Erasmus,** Richmond: John Knox Press, 1966.

5. Ibid., 57.

6. Cf. U. Gaebler, **Zwinglis Reformatorische Entdeckung,** 1977.

7. Z V. 563. Cf. **Antwort über B. Hubmaiers Taufbüchlein** (1525), Z IV, 587.

8. Cf. Z IV, 520-529. The brief advice to the monks of Rueti is dated 23 August 1525. Zwingli suggests daily readings of forty five minutes (one hour on Sunday), an exposition of what is read and daily meditation on three psalms.

9. Z V, 570.

10. Z III, 639.

11. Z IV, 536ff.

12. Z IV, 382ff. (see especially 395).

13. Z IV, 206ff.

14. The sermon was preached during the summer of 1522. Zwingli's Preface to the printed version is dated September 6, 1522.

15. Scripture derives its unique authority from the fact that it is the word of God, illuminated by his own spirit. Yet, as A. Rich, **Anfaenge,** 31ff. has clearly demonstrated, Zwingli does not adhere too closely to the Erasmian principle, "Den Buchstaben verachte, schaue vor allem auf das Mysterium". Nor does he follow Luther's "der natuerliche Sinn ist Frau Kaiserin". See also, Ibid, 48ff. and O. Farner, ZWA 111.12.

16. For an abbreviated version of the twelve points see Appendix A below.

17. Cf. **Von Klarheit,** $\underline{Z}$ I, 382.

18. Cf. **The Labyrinth,** lines 218 to 230. The same line of argument is pursued in the **Auslegen,** Article 39. See also A. Rich, **Anfaenge,** 66.

19. R. E. Davies, **The Problem of Authority** deals with many of these at some length.

20. <u>Ibid.</u>

21. The same approximate ratio may be found in other writings of this period. The **Archeteles** (1522) has 42 OT quotations and 183 NT quotations. **Von Klarheit** (1522) has 55 OT quotations and 121 NT quotations. **Von goettlicher Gerechtigkeit** has 51 OT and 129 NT quotations. The **Auslegen und Gruende** (1523) quotes the OT 182 times and the NT 737 times. In **De Vera et Falsa Religione** (1525) there are 277 OT quotations and 1007 NT quotations.

Ruth, Esther, Lamentations, and Obadiah are never quoted in the above-mentioned texts while Leviticus, Hosea, and Jonah are rarely quoted in some and never in others. More frequently cited books are: Isaiah, Psalms, Matthew, John, Luke, Romans, 1 Corinthians (see Appendix).

22. W. Thomas, **Das Erkenntnisprinzip bei Zwingli,** Leipzig Diss. phil., 1902.

23. Cf. <u>ZWA</u> 9.4 and 9.5.

APPENDIX A

Note: The following is a paraphrased version of the twelve points suggested by Zwingli to the nuns of Oetenbach taken from the text in Z I, 383/384.

1. Everyone ought to pray to God that the old nature may be overcome which lays great store by its own wisdom and skill.

2. That God may richly indwell the cleansed soul.

3. That God's initial work might be affirmed.

4. Note must be taken that God overlooks no one and chooses his instruments.

5. It is God's nature to humble the mighty and elevate the humble.

6. God's word always calls forth the poor and comforts the distressed and despairing.

7. One's own interests are always secondary.

8. It should be the intent of proclamation to make God known to humankind.

9. One ought to note that inner renewal takes place through God's word and not through human teaching.

10. A sermon must assure the listener of God's grace and eternal salvation.

11. It should put self in its place and elevate God.

12. There must be awareness of the fear of God which delights rather than threatens.

APPENDIX B

1. Table showing frequency of citations of Old Testament books in major writings of the period under discussion. The texts used are from the critical edition of Zwingli's writings.

2. Table showing frequency of citations of New Testament books in major writings of the period cited.

Appendix B - 1*

	Pentateuch	Historical Books	Psalms	Isaiah	Jeremiah	Ezekiel	Daniel	Minor Prophets	Apocrypha
Archeteles	4	1	5	8	12	6	1	3	
Von Klarheit	21	5	12	8	2	5			
Divine Righteousness	30	2	6	8		2		1	
Auslegen	56	14	21	36	13	6	2	5	7
Vera et Falsa Rel.	105	28	52	37	23	6	1	12	

Note: Leviticus and Micah are cited in **Divine Righteousness** and **Auslegen** only

Joshua, Judges, Jonah are in **Vera** only

Hosea is found in **Auslegen** only

Not cited at all: Esther, Ruth, Lamentations, Obadiah, Nehemiah, Zephania, Habakkuk

Appendix B - 2*

	Matthew	Mark	Luke	John	Acts	Romans	Other Paulines incl. Hebrews	Others	Apocalypse
Archeteles	44	7	23	38	14	5	41	15	
Von Klarheit	25	5	15	24	7	10	25	10	
Divine Righteousness	50	7	27	7	4	11	18	5	
Auslegen	177	36	96	141	39	90	209	45	5
Vera et Falsa Rel.	181	34	106	234	68	143	204	46	

Note: Cited in **Vera** and **Auslegen** only: 1 & 2 Thessalonians

Cited in **Auslegen** (1 x) only: Jude

Cited in **Auslegen** only: Apocalypse

Not cited at all: Philemon, 2 & 3 John

* I am grateful to Miss Heidi R. Furcha for gathering and tabulating the material in Appendix B, 1 & 2.

ZWINGLI IN THE YEAR OF DECISION - 1522 *

Ulrich Gäbler

A. Critical Preaching

Between 1519 and 1522 Zwingli's basic theological position changed in the direction of reformation, though stages in this change cannot be detailed before 1522. We know equally little about the content of his preaching during this time. The only thing that we can point to with certainty from the beginning of Zwingli's ministry in Zürich is his practice of expounding seriatim, entire books of the New Testament. According to comments by both friends and opponents the people's priest dealt with the normal topics of humanist criticism of the church from his pulpit. However, there is in addition a more far-reaching critique of the tradition of the church, as his discerning opponent, Canon Conrad Hofmann noted in 1522 in retrospect. Zwingli thunders against the common breakdown of morals and actually names a few individual citizens of Zürich for their offences. False preachers of the gospel and "speculative" scholastic theologians and ecclesiastical jurists are singled out. For one particular group of people, the monks, he reserves his special attention. He accuses them of idleness and of an excessive life-style. He recalls having had sufficient instances of their evil conduct in the confessional at Einsiedeln. Since monasteries had an important place in the church life of Zürich, such preaching was bound to stir more than normal attention.

More important still than his admonition directed to one specific group of people is his critique of ecclesiastical piety

* The translation of this article was made by E. J. Furcha from U. Gäbler, **Huldrych Zwingli. Eine Einführung in sein Leben und sein Werk.** Munich: C. H. Beck, 1983, 49-60. With kind permission.

and justice. In 1519, Zwingli expressly rejects the veneration of the saints, though he condones, for the time being, invocation of the saints (Z. VII 181, 7. June 7, 1519, to Beatus Rhenanus). He felt that there were too many feasts of saints, that one had to learn to distinguish between true and false narratives of the saints and purge all false legends. The people's priest doubts the existence of purgatory and maintains that unbaptized children would not be damned (should they die before baptism). He wonders whether the ban had any particular use. He clearly places preaching ahead of the celebration of the mass and waxes eloquent against prolonged celebration of the Feast of Corpus Christi.

Zwingli's attack on the tenth, however, was given most widespread attention, theologically as well as socially. Like some of the other critics, Zwingli objected to the tenth as an allegedly divine institution.

Its earlier intention as an ecclesiastical contribution had to be re-established. Zwingli allowed the practice of asking tithes to stand within economic life, for example, when credit had been granted. His criticism of the tenth had its special point in the fact that it was one of the stipulated duties of the people's priest of the Great Minster to "see to it and work toward the fact in preaching and confessional that the subjects of the Great Minster would honestly pay the tenth and all other contributions" (Farner: Zwingli 3, 31). Though Zwingli did not call directly for the abolition of the tenth, he nonetheless contradicted the immediate economic interests of the foundation which led to open conflict with his superiors.

Until the spring of 1522 there was no public reaction to this critical preaching. However, among the twenty-four Canons, opposition gradually arose against the sharp personal attacks from the pulpit as well as against the theologically far-reaching expressions on the authority of Scripture. These opponents were able to refer to a written complaint by the aged and highly educated Canon, Conrad Hofmann (1454-1525) who personally was above criticism. He himself had occupied the office of people's priest for several years at the beginning of the century and had become noted for his own critical sermons. Zwingli's opponents remained in the minority. When one of the positions of Canon became vacant, Zwingli was called to this position on the 29th of April, 1521 though he continued to carry out the duties of people's priest. This unusual combination broke with traditional practices at the Foundation since Zwingli combined in his own person executive duties and supervisory responsibilities. In any case, this new direction demonstrated clearly the growing respect his colleagues at the Great Minster had for Zwingli. Among this group of Canons he eventually found the greatest support for his reform ideas.

Later colleagues-in-arms and companions came out of this circle: Erasmus Schmid (in contact with Zwingli since 1518, died 1546), Dr. Henry Engelhart (simultaneously people's priest and Canon at the Fraumünster, died 1551), Henry Utinger (personally closely linked with Zwingli as godfather of his first child; the key role of Utinger at the Great Minster and in the reformation history of Zürich in general has not yet been studied, died 1536). We must add here the Chaplain Kaspar Grossmann (in Bern since 1528, died 1545).

It is possible that the Zürich magistrate reacted positively to Zwingli's preaching as early as the fall of 1520. There is a report in Bullinger's **Reformation History** of a mandate in which preachers are called upon to use Holy Scripture as the basis and yardstick of their proclamation. This magisterial order, however, is not verified in any additional source. Time and content of it therefore remain uncertain. Another political measure of the Zürich Council can hardly be related to Zwingli's activity. When in the spring of 1521 the agreement between the Confederates and the French king regarding the hiring of soldiers or mercenaries was to be renewed, Zürich refused to cooperate and stayed away from the new contract. In the summer of the same year, however, concession had to be made to the Pope for recruiting personnel. However, the general mood in the city of Zürich turned increasingly against mercenary service so that in January 1522 there was a general prohibition which, however, could not be carried through without flaws. These decisions by the authorities undoubtedly corresponded with Zwingli's convictions though he cannot have had direct influence upon their happening as has occasionally been assumed.

B. The Matter of Fasting

Public debate of Zwingli's preaching was kindled by the question whether and to what extent the ecclesiastical life-style, concretely in the matter of regulations for fasting during Lent would have to be observed. The impetus came from a demonstrative eating of sausages in the early evening of the first Sunday during the fast (March 9, 1522) in the house of the printer, Christoph Froschauer. As Zwingli himself concedes, the group of about a dozen participants transgressed the prohibition to break fast intentionally in order to proclaim Christian liberty (Z. II, 778, 11). Two smoked sausages were cut into small pieces and distributed among the participants. Is it merely happenstance that time of day, number of participants and manner of distribution remind one of the Supper in the New Testament? Among the participants was Zwingli himself (the only member of the group who did not eat), and two other clergy persons, one of whom was Leo Jud, Zwingli's successor in Einsiedeln and later pastor of St. Peter's in Zürich, who was to stand out by the radical notions he upheld which went beyond Zwingli. Among the lay persons named are several men who are known to us through other provocations too. Some of these later turned away from Zwingli because he did not go far enough. They joined the Anabaptist movement. It is conjectured that Zwingli held back, on the one hand, because he did not expect much of a publicly provocative deed--such actions contradict the picture we have of his manner of acting--and because he must have sensed, on the other hand, that a greater debate would follow for which he wanted to maintain the appearance of neutrality. The events in Froschauer's house became public knowledge very quickly. Other breaks of the fast followed. The Council was forced to intervene and began to make juridical inquiries. A tense atmosphere prevailed in Zürich.

Two weeks after the sausage incident in the house of Froschauer, Zwingli treated the subject of fasting from the pulpit-- clear proof, incidentally, that he could disregard the lectionary for a specific reason. In expanded form this sermon was published on April 16, 1524 under the title, Von Erkiesen Und Freiheit der Speisen (Z. I, 74-136). Zwingli justifies its publication by pointing to his responsibility as pastor. At a time in which several positions with regard to fasting had emerged he considered it his duty to make the intent of Scripture heard. After enumerating several biblical texts, especially from Paul's epistles, Zwingli observes that a Christian is entitled to eat any kind of food since food in itself is neither good nor evil. Only through abuse is a person harmed. Following this, Zwingli responds to four objections: 1. Though Christians are permitted to eat any kind of food there are times which are exceptions to this rule. 2. If one is permitted to eat meat during Lent, abstinence would soon come into disuse. 3. Though the directive to fast is a human commandment it is not permitted simply to annul such rule laid down by our forebears. 4. To eat meat during Lent would cause the weak in the faith to be offended.

Zwingli responds to these point by point. On the basis of Scripture--"God's law" (Z. I 99, 14f)--no generally valid regulations regarding food can be derived. Salvation does not depend on these. "If you like to fast, do so; if you prefer not to eat meat, don't eat it; but allow a Christian person his freedom in all of this (Z. I, 106, 15-17)." To transgress the regulation on fasting is not a sin. As a result it cannot be punished through ecclesiastical penalties. While it is correct to avoid offence and cause for stumbling, a preacher also has the task of educating the weak person. Evangelical freedom must be practiced. Such freedom can be curtailed only if the threat of public rebellion is present (Z. I, 123, 31f). In other words, Zwingli relegates the tradition of fasting to the private sphere. In conclusion, he offers to refute any objections on the basis of Scripture.

Whether Zwingli leaned on Luther's tract, On the Freedom of a Christian--with which he was familiar--cannot be said. In general his tract commands attention for its closely reasoned line of argument. It shows signs of a carefully thought out, precisely stated scientific dissertation. Its content, as was the case with Luther's, is the topic of freedom. However, while the Wittenberg professor speaks of a Christian's freedom from the law in general, Zwingli limits such exemption to human commandments and ordinances. The gospel contains the law of God, which naturally everyone must keep. Even this first of Zwingli's reform writings points to a fundamental difference between Luther and Zwingli on the question of law and gospel. When we assess his remarks we must furthermore emphasize their moderate tone. Monks and orders alone are caricatured. The authority of the scholastic teacher of the church, Thomas Aquinas is ridiculed: "they (the defenders of the commandment on fasting) cite Thomas right away as if one single mendicant has authority to prescribe laws for all of Christendom" (Z. I, 109, 2-4). How far Zwingli distances himself in this publication from his teacher Erasmus in the assessment of the ecclesiastical situation is shown by the latter's comment on the occasion of a breach of the fast rule in Basle. Erasmus shares the opinion that the commandments on fasting are untenable. But he demands that they be changed or set aside under the leadership of the princes of the church. As long as the ordinance is in existence it ought to be kept. As a result he criticizes sharply anyone who transgresses the law and condemns their action as an abuse of evangelical freedom. Zwingli, on the other hand, sees in the existing conditions clear abuse by ecclesiastical authority and denies its right to set up regulations in such matters (Z. I, 136, 1-7). This ought to be the concern of every individual Christian. Zwingli and Erasmus differ in their respective assessment of the responsibility of ecclesiastical authority; in other words, in their doctrine of the church.

During the three weeks which had passed between the preaching of the sermon and its publication, developments in Zürich had further heightened. The Council requested of the chapter of the Great Minster and of the three people's priests of the city an assessment on the problem of fasting. In the response, Zwingli's opinion on fasting as an exercise demanded by Tradition alone is shared, but at the same time a warning is issued not to discontinue the practice of fasting in order to avoid discontent. It is urged, therefore, that any transgression of the rules of fasting should be punished until a general clearing of the question is achieved. In general, the advice given goes in the same direction as the position of Erasmus. The Council is admonished to urge the preachers to appropriate proclamation. The right to concern itself with such ecclesiastical matters is clearly conceded to the Council by the above commission. In other words, the clergy of Zürich contributes to the breaking down of episcopal authority in favor of the Council. The bishop of Constance reacted to the events in Zürich by sending a delegation which stayed in Zürich between April 7-9, 1522. Zwingli prepared a report on the discussion (Z. I, 137-154). Characteristically, the episcopal delegation meets with the spiritual authorities of the city, the Great Minster and the people's priests as well as with the Small and Great Council-- the political authorities of the city. When talking to the magistrate the commission sought to limit itself to warnings and admonitions without entering into further discussion. This plan backfired since the Great Council insisted on the presence of the people's priests during the meeting. This enabled Zwingli to appear as opponent of the episcopal curia in the presence of the politically decisive Great Council and to justify his attack on ecclesiastical order. Though the Council condemned the breach of the tradition of fasting in an appropriate mandate of April 9, 1522 in its concluding agreement with the delegation it added to the agreement that this was to be merely a temporary decision. The ecclesiastical authorities were to issue a definitive position on how one ought to conduct oneself in this matter so that "nothing be done in the matter which would go against the ordinances of Christ" (Egli, Actensammlung 236).

The significance of this event for further developments cannot be overstated. The Council of Zürich accepts responsibility for ecclesiastical questions, recognizes Zwingli as of equal authority with the authorized representatives of the Bishop of Constance and places the burden of proof upon the ecclesiastical authorities. They are to justify traditional practice on the basis of the Scripture principle. Zwingli "could rightfully record success in the resolution of the matter concerning the fast" (Goeters 243). Internally, Zwingli had to come to terms in the spring of 1522 with the above-mentioned complaint of the noble born Canon Conrad Hofmann. Beyond that, an anonymous member of the Great Minster foundation submitted a complaint. These two admonitions found no public echo.

C. Confrontation With the Mendicant Orders

The question of the veneration of saints and the monastic life-style followed immediately after the problems concerning the fast as a matter of conflict in the post Easter period. The incentive to the public confrontation came once again from radical followers of Zwingli who interrupted the sermons of members of the orders. Apparently some of the members of these mendicant orders had criticized Zwingli's position on the veneration of saints toward the end of June or the beginning of July 1522. In these disruptions of services, Konrad Grebel had played a leading role. The intention of these provocative actions apparently was to cause the Council to take a decisive stance in favor of Zwingli's reform efforts. However, within the Council there was no clear majority in favor of Zwingli. As a result it was satisfied to simply forbid any form of agitation without expressing any opinion on the content. However, Zwingli later took dramatic advantage of the means of disrupting sermons.

He interrupted the traveling mendicant friar, Franz Lambert of Avignon when the latter preached in the Fraumünster on Mary and the Saints. Zwingli shouted: "Brother, you are in error." This time the intended goal was achieved. A disputation was arranged which included the entire theological leadership of Zürich and which was to deal with the content of the sermons preached by mendicant monks. As a result of this debate the delegation of the Council, which was appointed for that purpose, decreed on the 21st of July, 1522, that members of the orders had to preach according to Scripture along the lines of Zwingli's preaching. From now on they were to preach the gospel and to leave scholastic theologians, such as Thomas and Duns Scotus aside (Z. VII, 549, 3-5, July 30, 1522, to Beatus Rhenanus).

H. A. Oberman has rightly pointed out recently what a significant step this disputation and its outcome represents. This is the first time that a political authority assumes the office of judge on an ecclesiastical--theological question and decides on its own authority. One must keep in mind, however, that this was a decision merely of a delegation and not of the Council itself and that the directive referred to mendicant orders alone. It is not by accident that the civic authority undertook this measure over against the cloisters whose internal life it had attempted to bring under its control ever since the 15th century. We cannot as yet speak of a general mandate requesting preaching according to Scripture.

D. Rejection of Episcopal Authority

Upon the departure of the episcopal delegation the Bishop's next move came on May 24, 1522 in the form of a written admonition addressed to the Great Minster Foundation and to the civic authorities. Clarification in the matter of fasting such as was expected by the Council, the Bishop was unable to give, since such was beyond his authority. He simply repeats the traditional position and gives no indication of a new general ecclesiastical regulation.

Zwingli and ten sympathizers of the humanistic reform movement saw themselves forced to pick up another urgent problem of ecclesiastical life after this disappointing response. In a petition to the Bishop dated July 2, 1522 they request the abolition of celibacy. They combine this rather urgent demand for clerics with the request to permit scriptural, i.e. evangelical, preaching

(Supplicatio Ad Hugonem Episcopum Constantiensem: Petition to the Bishop of Constance Hugo, Z. I, 189-209). This petition addressed itself to the Bishop in form only but was actually intended to reach a wider public by drawing people's attention to the problem of celibacy, thus to serve in a publicly effective fashion the cause of reform propaganda. This writing appeared only two weeks later in German, albeit anonymously. (A Friendly Request and Admonition addressed to the Confederates, July 13, 1522, Z. I, 210-248). As the title suggests, the addressees were now the temporal authorities. In this respect it may be compared to Luther's pamphlet "To the German Nobility" of 1520. This appeal to the confederates expressly takes the side of Luther who in the meantime had been labelled a heretic. It urges the political authorities to permit the marriage of priests and to grant their women and children the normal juridical rights. The question of the marriage of priests for Zwingli himself was no longer a theoretical matter since from the beginning of 1522 he lived in secret marriage with the widow, Anna Reinhard (died 1538).

Apart from the broad consequences of the question of celibacy the matter was focused for the Episcopal chair by the fact that this petition did not come from Zürich alone but from priests in widely different areas of the Episcopal territory. With the appeal to the confederates to protect clerics from intervention by the Bishop a distinct political element was introduced. The Bishop responded in kind. In a mandate of August 10, 1522 he warned the Zürich magistrate to maintain ecclesiastical order and demanded of them to protect the church. With this the confrontation between Zwingli and his ecclesiastical superiors had reached the level of the confederacy. The Federal Diet, however, did not react for the time being. Zwingli and his associates received the support of the lower clergy instead. A gathering of clergy in Rapperswil agreed on August 19, 1522 to observe the scripture principle. In this atmosphere which was favorable to Zwingli he came to terms once and for all with his Bishop in the **Apologeticus Archeteles** (the "first and last word") of 22-23 August, 1522 (Z. I. 249-327). In painstaking fashion Zwingli countered the episcopal admonition of May 24, 1522 and objected above all else to the accusation of rebellion, schism, and heresy. The first accusation he countered by pointing to the actual calm and order which prevailed in Zürich as in no other locale of the Constance diocese or elsewhere in the confederacy. The public is in no way deceived when it is a matter of presenting to it evangelical teaching in order for it to leave behind human traditions and the whole matter of ceremonials. Such preaching cannot be schismatic or heretical since it proclaims Christ who is the sole foundation of the Church. To the demand that ecclesiastical ceremonies must be observed for the sake of order, it must be said on the contrary, that there is no way of speaking of order in the current situation of the church. Generally speaking Zwingli denies to the ecclesiastical hierarchy because of its own corrupt condition the right to judge at all in matters of proclaiming the gospel or with regard to ecclesiastical order. From his Bishop he does not expect anything anymore since he is found on the side of human ordinances while those who are reform-minded stand on the side of Christ. Erasmus reacted to this merciless attack with horror (Z. VII, 582, 8, September 8, 1522, letter to Zwingli). The rejection of the hierarchy becomes the distinguishing mark between humanist reform efforts and reform renewal.

This attack by Zwingli of August 1522 can be understood only against the background of the factual assessment of his position in Zürich since the early summer of 1522. Beyond the office as people's priest at the Great Minster he grows into the role of the influential preacher of Zürich with the aid of favorably inclined circles within the Council. This development is formally sanctioned in November 1522 when he is relieved of specific duties of his office (auricular confession and the reading of mass) and when it is expected that he should devote himself exclusively to preaching. We cannot determine precisely, however, to what extent Zwingli's legal position at the Great Minster Foundation had changed. It is certain in any case that besides the chapter, the civic authorities desired and brought about this change. Whether or not he can now be called the "city's preacher" (Locher, **Zwingli** 1982, 22) who received from the Council an "evangelical preaching office" (Walton, **Theocracy**, 131; Moeller, **Disputationen**, I, 293; II, 215) remains in doubt. What may be most readily stated is that the action of the Council is in line with a pre-reformation preaching appointment. This change does not allow us, however, to conclude in favor of a definitive change by the Council toward Zwingli; Oberman has rightly pointed this out (Oberman, Op.cit. 274).

An indication of Zwingli's increased authority is the demand by the Council that he preach in the Dominican monastery at Oetenbach though this task traditionally was reserved to members of the Order of Preachers.

E. Clarification of the Understanding of Scripture and the Veneration of Saints

The pamphlet, On the Clarity and Certainty of the Word of God, (September 6, 1522, Z. I, 328-384) is based on a sermon preached at the Dominican monastery of Oetenbach. Here for the first time, Zwingli refers extensively to the scripture principle. His starting point is the anthropological presuppositions for the hearing of the word of God. Since human nature in keeping with its god-likeness is spiritual, a human being must always look up to God. Therefore a person is capable of grasping the word of God which addresses the spiritual nature of humankind. God's word is spiritual and is transmitted neither through the text of the Bible nor through preaching, nor through the church fathers or Councils. God the Father speaks directly to a person through his spirit. In order to feel the spirit, one must trust that the spiritual relationship will be established, one must pray for the spirit and leave one's own "reason" behind. The "old nature" must be mortified. One can be sure of the word of God when one senses God's grace and eternal salvation yet looks upon oneself as small and insignificant. The inner being rejoices in the "law of God" (Z. I, 352, 7). One who is thus taught is capable of understanding all dark sayings of the Bible which at first glance might appear to be contradictory. No other authority can replace this authority of one's own feeling and one's own conscience, for the word of God as spirit has no other point of contact. In this immediate non-verbal communication between God and humankind the Biblical interpretation of an ecclesiastical teaching office or of a humanist exegete has no longer any place. Only the one who is taught by God, the believer, is capable of understanding and interpreting the Bible. From this interrelating of word of God and inner perception it becomes clear why Zwingli rejects so vehemently all ecclesiastical hierarchy. Its behavior demonstrates how little it is taught by God. Throughout his life Zwingli adhered to this understanding of the word of God.

In the very same month a second revised sermon appeared in print, a sermon on the eternally pure servant Mary (September 17, 1522, Z. I, 385-428). Zwingli expounds on a topic publicly on which in July he had held a disputation with the monks of the mendicant order. Undoubtedly, his critique which he made known orally in July, 1522 of traditional Mariology is reflected here. The sermon must have originated out of this context. It is hardly possible that this sermon goes back to Zwingli's participation in the Feast of the Dedication of Angels at Einsiedeln of September 15, 1522 as has often been presumed, since the printing would have had to be done within three days of that event. Zwingli's comments on Mary are non-polemical. They serve rather the defence against those accusations which charged him with having defamed the Mother of God in public and lowered her prominence. He clearly recognizes the term "Mother of God" as well as her permanent and unblemished virginity. However, he definitely rejects Mary's mediatorship and the religious veneration accorded her person. Faith in Christ is diminished when in the confessional the reciting of an Ave Maria (cf. Luke 1:28) is ordered. The right veneration of Mary is to see in her an example of strict morals, modesty and firmness in faith; "If you seek to honor Mary especially, follow her in her purity, innocence and firm faith" (Z. I, 426, 22f).

To review events in Zürich between spring and fall of 1522 we may observe firstly that the most burning problems of

the pre-reformation church such as rules on fasting, veneration
of the saints and Mary, the position of the monastic orders, the
marriage of priests were at the center of discussion. Their political,
economic, social, and human consequences were clearly at hand.
The central question is that of authority: who decides and on
what authority and by what criteria? Even without official sanction
by the Council the scripture principle, according to Zwingli, is
to be applied in place of ecclesiastical tradition. The relation
to the Bishop of Constance is tense but not yet broken. Zwingli
is not capable as yet to secure for himself a majority in the Council
but the process of forming opinion is clearly operating. The following two years will bring clarification of the relationship to the
Bishop and the final breakthrough of the reformed idea of Zwingli.

BIBLIOGRAPHY

Augustijn, Cornelis, "Die Stellung der Humanisten zur Glaubensspaltung 1518-1530",
in, **Confessio Augustana und Confutatio.** Der Augsburger Reichstag 1530
und die Einheit der Kirche, Münster 1980. Reformationsgeschichtliche
Studien und Texte, 118, 36-48.

Egli, Emil (ed.), **Actensammlung zur Geschichte der Zürcher Reformation in den
Jahren 1519-1533,** Zürich 1879 (Reprint: Aalen 1973; Nieuwkoop 1973).

Fast, Heinold, "Reformation durch Provokation. Predigtstörungen in den ersten Jahren
der Reformation in der Schweiz", in, Hans-Jürgen Goertz (ed.), **Umstrit-
tenes Täufertum,** 1525-1975. Neue Forschungen, Göttingen, 1975, Second
edition, 1977, 79-110.

Federer, Karl, "Zwingli und die Marienverehrung", in, **Zeitschrift für Schweizerische
Kirchengeschichte** 45, 1951, 13-26.

Figi, Jacques, **Die innere Reorganisation des Grossmünsterstiftes in Zürich von 1519
bis 1531,** Zürich 1951 - Zürcher Beiträge zur Geschichtswissenschaft
9.

Gäbler, Ulrich, "Huldrych Zwinglis 'reformatorische Wende' ", in, **Zeitschrift für
Kirchengeschichte** 89, 1978, 120-135.

Goeters, J. F. Gerhard, "Die Vorgeschichte des Täufertums in Zürich", in, **Studien
zur Geschichte und Theologie der Reformation.** Festschrift für Ernst
Bizer, Neukirchen 1969, 239-281.

Locher, Gottfried, W., **Zwingli und die schweizerische Reformation,** Göttingen 1982.
(Die Kirche in ihrer Geschichte, III, J 1.)

Moeller, Bernd, "Zwinglis Disputationen. Studien zu den Anfängen der Kirchenbildung und des Synodalwesens im Protestantismus", 2 parts, in, **Zeitschrift der Savigny-Stiftung für Rechtsgeschichte** 87, 1970, 275-324; 91, 1974, 213-364.

Nagel, E., **Zwingli's Stellung zur Schrift,** Freiburg i. B./Leipzig 1896.

Oberman, Heiko Augustinus, **Werden und Wertung der Reformation. Vom Wegestreit zum Glaubenskampf,** Tübingen 1977.

Pestalozzi, Theodor, **Die Gegner Zwinglis am Grossmünsterstift in Zürich,** Zürich 1918. -Schweizer Studien zum Geschichtswissenschaft 9, H. 1.

Walton, Robert C., **Zwingli's Theocracy,** Toronto, 1967.

THE PRESUPPOSITIONS OF ZWINGLI'S BAPTISMAL THEOLOGY

Timothy George

In June, 1525, a procession of rebaptized peasants from Zollikon entered the city of Zurich and paraded through its streets crying, "Woe, woe, woe, O Zurich." They pilloried Zwingli as "the old dragon" and, in the spirit of Jonah, gave the city forty days in which to repent. [1] This extraordinary demonstration followed a year of baptismal disturbances in and around Zurich, ranging from the refusal of certain individuals to submit their infants for baptism to the disruption of sermons, the smashing of baptismal fonts, and the gathering of (re-)baptized believers into separatist conventicles. The Zurich Council responded eventually to this crisis by banishing the obstinate offenders and by decreeing death by drowning as the penalty for rebaptism. [2]

Zwingli's baptismal theology was developed in the course of his struggle with these Täufer, and it has been studied primarily from this perspective. [3] His staunch defense of infant baptism places him, along with Luther and Calvin, in the front rank of Anabaptist opponents among the mainline reformers. This method is certainly justified given the paucity of Zwingli's early statements on baptism and the fact that his major writings on the subject were elicited by the radical challenge. Still, it has tended to obscure important emphases in Zwingli's overall sacramental thought, including his own unique baptismal theology.

Zwingli himself was well aware that his views on baptism flew in the face not only of the received tradition but also of other contemporary understandings: "We shall have to tread a different path." [4] Whereas Luther could rejoice that baptism was the one sacrament which had remained "untouched and untainted" by human corruption, Zwingli concluded that all the teachers of the church since the days of the apostles had been in error on baptism. [5] For his part Luther held that the Zwinglian view of baptism was worse than that of the Anabaptists, for it dissolved the sacrament into a "mere nothing." [6] So much attention has been given to the Abendmahlsstreit between Luther and Zwingli that a careful comparison of their baptismal theologies has yet to be made. It is beyond the scope of this paper to offer such an analysis. We must recognize, however, that Zwingli's doctrine of baptism was forged against two fronts: the ecclesiastical displacement of baptism by Anabaptist innovation and the sacramental objectivism of Roman Catholic and Lutheran practice. As theologian and churchman Zwingli was concerned with both the spiritual basis of baptism and its structural role in the Christian community.

THE IMMEDIACY OF GRACE

Zwingli frankly acknowledged his indebtedness to (and affinity with!) the Anabaptists on two crucial points. The first concerned the liturgical setting of the baptismal rite. Since 1523 a vernacular order of baptism, compiled by Leo Jud, had been used .in Zurich. Like Luther's Taufbüchlein of the same year, on which it was largely modeled, Jud's service retained many of the ceremonies of the old Latin rite including a double signing with the cross, blowing under the eyes, placement of salt in the mouth and spittle on the ears and nose, and anointment with oil which had been consecrated by a bishop. By 1525 Zwingli was repudiating such practices as a "form of magic," worthless "human additions" (menschlichen zusätz). [7] In May, 1525, he set forth a drastically revised order of baptism in which, as the title read, "all the additions, which have no foundation in the word of God, have been removed." [8]

What prompted this radical revision of the baptismal rite? We can discern at least three motives for Zwingli's severe pruning of the liturgical tradition. First, the principle of Scriptural authority relativized all extra-biblical practices. This is clearly expressed in the second of the Ten Conclusions of Berne (1528): "The Church of Christ makes no laws or commandments apart from the Word of God; hence all human traditions are not binding upon us except so far as they are grounded upon or prescribed in the Word of God." [9] Of course, this concern was also part of the larger program for a Christianismus renascens to which Zwingli was devoted along with other humanists before he came to Zurich. Already in 1518 Beatus Rhenanus complained to Zwingli about the "mere trifles" and the "ceremonies that do not pertain to the matter at hand." [10] The brevity and simplicity of Zwingli's rite derived in part from his desire to reproduce, as nearly as possible, the apostolic pattern.

Yet many of these ceremonies did go back to the early church, a fact of some embarrassment to Zwingli. He explained them as the trappings of paganism retained out of concern for tender consciences--precisely the same reason why substantial reform of baptism and the Mass had been delayed in Zurich until 1525. Still, this concession could not justify their continued usage: "Better to have abolished them entirely." [11]

In attacking the received baptismal tradition, Zwingli also disallowed the presumed salvific effect of the water. In June, 1523, he wrote to Thomas Wyttenbach: "You can wash an unbeliever a thousand times in the water of baptism, but unless he believes, it is in vain." [12] We touch here on one of the fundamental motifs in Zwingli's thought: the absolute separation between creature and Creator, a chasm which is deepened but not fundamentally altered by the condition of sin. No created thing can be a carrier of divine grace for the Spirit relates directly to the soul. It seemed preposterous to Zwingli, given his Neoplatonic-Stoic anthropology, that anything external, such as water, could effect an internal change. Sacraments have no power to cleanse the conscience; God alone can penetrate it. "How," he asked, "could water, fire, oil, milk, salt, and such crude things make their way to the mind?" [13]

A further, and more important, motive in Zwingli's critique of baptism was his fear that too much emphasis on the external rite would obscure the immediacy of God's grace in salvation. This soteriological concern was set forth in the third of the 67 Articles of January, 1523: "Christ is the only way to salvation for all who ever were, are and shall be." [14] If Christ is indeed der eynig Weg then there can be no salvation in external baptism. Zwingli draws this conclusion from the all-sufficiency of Christ's atoning death on the cross: "When he took upon himself the curse of the Law, Jesus Christ, the very Son of God, deprived us of all external justification . . . Christ abolished external things, so that we are not to hope in them or to look to them for justification." [15]

Zwingli felt that both the traditional emphasis on the opus operatum-character of baptism and the new-fangled Anabaptist exaltation of the sacrament denigrated the saving significance of Christ. Zwingli acutely observed that for many Anabaptists the act of rebaptism had taken the place of the sacrament of penance.

> They affirmed, however, that [in baptism] God had done something quite new towards them--the very experience which at one time we had in penance. For there, too, we were in great fear and distress before we made our confession: but the moment we had made it we said: God be praised, I feel a great joy and refreshing. [16]

For the Anabaptists it was indeed the adult's capacity to repent rather than to believe which formed the basis of their initial church-gathering (and also provided their strongest argument against infant baptism). But for Zwingli the whole experience smacked of a new legalism, a throwback to works-righteousness and monkish asceticism.

No one had taken a stronger stand for sola gratia than Luther, yet his sacramental realism seemed to run counter to his emphasis on the divine initiative in salvation. To be sure, he never lost the connection between baptism and faith, and Gott-schick was perhaps unfair in characterizing his later views on baptism as a reversion to a "medieval, magical way of thought." [17] Still, he did increasingly emphasize the inviolate connection between God and the material, sacramental signs. The baptismal water itself is no different from that with which a maid cooks, but once it is "sanctified" by the Word it becomes "a divine, heavenly, holy, and blessed water." In this sense faith "clings to the water and believes it to be a Baptism in which there is sheer salvation and life." [18] For Luther God is not only behind the sacramental signs, but in them as well. The water of baptism is thus "the true Aqua vitae," a "precious, sweetened water, Aromaticum and medicine [which] comes into existence because God himself is intermingled with it." [19] Karl Barth, in the tradition of Zwingli, speaks disparagingly of Luther's "Wassertheologie":

> To believe in Jesus Christ and in water consecrated by His presence is a dangerous thing and is not confirmed by any necessary relationship between the two. [20]

This was precisely Zwingli's fear: to focus on the external rite or the water was not only to elevate the creaturely to the level of the divine (idolatry); it was also to question the salvific suffi-ciency of Jesus Christ and to place an impediment in the way of grace (sacrilege). The work of God in salvation could not in any absolute way be tied to baptism as a medium salutis.

The primary soteriological significance of baptism in medieval theology was the removal of the guilt (culpa) of original sin though, of course, the tinderbox of concupiscence (fomes peccati) remained and would inevitably flare up into actual sins. Lutheran theologians also retained a connection between baptism and original sin. However, in keeping with Luther's doctrine of justification, for them baptism signified not so much the remission of original sin as its non-imputation. Both Melanchthon and Menius claimed that baptism removed the guilt of original sin in the sense that it was no longer computed against the individual who had been baptized. [21]

Zwingli admitted that he, too, had once harbored a similar

notion concerning baptism and original sin. "We also believed that the water of baptism cleanses children from a sin which they never had, and that without it they would be damned." [22] Zwingli claimed that this was one of the chief points which had been clarified for him by the controversy with the Anabaptists. We may assume, however, that his break with the traditional doctrine of original sin came even earlier. Erasmus's critique of the indelible "character" of baptism and his truncated doctrine of original sin may well have furnished the background for Zwingli's revisionist understanding, though his strong emphasis on personal accountability for sin probably owed more to his immersion in Pauline theology. [23]

Zwingli referred to original sin as a disparity or decrease, a fundamental breach in the natural order from which all suffering and mortality derived. He was far from approaching a Pelagian denial of original sin: he neither denied the seminal identity of the human race in Adam, nor the devastating effects of the Fall on each individual. There is within all persons an inclination to bestial ways, an apostasy from the divine (abfällig von der göttlichen) which issues in self-love and vices of every sort. [24] What Zwingli will not allow is the imputation of guilt before the conscious committal of sin.

> Original sin is a defect which is not of itself sinful for him who has it. This defect cannot condemn one--no matter what the theologians say--until he acts out of that defect against the law of God, and one can do that only if he knows the law. [25]

Zwingli's revised doctrine of original sin completely dissolves the necessity of baptism as the causa instrumentalis of regenerating grace. Again, Zwingli is concerned to safeguard the sufficiency and the uniqueness of Christ's atoning death on the cross. What was supposedly accomplished by the splashing of a little water at thousands of baptismal fonts throughout Christendom was in fact achieved once and for all by the sacrifice of Christ on the cross.

> So completely also did He obtain all things from the Father by His death that whatever we ask in His name is granted. Hence no created thing ought to be worshipped or held in such esteem as if it had any power for the cleansing of our consciences or the salvation of souls . . . Otherwise, the death of Christ were superfluous. [26]

Traditionally great care had been given to the "matter" of baptism, i.e. consecrated water, and to its "form," i.e. the Dominical words of institution. Zwingli betrays a studied nonchalance about these details. He criticizes those who stand in "awe of the water." [27] (As late as 1580 some church sextons were selling the baptismal water which was left over after the administration of the sacrament!) [28] It is a matter of little concern which words are used, for the apostles baptized only in the name of Jesus, without the full Trinitarian formula. Whether baptism was administered the first or the eighth day after birth was likewise adiaphorous, as was the mode of administration, although Zwingli seems to have preferred pouring. [29] Emergency baptisms were unnecessary and hence inappropriate. Zwingli's liturgical austerity derives from his belief in the immediacy of grace, understood as God's free and spontaneous favor, given by the Spirit alone without any material channel or vehicle,

> for He Himself is the virtue and energy whereby all things are borne, and has no need of being borne. [30]

THE SOVEREIGNTY OF THE SPIRIT

Zwingli discovered in the New Testament four distinct meanings of the word "baptism": water baptism, baptism of the Spirit, baptism of teaching, and baptism used as a short expression for the whole Christian economy. By far the most important of these is the baptism of the Spirit for without it no one at all could be saved. Zwingli defined this Spirit baptism as "the inward enlightenment and calling when we know God and cleave to him." [31] Baptism with the spirit is the unilateral act of God whereby individuals are drawn into the orbit of divine salvation. It is the means by which regeneration is effected, faith is begotten, and inclusion in the church as the one, holy, catholic, universal body of Christ is accomplished.

We have seen that Zwingli placed the sharpest distinction between this baptism and baptism with water. He found strong Scriptural support for his position in the very verse his opponents cited in favor of the indispensability of the latter, John 3:5: "Except a man be born of water and of the Spirit, he cannot enter into the kingdom of God." Luther's exposition of this text is typical: "For just as a child is drawn out of his mother's womb and is born . . . so one is drawn out of baptism and is born spiritually." [32] Zwingli argued that "water" in this verse did not mean material water at all for, as the next verse (John 3:6) teaches, material water cannot give birth to anything but material things. Rather, "water" here refers to that water which quickens the soul, which is nothing less than Christ himself who is the soul's only comfort and nourishment. Nor, Zwingli insisted, was he being fanciful in this exegesis. John the Baptist prophesied that Christ would baptize with the Holy Spirit and fire. Yet no one took him to mean material fire, except some Indian Christians who first baptize

with water and then burn a mark upon the head, perhaps a reference
to the baptismal ritual of the Malabar Church. [33]

To disclaim any correlation between water baptism and
baptism with the Spirit was to assert the sovereignty of God in
salvation. Not only was the Spirit not bound to external signs,
he was also free to bestow his gifts mysteriously and, from the
human point of view, indiscriminately: "God baptizes with His
Spirit how, whom, and when He will." [34] Zwingli belonged to
the radical Augustinian tradition which stressed predestination
and reprobation as gratuitous acts of the divine will. Zwingli
no less than Calvin believed in absolute, double predestination.
The reprobate no less than the elect are the objects of God's
will. Why did many who heard the gospel not believe? "Because
God did not move them inwardly: for he willed their rejection." [35]
However, Zwingli's emphasis on the freedom of the divine will
enabled him to contemplate the salvation of two groups which,
because deprived of water baptism, had generally been excluded
from eternal bliss: unbaptized children dying in infancy, and
the so-called "pious heathen" who were never exposed to the proclamation of the gospel.

From Augustine on the concept of a limbus infantium,
a form of modified damnation for children dying without the benefit
of baptism, played a central role in medieval eschatology. The
punishment of such unfortunates, Augustine conceded, was "omnium
mitissima": limbo was, so to speak, an air-conditioned compartment
of hell. Aquinas further speculated that children in this condition
could achieve a kind of natural happiness and even share to some
degree in the divine goodness. Still, they would forever be excluded
from the beatific vision. [36] By and large, the reformers abolished
limbo along with purgatory as a category of the afterlife. However,
the problem of infants dying without baptism still required some
explanation. Luther held out the possibility of salvation for unbaptized as well as for unborn infants. Concerning the latter, he
expressly forbade the (apparently common) custom of pouring
water onto the abdomen of a pregnant woman who threatened
miscarriage. Instead, the woman attending the mother should
commit the endangered infant to God who will doubtless receive
it for the sake of their prayers. [37] He also argued that, de
potentia absoluta, God was able to save infants who through the
neglect of their parents or some other mishap had not received
baptism. [38] Yet the church must be governed by God's potentia
ordinata and teach that without external baptism no one is saved.
The latter thought seems to be the dominant position for, in arguing
against the Anabaptists, he claimed that to keep infants from
baptism would make one responsible for "all the children who
were lost because they were unbaptized--a cruel and terrible
thing." [39]

In Zurich the death of unbaptized infants was first of all a serious pastoral concern. The custom had developed of burying unbaptized infants in a certain middle part of the cemetery, halfway between the profane and the holy ground--a vivid representation of limbo! Both Zwingli and Bullinger staunchly opposed this practice, urging that all children who died in infancy be given a full, Christian burial. [40] Zwingli is unequivocal about the children of Christian parents: they are saved whether baptized or not. Just as God's covenant of grace extended not only to Abraham but also to his seed, in like manner "our children are included in the covenant just as much as they were, for we are sons of the promise." [41] The basis of this inclusion is not the personal holiness of the parents, but the promise and election of God.

But what about the children of heathen parents who die in infancy, all of whom lack the rite of water baptism? Zwingli comes as close as possible to ascribing universal salvation to such infants, while in the end leaving the decision in the hands of God. If Adam's sin cannot be imputed for guilt to his adult descendants--"for who among us crushed with his teeth the forbidden apple in Paradise?"--how much less can it damn those who, by reason of their tender years, have never transgressed the law? [42] We must conclude that elect infants both within and outside of the pale of Christendom have experienced the inward baptism of the Holy Spirit whether or not they have received the outward rite. Whether this blessed number includes all who die in infancy or only those born of Christian parents remains a mystery for ultimately God's election is hidden from us.

Zwingli further held that even among heathen adults there were those chosen by God without benefit of the sacraments. They are our future neighbors in heaven; not only the Old Testament worthies but "Hercules too and Theseus, Socrates, Aristides, Antigonus, Numa, Camillus, the Catos and Scipios," indeed every pious heart and believing soul from the beginning of the world. [43] The presumed salvation of such heathen is not based on the universal revelation of God in nature nor on their own meritorious deeds, but rather on God's free decision to choose whom he will. Whether or not they ever come to faith in this life is a negligible consideration since faith follows election even as a blossom springs from a bud.

> For though those heathen knew not religion in the letter of it and in what pertains to the sacraments, yet as far as the real thing is concerned, I say, they were holier and more religious than all the little Dominicans and Franciscans that ever lived. [44]

By asserting so starkly the sovereignty of the Spirit Zwingli set himself against every form of sacramental imperialism.

His protest against baptismal regeneration was part of the general flight from secondary causality advanced by earlier theologians such as Thomas Bradwardine and Gregory of Rimini and reaffirmed no less strongly by John Calvin. This emphasis could well have led to the dissolution of external baptism altogether, as it did in certain radical reformers such as Caspar Schwenckfeld. That it did not is due to Zwingli's strong sense of the corporate nature of the visible church.

BAPTISM AS ECCLESIAL EVENT

Initiation and Identification. Zwingli defined a sacrament as an initiatory ceremony or pledge by which one was publicly bound to carry out the obligations of a certain office or order. Water baptism for him was essentially a human action made in response to God's prior act and word. By initiation he meant not simply a "beginning," but an induction into a new way of life. He drew out of his own experience two metaphors to describe the consignatio publica of water baptism. As the erstwhile novice at the Dominican monastery in Bern, he was well acquainted with the monastic rite of initiation. He compared baptism to the putting on of a monk's cowl: it signified a lifelong process of learning the rules and statutes of the order, of conformity to a distinct pattern of behavior. Again, as the veteran field chaplain of Swiss mercenary troops, he likened baptism to the white cross sewn onto the uniform of a confederate. Each year on the first Thursday in April the soldiers, clad in their white-crossed attire, gathered at Näfels to celebrate a military victory of their forebears and to declare their Swiss identity. Just so, baptism marked one off as a member of the militia Christi, a soldier of the gospel fighting under the direction of Christ the Captain. [45]

Neither the cowl nor the white cross imparted any special virtue or character to the one who wore them. They were public badges which identified one with a particular cause. Baptism is not primarily for the sake of the one who receives it; it is rather a guaranty for those who witness it. Its purpose is to inform the whole church rather than one's self of the faith which has been inwardly wrought by the baptism of the Holy Spirit. All the same, baptism with water does pledge the one who receives it to a lifelong mortification of the flesh. It is a testimony that one is now numbered among those who repent. It is our "visible (sichtbarlich) entry and sealing into Christ." [46] Still, the connection between baptism and repentance is of only marginal significance in Zwingli's baptismal theology. He never developed it as clearly nor as thoroughly as Luther.

Covenantal Continuity. Zwingli's description of water

baptism as a public pledge implied that it was applicable only to adults who could consciously make such a commitment. In fact, this is precisely what he seems to have believed in the early years of his reforming career in Zurich. He later admitted to having been "deceived" in believing that children should not be baptized until they came to the age of discretion. [47] Nor was he the only one to hold such an opinion. In the years before the Anabaptist crisis catapulted the issue onto a wholly different plane, Zwingli shared these doubts with several leading reformers including Erasmus, Farel, and Oecolampadius. [48] It is true that he never went so far as to advocate the abolition of infant baptism as the work of the devil, as did certain of his "green," inexperienced disciples.

Beginning in late 1524 Zwingli issued a series of writings in which he disabused himself of his earlier doubts about infant baptism, and defended the practice by means of a new argument: covenantal continuity between the people of Israel in the old dispensation and the visible church in the new. We can briefly identify three major strands in Zwingli's argument, each of which, with further elaboration by Bullinger and Calvin, became standard features in the Reformed doctrine of infant baptism. [49]

First, the analogy between circumcision and infant baptism: "baptismus sit Christianorum circumcisio." [50] This comparison was, of course, well worn by Patristic and medieval usage; Luther referred to it as well. No one, however, had developed it as thoroughly as Zwingli. The bloody Old Testament rites of circumcision and passover had been replaced by two "gentler" sacraments, baptism and the Lord's Supper. Baptism is gentler in another respect as well--it extends to female infants not just to boys, although even in the former dispensation the girls received the figure of baptism in passing through the Red Sea. We have seen already that Zwingli related election to infant baptism: salvation is assured for all children of Christian parents who die in infancy. He went so far as to claim that had Esau died as a baby, he would have been elect! Since Christian children so obviously belong to God, how can they be denied the sign of this belonging? Circumcision was not only a sign of Abraham's faith, but of the whole content of the covenant which God concluded with him and his seed. In this age water baptism is the external, collective sign of the New Israel, the church.

Secondly, Christian baptism derives not from the baptismal command of Matthew 28, but from the baptism of John the Baptist. Jesus submitted himself both to circumcision and the baptism of John, though of course he needed neither, thereby joining the rites of the two dispensations and signifying that they were of equal value. Medieval Catholicism, Anabaptism, and Luther agreed-- though for very different reasons--in drawing a sharp distinction between the baptisms of Jesus and John. [51] Zwingli, too, had formerly supposed the two baptism to be quite different. His new insight was based on the conviction that Scripture discloses not two covenants in which God acts differently for our salvation, but rather one covenant in two dispensations. The baptisms of the church and John are precisely the same because the gospel he preached is the very one we proclaim: "Behold, the Lamb of God who takes away the sins of the world!"

Thirdly, while the New Testament does not command infant baptism expressis verbis, it can be inferred from various passages. Zwingli cited the embrace of little children by Christ (Luke 18:15-17), household baptisms in Acts and the epistles, and the fact that Christ nowhere commanded infants not to be baptized as probable indications that the New Testament church practiced infant baptism. At points he appears to be skating on pretty thin exegetical ice, as in his surmise that John baptized infants in the Jordan, or his claim that the disciples of John who sought rebaptism (Acts 19) had only received a baptism of "teaching" not of water. Long ago, in his seminal study on Zwingli's doctrine of baptism, Usteri observed that whenever Zwingli had in mind adult baptism, he would quote copiously from the New Testament. But the moment he began to defend infant baptism, he would fall back on the argument from circumcision. [52] He could only secure the objectivity of infant baptism in the context of the unity of the covenant.

Baptism and Faith. We have seen that for Zwingli faith is the gift of the Holy Spirit and has no intrinsic connection with water baptism. Yet in the New Testament water baptism is invariably associated with faith; all doctrines of infant baptism must come to grips with the relation between the two. Luther toyed with the idea that the faith of the sponsors sufficed for the child, but abandoned this view of a fides vicaria for a full-blown doctrine of infant faith.

> A child becomes a believer if Christ in baptism speaks
> to him through the mouth of the one who baptizes, since
> it is his Word, his commandment, and his word cannot
> be without fruit. [53]

The fact that the intellective processes of the infant are in abeyance is no hindrance to the impartation of faith; if anything, it is easier for an infant to receive faith since whorish reason is not as likely to get in the way!

Zwingli will have none of this idea of an infant faith. "Baptism cannot confirm faith in infants because infants are not able to believe." [54] In Zwingli's baptismal liturgy of 1525, faith is mentioned only once, in the so-called "Flood Prayer" where the minister names the baptizand, and prays God to kindle "the light of faith in his heart whereby he may be incorporate into thy Son." [55] When and how the Spirit may choose to impart this faith to the individual being baptized is impertinent to the rite itself.

Zwingli did, however, place great store in the personal faith of the parents who offered the child for baptism. The whole concept of the covenant as the visible manifestation of God's purpose in history hinged on the fact that these were children of Christian parents. Only parents who were conscious participants in the covenanted community should present their infants for baptism: "We do not allow children to be brought to baptism unless their parents have first been taught." [56] The parents made a confession on behalf of their child, by proxy as it were, and the church accepted this confession presuming, in the judgment of charity, that the infant is truly elect. For Zwingli, though, the faith of the parents is secondary to the faith of the whole church. This is why he frowns on private baptisms and insists that baptism be administered "in the presence of the church" by a duly appointed minister of the Word. "The recipient of baptism testifies that he belongs to the Church of God, which worships its Lord in soundness of faith and purity of life." [57] Infant baptism is essentially an ecclesial event. The kind of faith which it presupposes is not the personal, subjective faith of the infants or the parents (fides qua creditur), but the whole content of the Christian message (fides quae creditur).

Baptism and the Social Order. In his **In catabaptistarum strophas elenchus** (1527) Zwingli summed up in one phrase his great fear of the Anabaptist movement: "They overturn everything." [58] Already in 1524 he had discerned that the real danger from the Anabaptists was not so much heresy as schism and sedition. Increasingly infant baptism came to be the fulcrum on which both the unity of the church and the integrity of the civic order turned. In 1526 Zwingli persuaded the Zurich Council to establish a Taufregister in every parish. This device, together with the decision to expel those citizens who refused to submit their infants for baptism, enabled the magistrates to make of infant baptism an instrument for political conformity. This policy went hand in glove with Zwingli's program of reform which presupposed the identity of the visible church with the populace of the Christian city or state: "a Christian city is nothing other than a Christian church." [59] The Christian civitas might be a corpus permixtum of sheep and goats, God alone knowing for sure who was which, but it could not be a company of baptized and unbaptized lest the civic order itself, and the proclamation of the gospel which depended upon it, be imperiled. It is ironic that water baptism which played at best an adiaphorous role in Zwingli's soteriology became the basis for his defence of the visible church.

CONCLUSION

Karl Barth once said concerning Zwingli's understanding of baptism: "Among his contemporaries he was a lonely figure." [60] We have noted several points at which his doctrine departed sharply from that of Luther. This difference persisted even after the Marburg Colloquy where the two reformers supposedly agreed on fourteen of the fifteen articles including one on baptism. However, Zwingli's marginal notes on this article reveal a continuing suspicion of Luther's sacramental realism. [61]

Zwingli's doctrine of baptism must also be marked off from later developments in the Reformed tradition. It is hardly conceivable that Zwingli would have endorsed the statement of the Second Helvetic Confession (1566) that to be baptized is "to be purged from the filthiness of sins, and to be endued with the manifold grace of God," much less John Knox's dictum: "We assuredly believe that by baptism we are engrafted in Christ Jesus, to be made partakers of his justice, by which our sins are covered and remitted." [62] Both of these statements represent the victory of Calvin's cognitive sacramentalism and his effort to lessen the separation of sign and thing signified. In his posthumously published **Exposition of the Faith** Zwingli himself seemed to be moving in this direction when he allowed that the sacraments could augment faith and recall the Christian to a deeper obedience and contemplation. [63]

The development of Zwingli's baptismal theology followed the course of his work as a reformer. If he seemed to undervalue water baptism as a salvific sign, he rallied to its defence as an indispensable symbol of ecclesial unity. We may applaud the later Reformed tradition for recovering a more incarnational theology of the sacraments, but Zwingli's appeal to the apriority and freedom of divine grace stands as a needed warning against every form of institutional idolatry.

NOTES

1. Z VI, 43, This incident is vividly retold by Fritz Blanke, **Brothers in Christ**, tr. Joseph Nordenhaug (Scottdale, PA: Herald Press, 1961), 60-65.

2. The decree was passed on March 7, 1526: **Quellen zur Geschichte der Täufer in der Schweiz**, eds. Leonhard von Muralt and Walter Schmid (Zurich: S.

Hirzel, 1952), I, 180-181. The severity of the decree is hardly mitigated by G. R. Potter's reminder that, after all, "the Anabaptists tended to rejoice in martyrdom," **Zwingli** (Cambridge: Cambridge University Press, 1976), 187.

3. The most complete study of Zwingli's baptismal theology remains Johannes Martin Usteri, "Darstellung der Tauflehre Zwinglis," **Theologische Studien und Kritiken** 55, No. 2 (1882), 205-284. Cf. also L. G. M. Alting von Geusau, **Die Lehre von der Kindertaufe bei Calvin** (Bilthoven: Uitgeverij H. Nelissen, 1963), 49-57, and John H. Yoder, **Täufertum und Reformation im Gespräch** (Zurich: EVZ Verlag, 1968), 13-42.

4. Z IV, 216, Unless otherwise noted I follow the translation of this treatise in LCC XXIV.

5. Ibid., 130. WA 6:526, cf. LW 36:57. In a later writing Luther lists "true baptism" as one of the benefits of Christ still present in the papal church: WA 26, 147.

6. WA 26, 173: "Denn die Sacramenter machen die tauffe ganz zu nicht."

7. Z IV, 247.

8. Z IV, 334-337. Zwingli's baptismal order is given in parallel columns with those of Jud and Luther in Fritz Schmidt-Clausing, **Zwingli als Liturgiker** (Göttingen: Vandenhoeck and Ruprecht, 1952), 143-165. Cf. also J. D. C. Fisher, **Christian Initiation: The Reformation Period** (London: S.P.C.K., 1970), 126-131.

9. **Creeds of the Churches**, ed. John H. Leith (Atlanta: John Knox Press, 1982), 129-130.

10. Z VII, 115. Cf. Charles Garside's discussion of this letter with reference to Zwingli's attitude toward church music, **Zwingli and the Arts** (New Haven: Yale University Press, 1966), 34-39.

11. Z IV, 247.

12. Z VIII, 85.

13. Z III, 759; Latin Works III, 181. Unless otherwise noted I follow the translation in **Latin Works.** On Zwingli's anthropological dualism see Christ of Gestrich, **Zwingli als Theologe: Glaube und Geist beim Zürcher Reformator** (Zurich: Zwingli Verlag, 1967), 25-27.

14. Z II, 30, "Dannen har der eynig Weg zur Säligkeit Christus ist aller, die ie warend, sind oder werdend."

15. Z IV, 216-217.

16. Z IV, 253.

17. D. J. Gottschick, **Die Lehre der Reformation von der Taufe** (Tübingen, 1906), 14. But cf. Adolf von Harnack's view: "In the doctrine of the sacraments Luther abandoned his position as a Reformer, and was guided by views that brought confusion into his own system of faith," **History of Dogma**, tr. Neil Buchanan (New York: Dover, 1961), 248.

18. "The Large Catechism of Dr. Martin Luther," in **The Book of Concord**, ed. Theodore G. Tappert (Philadelphia: Fortress Press, 1959), 438, 440.

19. WA 52, 102.

20. Karl Barth, **The Teaching of the Church Regarding Baptism**, tr. Ernest A. Payne (London: SCM Press, 1948), 23. Significantly, Barth characterizes his own baptismal theology as "Neo-Zwinglian" although he adds the disclaimer that he attempts "to understand Zwingli better than he understood himself or could make himself understood." **Church Dogmatics** IV/4, 130.

21. Cf. the helpful discussion in Alfred Vanneste, **De dogme du péché originel** (Louvain-Paris: Nauwelaerts, 1971). For Melanchthon and Menius, see John S. Oyer, **Lutheran Reformers Against Anabaptists** (The Hague: Martinus Nijhoff, 1964), 149-150, 186-189.

22. Z IV, 247.

23. This is the argument of Rudolf Pfister, **Das Problem der Erbsünde bei Zwingli** (Leipzig, 1939), and is supported by Gottfried W. Locher, **Zwingli's Thought: New Perspective** (Leiden: E. J. Brill, 1981), 53-54, 202-208.

24. Z IV, 197.

25. Z IV, 308.

26. Latin Works II, 30, 27.

27. Z III, 760.

28. Werner Elert, **The Structure of Lutheranism**, tr. Walter A. Hansen (St. Louis: Concordia, 1962), 296 fn. 9.

29. LW 35, 29 fn. 2. Bullinger allows sprinkling or dipping in accordance with the custom of the local church: **Sermons on the Sacraments** (Cambridge: Cambridge University Press, 1840), 155-156.

30. Latin Works II, 46.

31. Z IV, 219.

32. LW 35, 30.

33. Z IV, 251. How Zwingli would have known of this practice remains a mystery. The note in the critical edition lists several possibilities.

34. Z IV, 221.

35. Latin Works II, 186-187; Z IV, 262.

36. Augustine, **De peccatorum meritis et remissione**, I, 16 (PL 44, col. 120); Aquinas, **In Lib.** II **Sententiarum**, dist. 33, q. 2, art. 2.

37. WATR 6, No. 6763.

38. WA 43, 71; LW 3, 274.

39. WA 26, 166; LW 40, 254.

40. Z II, 455-456; Bullinger, **Sermons on the Sacraments**, 171-172.

41. Latin Works II, 21.

42. Latin Works II, 40.

43. Latin Works II, 272.

44. Latin Works II, 201.

45. Z IV, 231, 218. Significantly, Erasmus too compared baptism to military initiation: "If anyone through baptism becomes a soldier of Christ, it is just to fight with good faith under his standards." **Desiderii Erasmi Roterodami opera omnia** (Hildesheim, 1962), V, col. 934.

46. Z IV, 244.

47. Z IV, 228: "Denn der irrtumb hat ouch mich vor etwas jaren verfurt, das ich meint, es wäre vil wäger, man touffte die kindle erst, so sy zu gutem alter komen wärend." Cf. Hubmaier's reminder to Zwingli that "in the year 1523, on the day of Philip and Jacob, I personally conferred with you on Graben Street concerning the scriptural teaching on baptism. Then and there you said I was right to hold that children should not be baptized until they were instructed in the faith." **Balthasar Hubmaier, Schriften**, eds. Gunnar Westin and Torsten Bergsten, **Quellen zur Geschichte der Täufer**, IX, 186.

48. Erasmus held that baptism might be postponed until adolescence at the discretion of the parents: **Opus epistolarum Des. Erasmi Roterodami**, eds. P. S. Allen, H. M. Allen (Oxford, 1906-1957), X, no. 2853, 39-42. For Oecolampadius see Z IV, 195-196; for Farel, **Correspondence des Réformateurs dans les Pays de langue française**, ed. A. -L. Herminjard (Geneva and Paris, 1866-1897), II, 48. Cf. also the article on "Guillaume Farel," in **Mennonite Encyclopedia**, II, 301.

49. The originality of Zwingli's covenantal theology has been challenged, but see the authoritative study of Jack Cottrell, "Covenant and Baptism in the Theology of Huldreich Zwingli," unpublished Th.D. dissertation, Princeton University, 1971. J. Wayne Baker, **Heinrich Bullinger and the Covenant** (Athens, Ohio: Ohio University Press, 1980), 1–25, has demonstrated that Bullinger differed from Zwingli in stressing more fully the soteriological unity and bilateral nature of the covenant.

50. Z VIII, 271.

51. Cf. David Steinmetz, "The Baptism of John and the Baptism of Jesus in Huldrych Zwingli, Balthasar Hubmaier and Late Medieval Theology," in **Continuity and Discontinuity in Church History: Essays Presented to George Huntston Williams on the Occasion of his 65th Birthday**, eds. F. F. Church and Timothy George (Leiden: E. J. Brill, 1979), 169–181.

52. Usteri, "Darstellung," 225.

53. LW 40, 245–246; WA 26, 159.

54. Z IV, 228. Cf. also Z V, 649.

55. Fisher, **Christian Initiation**, 130.

56. Z IV, 238. Cf. Bullinger's view: "It is lawful to require faith of them that are baptized of perfect age, or else of them which bring the infants to be baptized." **Sermons on the Sacraments**, 149.

57. Latin Works II, 48.

58. Z VI, 46: "Omnia turbant inque pessimum statum commutant."

59. Z XIV, 424. Cf. the excellent analysis of Robert C. Walton, "The Institutionalization of the Reformation at Zurich," **Zwingliana** 13 (1972), 497–515.

60. **Church Dogmatics** IV/4, 128.

61. Cf. Susi Hausammann, "Die Marburger Artikel--eine echte Konkordie?" Zeitschrift für Kirchengeschichte 77 (1966), 288–321.

62. **Creeds of Christendom**, ed. Philip Schaff (New York: Harper and Bros., 1877), III, 290, 468.

63. To be sure, this is a small step toward any kind of sacramental mysticism. Locher is surely right in denying that the phrase "water rich in grace," found in the Zurich Church Order of 1532, could have come from Zwingli's pen. **Zwingli's Thought**, 218 fn. 331.

EXEGETICAL PROJECTS AND PROBLEMS:
A NEW LOOK AT AN UNDATED LETTER
FROM BUCER TO ZWINGLI

Gerald Hobbs

I

The correspondence of the evangelical reformers of the upper Rhine valley, even in its imperfect state of survival, offers interesting insight into their activity as biblical teachers and commentators. In Basel, Zurich, and Strasbourg, the leaders of the Reform movements were among the best-equipped biblical scholars of their generation. Given in addition their ideological commitment to the authority of Scripture in the church, it is not surprising to find them engaged in public lectures of serious scholarly merit on the biblical text. In Basel, this could find its natural setting within the university, where Konrad Pellican and Johannes Oecolampadius taught Old and New Testament respectively. In the other two cities, a framework had to be developed within which a largely, albeit not exclusively, clerical audience could acquire some of the exegetical skills desirable in the Reformed preacher. [1]

The desire to give more permanent form to the fruits of these labors as well as the hope of access to a wider public, stimulated the transformation of these lectures into published commentary. Further, this wider audience encouraged an increasing sophistication of method; it meant the facing of traditional problems that had confronted earlier exegetes in the same texts, and inevitably, disagreements over the resolution of these issues. The commentaries themselves afford lively glimpses into contemporary debates, for those able to read between the lines. [2] The same themes are picked up and aired in the correspondence.

Such concern for the substance of the letter of Martin Bucer to Zwingli which, edited by Walter Köhler, appears as document 871 in the Zwingli Briefwechsel. [3] The original of the letter, which is undated, is in the Zurich Staatsarchiv (E II 339). Following the lead of Schuler and Schulthess, [4] Köhler assigned it to the beginning of July, 1529. [5] The year is certainly correct, as we shall see; but close examination of the letter's contents within the framework of the exegetical activity of both author and recipient, as well as within the sequence of their correspondence, makes imperative the ante-dating of this ascription by about three months, to late March or early April. Located properly, the letter casts interesting light upon the exegetical labors and concerns of Zwingli and Bucer, and shows the degree to which these were shared between exegetes of the two cities.

The following discussion will demonstrate what I believe to be compelling reasons for the redating of this document. In view of the intrinsic interest of the text, and to facilitate understanding of the argument of this paper we begin with a translation of the letter in question.

II

Greetings in the Lord, respected Zwingli! [6]

[i] I have sampled your Isaiah during one evening. Christopher [7] has promised that upon his return from Frankfurt he will leave with us whatever portion he brings back with him; from which I shall derive great pleasure as well as benefit. For I certainly disapprove of that practice, more superstitious than scrupulous, of translating the Scriptures word for word, viz., in such a way that they are incomprehensible to everyone. Of course those desirous of coming to a sure judgment ought to consult the sources themselves; but what of those for whom this is not possible? Is it not better that some part at least of the sacred texts be understood properly, rather than none at all? If the translation is made according to sense, the translator may here and there intrude something of his own thought; but if he slavishly clings to the letter, [8] the result is utter nonsense, and the readers are left to invent meanings for themselves, which rarely, as experience has shown, conform to the proper sense.

[ii] For my part, with what small talent I possess I have attempted the same thing as you, but in the Psalms. Moved by the brothers and sisters of France and Lower Germany, I have decided to issue a commentary on the Psalms, using a different name so that the work may be purchased by booksellers there. For it is a capital offence to import volumes bearing our names into those regions. So I pretend to be a Frenchman, and take pains

to put across the truth in the various commonplaces under the authority of the Fathers--admittedly stuffing in a good deal out of context! Unless I change my mind, I will make it the work of one "Aretius Felinus," which is, for that matter, my name in Greek and surname in Latin. [9]

I intend three things by this subterfuge: first of all, to encourage by this means a more genuine method of biblical interpretation among those sisters and brothers in captivity; secondly, to take away that inopportune sense of alienation they feel with respect to the dogmas of our religion, as well as that barbarous frenzy for ranting and raving [10] in such things that has been introduced by the Lutherans; and thirdly, that from this these folk may be the more surely confirmed by these sacred consolations in the persecution which they are undergoing. For this reason, too, I have undertaken to expound everything in great detail in the first section; the remainder will be more concise.

When you have the time, I beg you to do me the kindness of sampling one or two of the psalms, and of drawing to my attention as soon as you can, those ways in which I can make the work of greater benefit. Only twenty-two psalms have been printed to date, which portion I am sending you. Many of those that remain to be done are on similar themes. It will therefore be possible to emend and repair what is amiss in the part not yet printed. Likewise, should you find ill-advised my decision to publish these, let me know at once. For I have no other purpose than to be of service. Now I know how much the Lord has given you, to despise whatever is of this character!

I hear that you are already at work on the Psalms. The advice I am looking for with respect to my own commenting upon them will therefore be neither far removed from your own pursuits nor an extra burden.

On other matters, Christopher will give you a full account. Farewell, and press vigorously on in advancing the kingdom of Christ and shedding light on the Scriptures. For you have received great gifts to which ours cannot compare; we simply do what we can.

[iii] The wickedness of the Catabaptists has compelled our Senate to take somewhat harsher measures against them. There Satan has been confounded in wretched fashion. For only the pain of exile has softened the steel of certain ones, while for others it was a sojourn in harsher confinement. Those whom admonitions proffered in friendship and drawn from Holy Writ have always rendered more fierce were tamed by the abrupt sentence of the Magistrate: Become an exile! I dispatch you to

the lower dungeon! Hitherto the eyes of many have been blinded by the slightly more rigorous words of these persons and by their melancholic tears, [11] which have furnished material for Satan's mockery. But we must be troubled in this way, so that we finally realize that there are also spiritual evils, more terrible than those that merely touch the body. [12]

Farewell. Greet the brothers, and ask Pellican for what sin I am being punished in having no reply to so many letters. What I have written concerning my plan for issuing a Psalter, I write for you alone.

M. Bucerus

[Overleaf] To Huldreich Zwingli, most faithful and watchful pastor of Zurich, and honored preceptor.

III

The year 1529 saw an important development in the exegetical work of both Zwingli and Bucer. The months between the Diet of Speyer (March-April) and the Marburg Colloquy (October 1-3), charged with a flurry of activity whose goal was the realization of a common theological and diplomatic front among territories and cities embracing evangelical Reform, also saw the appearance of a major Old Testament commentary by each: Zwingli's **Isaiah** [13] and Bucer's **Psalms.** [14]

In the case of Zwingli, this was his first formal biblical commentary, although previous biblical lectures had appeared in print through the labors of Zurich colleagues. [15] It was also to prove his most substantial contribution to exegesis. There is no indication whether, when the Zurich Prophezei turned to the interpretation of Isaiah on September 2nd, 1527, Zwingli had this end already in view. That study in the Prophezei just completed (February 27th, 1528), he launched, as was his custom, into a series of sermons on the same texts in the Grossmünster which lasted until Christmas week 1528. [16] In these, according to one listener, Zwingli stressed the present-day relevance of the prophetic note of judgment upon those who failed to heed the divine Word.

Our Zwingli cries out faithfully, anxiously and constantly; he rages with great distress indeed but with less result against the ancient vices. Moved by the Spirit he has begun Isaiah. I fear, after the prophecies of Isaiah and Jeremiah, that captivity is imminent for us; for even so God is wont to bring his judgments upon those who have been forwarned! Yet meanwhile we always hope for better things. [17]

From this period comes the first mention of a projected commentary. In a letter, now lost, to Wolfgang Capito of Strasbourg, probably written in early summer 1528, Zwingli apparently included within a discussion of issues arising from the exegetical labors of the Strasbourgers, advance notice of his own "planing smooth" (complanatio) of the prophet. [18] Capito, Gaspar Hedio and Bucer all replied encouragingly; [19] and the latter spread the word among friends of its imminent appearance. [20] This was somewhat premature, and caused mutual embarrassment; for it was not until the 9th of December, 1528, that Zwingli reported to Vadian that at last a part of the work was in press:

> Our **Isaiah** is now groaning under the press. It can expect the attacks of the ignorant--even the fate of Hippolytus' chariot [21]--when it appears, unless things turn out better than Pellican predicts they will (although he himself approves the work). [22]

With due allowance for humanist hyperbole, it is clear that Zwingli was concerned for the reception of his work. Pellican, veteran of Erasmus' campaigns against scholastic opponents of humanist biblical scholarship (as these "ignorant" persons of Zwingli's letter are probably to be understood) could rightly anticipate that a departure from the received translation as radical as that of Zwingli's "planed and smooth" rendering would certainly arouse opposition. Indeed, when the volume eventually went to press, Zwingli yielded to Pellican's concern, and had his new translation printed in parallel columns with the traditional version "of Jerome." [23] For his part, Pellican furnished a letter of commendation "to the pious and learned reader," which was printed at the conclusion of the commentary. In it he gave elegant praise to Zwingli's demonstration of the faith, gift of languages, scholarship, discernment, modesty and wisdom requisite in a biblical commentator. [24]

The completion of the volume took another six months, judging from the dates of the preface (May 22) and the dedicatory epistle to the cities of the Swiss evangelical coalition (July 15, 1529). [25] In all likelihood it first appeared before the public in its entirety in Christoph Froschauer's stalls at the Frankfurt autumn fair of 1529. Meanwhile, on his way to the Easter fair in mid-March, Froschauer paused in Strasbourg with the usual correspondence, [26] and showed the Strasbourgers a sample of the work. On March 15th, Capito sends Zwingli a mixed reaction:

> We have seen a sample of your **Isaiah**, and approve it. I beg you however not to neglect too much the commentaries of the Hebrews, which maintain extremely well that simplicity of spirit that is your own as well. [27]

This gentle reminder to Zwingli of the merits of medieval rabbinic commentaries was not particularly appreciated in Zurich, to judge from Capito's subsequent qualifications and retractions. [28] On the question of the value of Jewish exegesis for the interpretation of the Old Testament Zurich and Strasbourg remained in friendly disagreement. In this case, however, the apparent sensitivity of the subject is probably the aftermath of the vigorous and at times sharp debate of 1528 that had pitted Capito and Martin Cellarious against Bucer and the Zurichers, on the question, amongst others, of the eventual return of the Jews to Palestine. [29]

The comments contained in the letter from Bucer that is our present concern will have been more welcome to Zwingli. This letter touches upon several matters of interest; three of these shall briefly retain our attention here.

In the first place, although Bucer shared as a rule Capito's predilection for rabbinic commentaries and would give them a large place in his own **Psalms**, [30] he breathes not a word of criticism on that score. Instead, he chooses to offer encouragement to Zwingli's decision to translate freely, according to sense, rather than to remain attached to the letter of the original. Behind Bucer's opening paragraph lies an old controversy concerning the nature of translation, and particularly of biblical translation. [31] St. Jerome, patron and prince of biblical translators, had left an ambiguous heritage to his successors in the field. In his best-known statement on the subject, the <u>Letter to Pammachius on the best kind of translation</u>, Jerome had cited approvingly the dicta of Cicero and of Horace against slavish emulation of the original. To these, however, Jerome prefaced a key qualification -

> save in holy Scripture, where the word order also contains a mystery. [32]

This rigid circumscription of the role of the "faithful translator" (<u>fidus interpres</u>) of Scripture could only encourage the practice of literalism; and such characterizes the work of the mediaevals, as well as of early 16th century scholars like Sanctes Pagnini, whose complete Latin Bible appeared in 1528 [33]-- although in Pagnini's defence one must add that he did permit himself on occasion to paraphrase for the sake of sense. Closer to home, literalism was very much the hallmark of the translation of Isaiah which accompanied the 1525 commentary by Bucer and Zwingli's Basel colleague, Johannes Oecolampadius. [34] The latter indeed argued for the utility of such a rendering even when it contained barbarous solecisms, for persons making a beginning in the Hebrew tongue.

> Once upon a time I thought that Jerome had translated the entire Old Testament according to the Hebrew truth.

But in fact--though how it came about I am unaware--we have a great deal from the Septuagint stuck in [our Latin Bible] in place of the Hebrew.

Accordingly, since a number of my listeners had begun Hebrew studies, I wished to be content with the Hebrew text, and be tied to no other translation; even though I did not despise the others, but consulted and even on occasion adduced them by way of commentary. For this same reason, anywhere that idioms of the Hebrew people sounding somewhat harsh in Latin have been retained, this was deliberate, consideration having been taken of the students who might thereby read Hebrew more easily; and wherever the examination of the individual words is anxiously sought, the proper signification of the words is manifestly at hand.

On the other hand, as far as pertains to the elegance of the Latin or German language, one may hope that even as I think that I have satisfactorily fulfilled my office if I am not convicted of having been an unfaithful translator, so others endowed with more and varied gifts of the Holy Spirit particularly for this type of translation will thus render with fidelity the lively fulness of the speech according to its tropes. [35]

In his desire not to give offense unnecessarily, Bucer does not mention their mutual friend by name; yet there can be no doubt that the practice of Oecolampadius (amongst others) is in mind. Both here, and in his more fully developed statement that prefaces his **Psalms,** [36] Bucer brings considerations both pastoral and theological to respond to the argument of Oecolampadius for literal translation. For Bucer, the translator must have primary concern for those who have no access to the Hebrew original--not for students of Hebrew. If simple, unlearned Christians are to fulfill their responsibility to judge the meaning of Scripture for themselves, [37] they must be served with a rendering whose sense is readily apparent. Failing this, they will perforce fall into all sorts of interpretations invented without foundation in the proper sense of the passage. Here Bucer is certainly thinking of the (to his mind) perverse readings of Scripture prevalent among many radical groups as well as of the more fanciful allegories of mediaeval exegetes. Rather than this outcome, better let the translator rely upon the promised gifts of the Spirit--the charismata of the knowledge of tongues and of prophecy--and render clearly the sense as he discerns it.

Bucer's words strike a common chord with the sentiments of Zwingli as these are expressed at some length in his preface to the Isaiah. There the reference to the work of Oecolampadius is made explicit.

After these [the Septuagint and Jerome], Oecolampadius
(a man in every respect more perfected than is the common opinion) has also given us an Isaiah, one so illuminated
with commentary that as far as pertains to the sense
and the comparison of the sacred text, no work has
ever issued from anyone which can with equal right be
termed a cornu copiae. But he has left the speech itself
of the prophet, and the expression of the Hebrew tongue
to be smoothed out (complanandum) by others in the
Latin tongue, either because the occasion required this
for the reason that up till the present the novices in
the sacred tongue were more inexperienced, or because
the superstition of some persons dared to be more undeservedly angered when word did not correspond to word,
even if nothing was wanting for the sense . . . Thanks
to God, who has given us these teachers [Jerome and
Oecolampadius], by whose labor we have been both stimulated and helped. so that we might translate more collo-
quially and popularly for the general good of all, those
things that they were unwilling to say more plainly, being
held back by scruple. Not that we disagree with them,
but that we speak more in the language of the people . . .
[38]

It is the overscrupulous respect for the letter of the
Hebrew that has engendered confusion; to this are attributable
the rise of theological definitions having no basis in Scripture,
foolish allegories to make sense of nonsense, and much attendant
strife. In the light of the needs of the age, and the practice of
so many commentators, Zwingli has concluded it would be worth-
while "to render for students of sacred letters that sense plain
and obvious which I believe to be the certain and unquestionable
meaning of the prophecies of Isaiah." [39]

From this subject Bucer makes a natural transition to
his own exegetical project, the **Psalms**. The volume is well under-
way, twenty-two of the Psalms having already been printed; and
a copy of these is being sent to Zwingli together with this letter.
Knowing that Zwingli himself is treating the Psalms in the Prophezei, Bucer feels less reticent about soliciting his colleague's
comment upon his work. From the concluding remarks, it would
seem that Pellican, too, has been approached for advice. Bucer
is making his first major venture into Old Testament exegesis;
his only previous publication in Hebrew Scriptures was a commentary
on the minor prophet Zephaniah, (fall, 1528), which he had undertaken as a limited trial run before tackling the more formidable
Psalter. [40] We should therefore take his request for Zwingli's
advice at face value. His will be the first commentary on the
full Psalter by an evangelical Hebraist; [41] if there are manifest
errors or omissions, if his interpretation is off course in any area,

there will be opportunities yet for corrections and redirection in the large number of Psalms yet to be printed. In Zwingli's **Isaiah**, as noted above, his new translation of the entire prophetic book is printed in parallel columns with Jerome's at the beginning of the volume--a prudent concession to tradition--separated by his introductory apologia from the body of the commentary. In the case of Bucer's **Psalms**, however, translation is integrated with commentary, the new paraphrastic rendering appearing at the head of each Psalm. Thus if changes to the first twenty-odd psalms would now be difficult, there were numerous opportunities to alter both translation and commentary in psalms of similar theme occuring later in the volume.

In our letter, Bucer gives considerable space to an explanation of his motivation and consequent decision to issue the volume pseudonomously. The Gallican mask that Bucer will adopt--with considerable success as it turned out--for the purpose of evangelical propaganda in that kingdom and elsewhere, is only the latest manifestation of a longstanding interest for the church in France and its reform in faithfulness to the Gospel. [42] His earliest translations of Luther, as well as his Synoptics commentary of 1527, bear dedicatory references to French evangelicals. [43] Zwingli, too, was not unmoved by the French connection; two of his more systematic theological treatises were addressed to Francis I, in whom he like other evangelicals of the 1520's apparently set what turned out to be unrealistically high hopes. [44]

From even before the 1524-25 sojourn of Lefèvre d'Etaples and Gerard Roussel in Strasbourg, there was a lively interest in French evangelicalism in the city; and it was these correspondents who most consistently admonished of the noxious effects for the evangelical cause of the Supper strife. [45] We find a reflection of this in Bucer's censure in our letter of the evangelical in-house quarreling over points of doctrine. The modern reader may find this somewhat ironic, evidence of a belated conversion, on the lips of one who had played so prominent a part in the public acrimony. One is not surprised to discover that it is the Lutherans who must bear principal responsibility for troubling the peace of Israel! [46] Nonetheless, the choice of pseudonimity is recognition by Bucer that the ink spilled between himself and both Luther and Bugenhagen has given him a sectarian image, and that the commentary will find much wider readership if Bucer's association with it is not suspected, both among evangelical partisans and those still firmly attached to Roman obedience.

The claim by Bucer that the booksellers of France and the Low Countries face the supreme penalty for importing the works of known evangelicals is difficult to substantiate. Royal and imperial decrees which menace with severe punishment those printing or selling heretical literature are known from 1521 on. [47]

But the capital penalty does not seem to have been imposed on a bookseller in either realm before 1529, although such is known to have occurred elsewhere, for example in the ancestral Hapsburg lands. [48] On the other hand, there had been several executions for heresy in France, and notably in the Low Countries under the regency of Marguerite of Austria; and unauthorized possession of proscribed heretical texts was prima facie evidence of heresy. [49] From his French correspondents moreover, Bucer may have been aware of the slender thread by which the life of Louis Berquin was maintained. Royal favor failed in fact to rescue this imprudent "Lutheran" from the stake on April 17, 1529, following his third trial for heresy. [50]

Apparently as an afterthought, Bucer adds a report on the latest stage in the struggle of preachers and magistrates with the radical Anabaptist element in Strasbourg. Although several confrontations between Bucer and his colleagues on the one hand, and various radical elements on the other had occurred in the period 1526-28, and one Thomas Saltzmann was beheaded for denial of the trinity and the divinity of Christ in 1527, [51] in general the magistrates had taken a soft line with these opponents of the city preachers. [52] The definitive vote by the Council on February 20th, 1529 for the abolition of the last vestiges of the Mass in the four collegiate churches seems to have given impetus, however, to a more vigorous prosecution of radical dissent as a part of giving some shape to the new religious establishment.

Bucer has clearly some satisfaction in informing Zwingli of the magisterial action, the more so that the unexpectedly severe sentences have succeeded in bringing about recantations in several cases. [53] He admits ruefully that the severity of message and lugubrious demeanor of the radicals have made sympathizers of a number of Strasbourg citizens. At the same time, adherents of the old ways (for these he intends when he speaks of Satan's mockery) have not failed to exult over this evident confusion among evangelicals, and their recourse to the sword of the magistrate to enforce conformity. This was no light matter, for Bucer well knew that disunity was a traditional proof of apostasy; [54] and this explains his comforting allusion to St. Paul's teaching on the inevitable presence of heresy amongst the faithful.

IV

We may turn now to the matter of the dating of the letter. That the year is 1529 may be accepted with certainty from the advanced state of preparation of the Isaiah and Psalms commentaries. This is confirmed by the reference to Zwingli's own work on the Psalter. Pellican's **Chronicon** sets this in the period February 23rd - June 17th, 1529. [55]

It would seem to have been the July date of the dedicatory epistle of Zwingli's Isaiah that prompted the Zwingli editors to assign the letter to that month. Yet as Köhler observed, another letter from Bucer to Zwingli, of July 10, 1529, [56] assumes the present letter, and must therefore fix a terminus ante quem. In fact, a July date is quite impossible, as the following will show.

At the moment of the writing of our letter, Christoph Froschauer is in Frankfurt. The July 10th letter just referred to makes it clear that this was to attend the Frankfurt Easter book fair, and confirms that the arrangement was carried out as intended:

> Of the commentary which I began quite some time ago for the sake of certain sisters and brothers in France and lower Germany--I sent certain parts to you by means of Christopher, on his return from the last Frankfurt fair, and asked that, having looked over one or two psalms, you should advise what you think I should pursue in the remainder. But you have been so occupied by affairs that I can easily believe you have not had the time to give this matter attention even once. God knows, had I ever dreamed you were going to treat this book of Psalms, I should not have set my hand to it . . . But because I sent you a part, I think it fitting that I send the rest as well. Therefore I am now dispatching what is lacking in what was already sent, up until the third book. [57]

The date of the Frankfurt spring fair in the 16th century seems to have varied somewhat according to circumstances, but was in general fixed in relation to Easter, which in 1529 fell on March 28th. [58] Froschauer's passage through Strasbourg towards the fair can be dated as no later than March 15th, on the basis of Capito's letter of that day, which likewise confirms reception of the Isaiah samples in terms similar to those of Bucer. [59]

On March 29th, Easter Monday, Bucer indicates in yet another letter that Froschauer has not yet returned. If the surviving correspondence does not permit a more precise dating of the Zurich printer's return journey, there is in the affair of the crackdown on the Strasbourg Anabaptists, evidence pointing to the beginning of April for the composition of the letter. Within the collection of sources published by Krebs and Rott, there occurs a series of documents relating the dramatic action of the Strasbourg "Rat" in March, 1529 against a number of known radicals. [60] Among these was Fridolin Meyger, a notary in the episcopal service and one of the more prominent Anabaptists of the city. [61] Already in October, 1528, Meyger had been arrested together with several other Anabaptist leaders, and after a hearing, released on his bond. [62] On March 16th, he and others appear anew for a hearing, having been apprehended at a house-meeting a day or so previously. This time the action of the Magistrate is more extensive and severe; the documents list several dozen persons arrested and interrogated, and torture is used to expedite the latter. Sentencing took place on March 30th for a number of the Anabaptists--Meyger is banished from Strasbourg territory, others are sent back to incarceration. [63] The documents further show that, upon his humble plea, Meyger was pardoned. When one notes that Meyger was well-known to Bucer--having served as his notary, and having written a lengthy memorandum to Bucer on the subject of usury [64]--and that on this occasion Bucer and other preachers of the city requested the Magistrate to permit a formal debate between themselves and the arrested Anabaptists, (which request was denied); [65] it seems quite evident that these are the persons and events referred to in Bucer's letter. In confirmation of this identification, note, too, similar references in the March 29th letter of Capito to Zwingli. [66]

These indices of a date not long after Easter for our letter also correspond much more appropriately than does a July date to the progress of the printing of the Bucer **Psalms**. As we have seen, the letter is to be accompanied or shortly followed, by the first twenty-two psalms, namely 131 ff. in-4o in the 1529 edition. On July 10th, however, Bucer dispatches a second bundle slightly longer than the first, bringing the total up to 268 ff., to the end of Psalm 72. While there are several imponderables that prevent any accurate calculation of the rate of printing--the size of the press run, the number of presses, other work being done concurrently--it is quite improbable that George Ulricher Andlanus, a printer of modest means, [67] should have been able to complete some 130 ff. in 8-10 days. [68] Moreover, were the work proceeding at such a pace, Bucer's request to Zwingli for suggestions that could be incorporated into the latter parts of the work, a request that is repeated with the reminder to Pellican in the July 10th letter, becomes meaningless.

That considerable time has in fact elapsed between our letter and that of July 10th is evident from the latter. Bucer is manifestly uncomfortable with Zwingli's failure to respond to the earlier request; he repeats much of what he wrote in the earlier letter, and excusing Zwingli from the role of advisor, requests him to give the entire package to Pellican, who will do so instead. More responsive than Zwingli, Pellican in fact sent a critique in early August, [69] although by that date, there can have been little of the work still to be written.

Finally, a spring date for our letter and thus for the dispatch of the first lot of the commentary on the Psalms is encouraged by the correspondence with two other colleagues in Switzerland. On May 10th, Guillaume Farel writes, acknowledging receipt of a portion of the commentary; [70] and one week later, Berthold Haller of Berne reports that Farel has passed along to him the portion of the **Psalms** already in print. [71] It is reasonable to conclude that this packet was similar to that sent off to Zwingli.

Thus the letter # 871 will have been penned by Bucer at the end of March or in the first half of April, following Froschauer's stop in Strasbourg en route to Frankfurt and in the aftermath of the sentencing of the Anabaptists on March 30th, but before Froschauer's return from the Frankfurt fair. Understood in this setting it cast interesting light upon the course of events in both cities in the first half of 1529, and in particular, upon the on-going working relationship in biblical exegesis of the Zurich and Strasbourg reformers.

NOTES

1. On the biblical work of these reformers, cf. Bernard Roussel, "Martin Bucer exégète", in **Strasbourg au coeur religieux du XVIe Siècle** (Strasbourg 1977, Société Savante d'Alsace et des Régions de l'Est, 12), 153-166; O. Farner, **Huldrych Zwingli** (Zurich, 1943-1960), t.3, 29-45, 551-563; Chr. Zürcher, **Konrad Pellikans Wirken in Zürich** (Zurich, 1975, Zürcher Beiträge zur Reformationsgeschichte 4), esp. chs. 1-3; E. Staehelin, **Das theologische Lebenswerk Oekolampads** (Leipzig, 1939, QFRG, 31), esp. chs. 8 & 14. For an examination of the genesis and evolution of this activity, see R. Gerald Hobbs, "Prophecying in Zurich and Strasbourg", in press.

2. For an example of one such discussion, see Hobbs, "Monitio amica: Pellican à Capiton sur le danger des lectures rabbiniques", in: **Horizons Européens de la Réforme en Alsace**, ed. M. de Kroon & M. Lienhard (Strasbourg, 1980), 81-93.

3. Corpus Reformatorum, 97 (Leipzig, 1929).

4. **Huldrichi Zuinglii Opera:** t.8, Epistolarum pars secunda (Zurich, 1842), where it appears as Document 62, between letters dated respectively July 1st and July 3rd, 1529.

5. A dating likewise accepted by A. -L. Herminjard, **Correspondance des Réformateurs . . .** t.2 (Genève-Paris, 1868), 194, n. 2; C. Hopf, **Martin Bucer in England** (Oxford, 1946), 208 and n. 2; and M. Krebs and H. G. Rott, **Quellen zur Geschichte de Täufer: Elsass I** (QFRG, 26 = QGT, 7, Gütersloh, 1959), 240-241. All these reprint portions of the letter.

6. The text given in the Köhler edition has been compared with a photocopy of the original. Our punctuation and paragraphing vary from that given in Köhler, to conform to the sense presented here.

7. Christoph Froschauer, the Zurich printer. Cf. infra n. 26.

8. Si autem adnumerentur verba: a reminiscence of Cicero (**De opt. gen. orat.**, 14) as quoted in Jerome, **Epistola** 57, De opt. gen interp., 5.

9. Thus, **Aretius** from "Aρη s (as <u>Martinus</u> from <u>Mars</u>). On <u>Felinus,</u> probably relating <u>Butzer</u> to <u>putzen</u> (Alsatian <u>butzen</u>): cf. **Martin Bucers Deutsche Schriften** t.1 (Gütersloh, 1960), 14.

10. **Scythica rabies:** a proverbial use of the popular belief that the Scythians exceeded all bounds of good behavior when enraged. Cf. Erasmus, **Adagia** II, iii, 35, LB 2, 495E.

11. <u>ex atre bila:</u> from excessive influence of the black bile or <u>melan-cholia</u> were believed to come such personality traits as gravity, and religious enthusi-asm, inter alia. Cf. the later application of this to English Puritans in: John F. Sena, "Melancholic madness and the Puritans", <u>Harvard Theological Review</u> 66 (1973), 293-309.

12. Cf. 1 Cor. 11:19.

13. **Complanationis Isaiae prophetae foetura prima, cum apologia qur quidque sic versum sit, per Huldrychum Zuinglium,** (Tiguri, 1529). Reprinted in **Zwinglis Sämtliche Werke,** CR 101, 1-412.

14. **Sacrorum Psalmorum libri quinque, ad ebraicam veritatem versi et familiari explanatione elucidati. Per Aretium Felinum Theologum** (Argentorati, 1529). A critical edition of this text is under preparation by R. Gerald Hobbs for eventual appearance in the **Martini Buceri Opera Latina** (SMRT, Brill, Leiden).

15. Leo Jud and Caspar Megander, colleagues in the Zurich <u>Prophezei,</u> issued a Genesis and an incomplete Exodus in 1527, as "annotationes ex ore Zwinglii exceptae": cf. CR 100, 287-288 & 294-295; likewise Leo Jud published notes on the Corinthian letters in 1528, as **Annotatiunculae . . . ex ore Zuinglii in utranque Pauli ad Corinthios, publice exponentis conceptae.**

16. The **Chronikon** of Konrad Pellican, who participated in the <u>Prophezei</u> from his arrival in Zurich in late winter 1526, is an important source for the precise workings of this institution: ed. B. Riggenbach, **Das Chronikon des Konrad Pellikan** (Basel, 1877), 115. On the chronological sequence of exposition and preaching, see E. Künzli, "Zwingli als Ausleger des Alten Testaments" in CR 101, 872-873.

17. K. Pellican to A. Blarer (26.3.1528): ed. T. Schiess, **Briefwechsel der Brüder Blaurer,** (Freiburg i.Br. 1908-1912), t.1, #117. O. Farner in his "Nachwort zu den Esaja-Erklärungen" (CR 101, 412), seems to have misunderstood this passage, in construing some dissatisfaction on Pellican's part with Zwingli's preaching. Farner

attributes this to a letter of Pellican to Vadian of March 22nd, 1528; but no such letter is known to the editors of the correspondence of either. Cf. also Zürcher, op.cit., 44-45.

18. Zwingli's letter is referred to in Capito's reply of 31.7.1528 (CR 96, # 743). Bucer, writing a fortnight earlier, likewise mentions the news (19.7.1528, CR 96, # 735). For the context of this correspondence, see my article cited above n. 2.

19. In addition to the correspondence cited in the previous note, cf. Hedio to Zwingli (2.8.1528), CR 96, # 746.

20. Bucer claims to have been misled by other Zurichers into expecing its appearance for the autumn fair of 1528: 26.9.1528, CR 96, # 762.

21. When his team was afrighted by a sea monster sent by the offended Poseidon, Hippolytus's chariot was overturned, and he was dragged to his death along the sea shore.

22. CR 96, # 783; and ed. E. Arbenz & H. Wartmann, **Die Vadianische Briefsammlung** (St. Gall, 1890-) t.4, # 546.

23. The editors of the CR seem to have overlooked a brief "Ad lectorem", in which Zwingli reports this decision. "Pellicani nostri consilio factum est, candide lector, ut Hieronymi interpretatio nostrae e regione opponeretur. Eam ergo qum verisimile sit, non aliunde emendatiorem quam ex Frobenii officina peti posse, huc adsociavit, addita interdum lectionis varietate, Quae omnia quo consilio fecerit, mox qui conferet intelligit. Vale." (**Complanationis Isaiae Prophetae Foetura Prima** . . . Zurich, 1529, Sign. [& vi] v.). That Pellican remained a conservative in biblical translation, and resisted the position taken by Zwingli and Bucer as outlined in this article, is confirmed by his comments and practice in his **Commentaria Bibliorum** (Zurich, 1532+) t.1, Sign. B 2 v. -3 r.

24. CR 101, 410.

25. The Christliche Burgrecht was a defensive alliance, promoted by Zwingli, among evangelical cities of Switzerland and upper Germany. Begun Dec. 25, 1527 with the alliance of Constance and Zurich, it finally comprehended Strasbourg along with seven other cities when Strasbourg's adherence was secured January 5, 1530. The sealing of this alliance was the subject of anxious correspondence, with cryptic allusions (often in Hebrew), among the Zurich and Strasbourg reformers: cf. CR 96 # 785; 97, ## 794, 827, 827a, 835, etc. Cf. René Hauswirth, **Landgraf Philipp von Hessen und Zwingli** (Tübingen-Basel, 1968 = Schriften zur Kirchen- und Rechtsgeschichte 35), 86-95.

26. On the important role of Froschauer as communications link between the several upper German and Swiss reformers, cf. Paul Leemann-van Elck, **Die Offizin Froschauer** (Zürich, 1940 = Mitteilungen der Antiquarischen Gesellschaft in Zürich, 33/2), 76-77. The relatively small number of letters from Zwingli to the Strasbourgers may be explained in part by Zwingli's willingness to let Froschau-

er's messages stand in place of written missives: cf. Zwingli to Pirckheimer, 24.10. 1524, CR 95, # 349.

27. CR 97, # 821.

28. CR 97, ## 827a, 835.

29. Cellarius or Borrhaus, an ardent defender of rabbinica, was particularly persona non grata with Zwingli: cf. the article cited supra, n. 2., esp. 84-85. Cf. also Irena Backus, **Martin Borrhaus (Cellarius)** (Repertoire des non-conformistes religieux des seizième et dix-septième siècles, 2, Bibliotheca Bibliographica Aureliana, 88, Baden-Baden, 1981).

30. For a discussion of Bucer's use of his Jewish sources, cf. Hobbs, "Bucer on Psalm 22," in **Histoire de l'exégèse au XVIe Siècle**, ed. O. Fatio & P. Fraenkel (Genève, 1978, EPH 34), esp. 149-159.

31. Cf. W. Schwarz, "The meaning of 'Fidus Interpres' in medieval translation", JTS 45 (1944), 73-78.

32. **Epistulae** 57/5; CSEL 54, 508; MPL 22, 571.

33. **Biblia habes in hoc libro . . . utriusque instrumenti novam translationem aeditam a . . . Sancte Pagnino** (Lyon, 1528). In his dedicatory epistle to Pope Clement VII, Pagnini states: "Verbum verbo reddimus--ubi reddi potuit--ut arcanis (quantum fas est) literis deferremus, simul ac iis qui hebraeas perdiscere cupiunt literas, faceremus satis. Perphrasi tamen nonnunquam uti opus fuit, quod sensus alias commode exprimi non potuerit" (Sign. d iii v.-d iiii r.).

34. **In Iesaiam prophetam hypomnematon . . . libri VI** (Basel, 1525).

35. Ibid., Sign. a 3v.-4r. Cf. also f.3r.: ". . . ipse mihi bene sum conscius, infidelitatis me non posse coargui, atque adeo, ut in nonnullis manifestarios et inexcusabiles barbarismos et soloecismos non abhorruerim, ut ante oculos ponerem qua phrasi propheta sit usus . . . "

36. Edition of 1529, Sign. α5-6. The germ of the argument is found already in his preface to the **Epistola D. Pauli ad Ephesios** (Strasbourg, 1527), Sign. A 5 r.-v.

37. Cf. 1 Cor. 14:29-32.

38. CR 101, 87-88.

39. Ibid., 90.

40. The **Tzephaniah, quem Sophoniam vulgo vocant . . . ad ebraicam veritatem versus et commentario explanatus**, (Argentorati, 1528). Cf. Bucer's remarks in the preface: "Pridem proposui hac hyeme . . . Psalmos quoad licebit pura et genuina enarratione explanare; cui minime vulgari operi paratiorem me redditurus,

consilium nuper coepi, explanatione Prophetae alicuius brevioris velut praeludere · · · Desumpsi ergo mihi Tzephaniah . . . " (f. 10 r.-v). Prior to this, Bucer had worked primarily in New Testament exegesis.

41. The **Operationes in Psalmos** (1519-1521, WA 5) of Luther cover only Psalms 1-22; the **Interpretatio in librum Psalmorum** (Basel, 1524) of Johannes Bugenhagen did not pretend to work from the Hebrew text.

42. On the ties between Strasbourg and France in the early years of the Reform, cf. R. Peter, "Strasbourg et la Réforme Française vers 1525", in **Strasbourg au coeur religieux du XVIe Siècle**, 269-283.

43. Between 1525 and 1527, Bucer published six volumes of Latin translations of Luther's **Kirchenpostillen;** his Synoptics commentary was entitled **Enarrationum in evangelia Matthaei, Marci et Lucae libri duo.** All were published in Strasbourg. Cf. Josef Benzing, **Lutherbibliographie** (Baden-Baden, 1966), # 1733; and R. Stupperich, **Bibliographia Bucerana** (Gütersloh, 1952), # 14.

44. The **De vera et falsa religione** (1525) and the **Christianae fidei expositio** (1531). Cf. G. R. Potter, **Zwingli** (Cambridge, 1976), 204-206, 395-396.

45. Cf. A. -L. Herminjard, **Correspondance des réformateurs . . .** (Genève, 1866-1887); e.g. the letter of Roussel to Farel of 27.8.1526 (# 182).

46. Bucer expresses himself similarly in the preface to the Zephaniah commentary of late summer 1528, and there too, faults principally his Lutheran adversaries.

47. For the Empire: Paul Fredericq, **Corpus Documentorum Inquisitionis Neerlandicae** (Gent, 's Gravenhage, 1903), t.5, ## 529.541.551.735, where the penalty was banishment. For France, Ch. Duplessis d'Argentré, **Collectio Iudiciorum** (Paris, 1755), t.2, 8-9 & passim, and Isambert, Jourdain & Decrusy, **Recueil général des anciennes lois françaises** (Paris, 1828), t.12, 231-237.

48. Cf. Wm. Toth, "Luther's frontier in Hungary", in **Reformation Studies in honor of Roland Bainton,** ed. F. H. Littell, 82.85f.

49. On the vigorous policy of the Duke of Lorraine, cf. Peter, op.cit. 270; on burnings in France, **Journal d'un bourgeois,** ed. Bourrilly (Paris, 1910), 190.363-368; on the policy of Marguerite of Austria, see Fredericq, op.cit., passim.

50. Cf. **Declamation des Louenges de Mariage** [1525], ed. Emile Telle (Geneve, 1976), 45-49.

51. Cf. Krebs & Rott, op.cit., I, ## 110-111.113-114

52. For a careful discussion of the evolving position of the Strasbourg authorities, cf. Marc Lienhard, "Les Autorités civiles et les Anabaptistes: attitudes du Magistrat de Strasbourg (1526-1532)", in: **The Origins and Characteristics of Anabaptism . . .** (International Archives of the History of Ideas, 87, The Hague, 1977), 196-215.

53. For the argument that Bucer's attitude to Anabaptists was hostile from the beginnings of the Strasbourg Reform, cf. Henry G. Krahn, "Martin Bucer's strategy against sectarian dissent in Strasbourg" MQR 50 (1976), 163-180. In my judgment, Krahn overstates his case, generalizing from the 1532-1533 Synod period, and overlooking evidence that disputes his case in the 1520's, e.g. the case of Michael Sattler.

54. Cf. Johannes Eck, **Enchiridion locorum communium**, ch. 1, De ecclesia (Münster, 1979, Corpus Catholicorum, 34), 22-23.

55. <u>Op.cit.</u> 117.

56. CR 97, # 874.

57. <u>Loc.cit.</u>

58. From 1349 on periodic regulations attempted to fix the dates of the spring fair to a period before Holy Week. In fact until 1727 the dates vary widely, depending upon travel conditions, wars, etc. In particular an early date for Easter could mean that the fair took place during and after the Easter celebrations. Cf. Alexander Dietz, **Frankfurter Handelsgeschichte** (Glashütten im Taunus, 1910-1925) t.1, 37f.

59. V. supra n. 26.

60. <u>Op.cit.</u>, I, ## 174-182.

61. Cf. <u>op.cit.</u> 132, n. 8.

62. <u>Op.cit.</u>, # 153. ". . . Meiger ist auf urphed des thurms wieder erlassen." I am grateful to Professor Christopher Friedrichs of the University of British Columbia for the information that such an oath customarily bound the individual not to seek vengeance. One must assume that Meyger's Anabaptist beliefs did not prevent his taking this oath.

63. ". . . inter quos Fridolinus Meyger, cui interdicitur terra Argentinensis; duo in foveam reponuntur . . ." from Nicholas Gerbel's **Tagebuch,** in Krebs & Rott, <u>op.cit.</u>, # 181. Note the similarity to the expressions employed by Bucer in the letter.

64. <u>Op.cit.</u>, # 172.

65. <u>Op.cit.</u>, # 178.

66. CR 97. # 827a.

67. Cf. François Ritter, **Histoire de l'Imprimerie Alsacienne** (Strasbourg-Paris, 1955), 316-317.

68. Andlanus will have had two presses at most. On calculations of the possible output of a printer, cf. L. & W. Hellinga, "Regulations relating to the planning and organization of work by the Master Printer in the ordinances of Christopher Plantin" **The Library** Series 5, vol. 29 (1974), 52-60; cf. also Erasmus, **Epistolae** ed. P. S. Allen (Oxford, 1906-), t.6, # 1683.

69. Letter of 6 August 1529, unpub. Zurich Staatsarchiv, E I 1, 1 # 216, Zürcher # 55.

70. Herminjard, t.2, # 256. Herminjard's assumption that this packet is already dispatched and referred to in a letter of Bucer to Farel on 7 March 1528 is incorrect; this reference will almost certainly be to a portion of Bucer's **John** which he was engaged in writing at that point.

71. Unpublished, quoted by Herminjard loc.cit.

THE MESSAGE AND IMPACT OF HULDRYCH ZWINGLI: THE SIGNIFICANCE FOR HIS TIME [1]

Gottfried Locher

I

We are a festive gathering here this evening. Yet, closer examination suggests that the Reformer Zwingli is poorly suited for purposes of such a jubilee. According to present-day judgment he committed serious errors. Well-known faults and inner contradictions in character and work are evident. The anxious, violent severity against the peaceful Täufer among whom were some of his initially most devoted followers, repulses us. And the death of this erstwhile pacifist, with halberd in hand, may appear tragic to us, but hardly worthy of honor.

Further considerations come to mind. First, must we not assess his life's work, judged according to his proud goals and hopes, namely the conversion in a short time of the dearly beloved confederacy to the newly discovered Gospel, and all of Germany and France in a few years, [2] as pathetically limited, hence as failed? The gifted free Ammann's and farmer's son from the Toggenburg, chaplain of the Glarus troops, reformed humanist and respected educator, was called to Zurich in 1519 as an opponent of the corrupting mercenary service and papal pensions. Together with his friends, he led this outpost of the confederacy to a thoroughgoing renewal in one decade through his high diplomatic skill and his learned biblical preaching which had developed into the reformation message, informed by Augustine, Paul, the Letter to the Hebrews and the prophets. To be sure, all this led into a dangerous political isolation. However, this was overcome. St. Gall, Berne, Basel, Schaffhausen changed over; all of Eastern Switzerland was stirred into action. Constance, Strasbourg, the landgrave of Hesse, joined the alliance of the Christian Civic Union and powerful imperial cities like Augsburg and Ulm sought to join it. The reformer participated as advisor in the pressure which, in the hate-filled, often bloody tensions, Zurich from then on brought to bear on loyally catholic Inner Switzerland. He wanted to prevent any rearguard action in the generally expected confrontation with the Emperor, with Hapsburg Spain. He aimed to obtain through legal means permission for evangelical preaching in the entire region of the confederacy. His opponents and the people understood, of course--this is true to this day--that the "new faith" was pressed upon the original Swiss by force. When in the surprise outbreak of the Second Kappel War of 1531, shortly before the battle, the baker Lienhard Burkart, no friend of the Reformation, addressed "Meister Ulrych, How do you like this affair? Are the beets seasoned? Who wants to eat them?" The answer was, "I and many an honest man who are here in the hand of God, whose we are in life and death." Whereupon Burkhart answered, "And I too, want to help clean the plate and will risk my life and limb cheerfully." [3] That sounds noble, but can one celebrate that?

Secondly, it belongs to the character of Zwingli that he always appears in community with his co-workers; he does not strongly stand out himself. "I ask all brothers in Christ that they place no weight on my name, but that everything be weighed on the scales of the word of God." [4]

Thirdly, to be sure, it applies that in the last few decades we have again discovered how the impact of the Zurich Reformation did by no means come to an end on that 11 October 1531, and that it did not remain limited to the sphere of influence of the five Protestant cities. [5] Much more, the Swiss Reformation type, together with the closely related Strasbourg type of Martin Bucer and the Constance type of Ambrosius Blaurer, and spiritually entwined with the social and political endeavors of the guilds, found its widest expansion in approximately fifty south German free and imperial cities. In many places, as in Ulm and Augsburg, it prevailed for the better part of two generations. Not until the Schmalkaldic War of 1545 and with the introduction of the Formula of Concord in the 80's did it give way, either to recatholicizing or relutheranizing--in part, quite often, against long, tenacious resistance.

Surprisingly, clear traces of Zwinglian influence are encountered among the French humanists and in the early Huguenot congregations, not least of all under the impact of Guillaume Farel, who was an enthusiastic supporter of Zwingli until he later became the most significant combatant-in-arms of Calvin. Quite unexpected were the translations and numerous editions of Zwinglian writings in England and the numerous proofs of their broad and deep effect in the Inquisition processes.

Particularly astonishing, however, are the results of a more careful consideration of Scottish Reformation history. Biographies and writings of leading personalities, the revolutionary removal of Mary Stewart and an analysis of the Scots Confession show that the movement there was overwhelmingly inspired by Zwingli until the return of John Knox.

Nevertheless, it is well-known that in the sixteenth century already the Zwinglian traditions in France, England and Scotland were covered over by the modern influence of Calvinism, armed against the attack of the Counter-Reformation. For all that, Heinrich Bullinger enjoys high authority in the Church of England right to this day.

Now, if the "significance" of Zwingli "in his own time" was of this nature, what then brings us to commemorate him today?

II

This question forces us to direct our attention away from Zwingli's person and from the geographical reach of his influence, be it Switzerland or Europe, and onto several content-oriented themes of his efforts. Indeed, we think that it is precisely those indications of the failure, limitations and set-backs of this previously highly successful preacher that should open our eyes to the significance of his impact, in the uniqueness of the commission bestowed on him and his own peculiar insights and gifts. Thus, the honest admission of questionable impressions leads us from a mood of celebration to contrite reflection, which is well-suited for a reformed congregation on a day of commemoration.

We name five themes, which were already controversial in his time, as well as in the Reformation, but which received their illuminating power and have unfolded to this day precisely because they were in the shadow of failure, error and persecution.

1. Reformed Theology

Zwingli was the first reformed theologian. [6] We do not forget, of course, the intellectual exchanges with Bucer, Oecolampadius, Leo Jud, Vadian, Francis Lambert, Blarer, Farel and many others. However, through energy in word and deed, and in his political ability, he stands out. For our purpose here, allow me to characterize his reformed theology through several quotations.

The second thesis of 1523 reads, "The sum of the Gospel is that our Lord Christ Jesus, true Son of God, has made known to us the will of his heavenly father, and with his innocence has redeemed us from death and reconciled us to God."

The third thesis, "Therefore Christ is the only path to salvation for all who were, who are, or who will be." [7]

That is obviously the general reformation assertion. Nevertheless, the formulation which ties the work of reconciliation of the Lord immediately to his authority enters into the reformed tradition and will through Calvin and the Heidelberg Catechism shine forth with unprecedented power. [8] However, Zwingli risks the extremest consequences: the validity of the sacrifice and therewith the lordship of Christ lift him above the boundaries of that which we know as faith, church and christendom. One day "you may hope to see the fellowship, the union and the gathering of all saints, the wise, the believers, the brave, the steadfast and the virtuous, who have lived since the beginning of the world." [9] Speaking theologically: salvation history is bound to the Lord, not the Lord to salvation history. With that the freedom of God leads to liberated thinking. God gives light and knowledge where he wants.

Related to this freedom of the exalted and of his spirit is the following: the truth of God about the world, humankind and me is to be perceived not according to previously designated dogmatič or liturgical tenets, but from the great perspectives of the biblical witness, which reveal themselves only to one who is absorbed in the context of Holy Scripture. For this reason, Zwingli the preacher did away with the pericopes when he entered the pulpit on New Year's Day, 1519. He will "preach with God's help the entire Gospel of St. Matthew, seriatim. He will not cut up into little pieces the Lord's Gospel." [10] The emancipating effect, which begins with the reformed practice of the continuing exposition of biblical books, was established. This method educates the listeners to reading in their own comparative and critical way and with that, to autonomy at the religious core of their personality. Exposition and reading of this kind, if pursued honestly and earnestly, automatically prove their nearness to life. "Don't be afraid . . . God will direct his word so powerfully toward the breaking forth of all that is good and the demise of all that is evil, that all the world will see the salvation of the Lord." [11]

An important result of this prioritizing of the biblical witness in its own context was the relativization of dogma and official credo. In 1523 Zwingli sent his theses out with the rider that, "in case I have not understood the Holy Scripture correctly, let someone instruct me, but only out of Holy Scripture." [12] This reservation to better instruction later entered into almost all reformed confessional writings. It means that confessions can and must be revised or supplemented according to time and circumstances.

2. The Church

With Zwingli the building up of the church is principally not brought about by the hierarchy, nor does it proceed from the office of the clergy. Rather, it comes from the heard word, i.e. from the congregation itself, from its very foundation. In German Switzerland the introduction of the Reformation did not succeed by virtue of visiting commissions, but through laborious votes, from guild to guild and village to village. To be sure, these votes had their political side, especially since the Reformer held that the disenfranchised, who normally had no vote, could participate in the decision-making. The laity had the word. That Zwingli consulted the magistracy and thereby conceded a certain ecclesiastical competence to the Council must also be seen in the light of this incorporation of the laity. They were given the functions the bishop had earlier exercised over them. On the basis of certain passages in Jeremiah the Reformer charges councillors and princes that they too are, "shepherds over the sheep of Jesus Christ." [13]

3. Political Responsibility

With that we have come to the third theme which the Zurich reformer has imprinted on Protestantism with his teaching and his often good, toward the end unhappy, but always impressive example: political responsibility. "A Christian is a good citizen and a Christian city is nothing other than a Christian church." [14] That is a medieval conception. But the reminder that political activity and political decision-making is an external manifestion of Christian faith is still relevant. Already in the sixteenth century Zwingli's doctrine that God the Lord was well-disposed toward political freedom and that there was clearly a connection between Christian freedom, freedom of belief and political freedom, was of powerful significance. "The kingdom of Christ is also external," [15] he says, among other things, against the Lutheran judgment of the Peasant's War. That significance is already apparent in the uprising of the Huguenots and in the wars of independence in the Netherlands.

The Reformer expresses a lasting problem, however, with his best-known word, "Do something bold for God's sake." [16] He meant by it, "demand from the Confederates the freedom for evangelical preaching." That was interference in the sovereignty of the Confederates and the Reformer knew that. He saw clearly that there are cases in which the word of God and human rights collide with legal constitutions and laws. That is a universal experience today.

In any event, the Zurich branch of the Reformation taught that all political work takes place in responsibility before God. The conscience remains indivisible. To distinguish between a religio-ethical motif on the one side and a political on the other, remains impossible.

4. Social Responsibility

Closely related to the above theme is the social responsibility of Christian life. If the immediate relationships of the Christian community to the civil community have become alien to our pluralistic age, the reformed-puritanical values of industry, thriftiness, selflessness, and honesty have, by no means, become so in the work arena. They are, as Wittenberg also taught, the secular worship of God. However, Zurich and Geneva say still more: they ought to build up a commonweal in which the honor of Christ shines. The contradiction against the suddenly arising phenomena of early capitalism in that time was well understood. The principle of pure profitability is directly excluded. "You ought not consider your earthly goods as your own possessions; you are only a steward thereof." [17] Work especially must serve humankind for it belongs to our humanity. "The human being is created for work as birds are for flying," [18] Zwingli writes.

5. Failure

We return now to the beginning in the attempt of decoding somewhat what is imparted to us in those symbols of the failure of his life work. In any event, there were here on both fronts higher, more earnest stakes in play. When in the battle at Kappel on Albis two thousand Zurich men were defeated by eight thousand men from Inner Switzerland the first victory of the Counter Reformation had taken place. This was immediately understood as such throughout the whole of Europe. Yet, the battle bears still another distinctive element which has only rarely been repeated. Here true Catholics fought--the bishops had failed them--for their ancestral church, and there evangelical Christians stood up for their, only recently won, evangelical faith. On their own. Thereupon for centuries, religious wars in all of Europe were to be fought almost exclusively by mercenaries; even in France and the Netherlands. Churches themselves were affected since villages were burned down and cities besieged.

In addition to numerous individual executions and banishments of heretics, the first mass escape had taken place two years earlier. Approximately one hundred families from the imperial city of Rottweil, [19] fled to Switzerland which, by the way, indicates of what Spirit they were. The meetings of the Christian Civic Union were for a long time at a loss as to what they should do with these people. In Bullinger's time the reformed church learned how one had to receive refugees (citizen of Locarno, Italians, French and English).

We don't want in any way to elevate Kappel 1931 to the level of a martyrdom. Nonetheless, men stood up there for their faith and mistakes--valiantly. All this means that the people of the Zurich and the Swiss German Reformation, among whom until now, as a result of Zwingli's work and skill everything had run its course fairly smoothly, had to learn and demonstrate it for all of Europe that christendom and faith are for community and individuals alike, things for which one must risk one's life. That too belongs to the "significance of the Zwinglian Reformation" in the sixteenth century and to its legacy. "The less you fear death, the stronger is faith in you," says Huldrych Zwingli. [20]

LITERATURE

Bernd Moeller, **Reichstadt und Reformation,** Gütersloh, 1962.

Fritz Büsser, **Huldrych Zwingli. Reformation als prophetischer Auftrag,** Göttingen, 1973.

Gottfried W. Locher, **Die Zwinglische Reformation im Rahmen der europäischen Kirchengeschichte,** Göttingen, 1979.

Martin Haas, **Huldrych Zwingli und seine Zeit,** 3rd edition, Zurich, 1983.

Ulrich Gäbler, **Huldrych Zwingli, Leben und Werk,** Munich, 1983.

NOTES

1. This paper was first read on the occasion of the celebration of the 500th anniversary of the birth of Huldrych Zwingli in the Grossmünster, Zurich, Switzerland, 28 January 1984.

2. Z IX: 130.

3. Bullinger III: 137.

4. Z I: 621.

5. Locher, chapters 18 and 24.

6. See G. W. Locher, "The Characteristic Features of Zwingli's Theology in Comparison with Luther and Calvin," **Zwingli's Thought. New Perspectives** (Leiden, 1981), 142–232.

7. Edwin Künzli, **Huldrych Zwingli: Auswahl seiner Schriften** (Zurich, 1962), 69f. Z I: 458. H III: 3.

8. As early as question and response number 1 of the catechism.

9. S IV: 65, H XI: 349.

10. Bullinger I: 12.

11. Z III: 407.

12. l.c. note 6.

13. S IV: 58. S VI/I: 88.

14. Z XIV: 424.

15. Z IX: 454.

16. Z X: 165.

17. Z II: 451.

18. S VI/I: 209 (After Job 5:7, Vulgate).

19. Locher, 436ff.

20. Z III: 40. H I: 210.

IN SEARCH OF TRUE RELIGION
THE SPIRITUALITY OF ZWINGLI AS SEEN IN
KEY WRITINGS OF 1523/24

H. Wayne Pipkin

On this occasion of the celebration of the 500th anniversary of the birth of Zwingli the effort is being made to understand the Swiss Reformer from many different perspectives. Zwingli was a complex man with far-reaching influence in Zurich and beyond, a multi-dimensional person. The fact that he died on the battlefield, coupled with his obvious concerns for the whole life of the city, leaves an impression with the modern person of a predominantly political and social reformer. His training as a humanist, and especially his close relationship to Erasmus, as well as his radical biblical exegesis in the eucharistic controversy with Luther, have led some to dismiss Zwingli as merely an intellectual, if not a rationalist. Such images of Zwingli likely linger in the English-speaking world owing to the paucity of Zwinglian writings readily available in modern translation. Such views are unfortunate, though understandable. For, however much he concerned himself with the questions of the polis, or however much he was a scholar, he was first of all a religious reformer and his concerns were religious concerns.

The purpose of this essay is to describe the essential elements of the spirituality of Zwingli through an examination of three treatises associated with the theological working-out, and the official acceptance of, that spirituality. We shall then draw several conclusions about the spirituality of Zwingli based on what these writings reveal.

By "spirituality," we mean the religious and specifically Christian framework of Zwingli's thinking and reforming work. In an attempt to understand Zwingli as homo religiosus, the effort will be made to observe Zwingli's grasp of the nature of sacred or divine reality, how one participates in it, and what the implications of such participation are for Christian existence. [1]

117

The three treatises I wish to examine are related to 1523:

(1) **The Exposition and Basis of the Conclusions or Articles.** [2] Published in July 1523, this was Zwingli's most complete theological writing. It laid the theological foundation for the Zurich reform in its most comprehensive form. (2) **The Short Christian Instruction.** [3] Published in November, 1523 with an official mandate of the Zurich Council, the **Instruction** was the most concise statement of the spirituality of the Zurich Reformation. (3) **The Shepherd.** [4] A sermon preached during the Second Disputation, but written and published only in 1524, **The Shepherd** contained Zwingli's notions on the true spirituality of the minister and his people. It is the most personal religious statement of the three, and is an excellent compliment to the **Instruction.**

I

The sixty-seven articles prepared for the First Zurich Disputation of January, 1523, contained the essential outline of the Zwinglian position. It was, however, only with the July publication of **The Exposition and Basis of the Articles** that Zwingli articulated in full detail his position on every issue facing the reform in Zurich. After the First Disputation it was clear that the Council had full authority over the church in Zurich and would be finally responsible for the reform. The fact of Reformation was assured. [5] What had not yet been fully determined was the exact nature of the reform. To this point, the theological basis of the Reformation had not yet been set forth in detail; thus, the **Exposition** was to provide the most detailed statement of the reformed position to date. It was a mature reflection of Zwingli's evangelical position, although it would be expanded significantly later on the matters of baptism and the Lord's Supper. In addition to providing a statement of Zwingli's doctrine, the **Exposition** provides several clues to an understanding of his spirituality.

In the epilogue to **The Exposition of the Twentieth Article** Zwingli reveals a striking insight concerning the core of his religious perspective. He refers to his earlier reading of the poem by Erasmus in which Jesus takes to task a man who has turned away from him, the one true source of salvation, and now perishes through his very own fault. [6] The dating of the experience and whether or not it was Zwingli's "evangelical experience" is not the point here. What is significant is Zwingli's interpretation in 1523. The basic religious insight which Zwingli relates in this context is that Christ is " . . . the sole treasure of our benighted soul." (II 217: 18-19) [7] It is not the saints, which is to say, it is not creatures. He recognizes that one's God is that in which one has confidence and in which one trusts. (219: 13-14) Therefore one should turn only to the Creator, "for God is ever the good in whom one ought to put one's trust; he alone knows our hearts." (219:36-220: 2) This insight is very near to the center of Zwingli's reformed vision. It is the contrast between false and true religion. This contrast runs through the whole of his reforming work and is at the root of his spirituality. Important at this point is the notion of faith and its object.

Faith is for Zwingli confidence, assurance and total trust in God alone. (182: 4-8; 193: 7-8) It is to place confidence in whatever becomes one's God. True religion is the act of placing all one's confidence in the Creator. It is following the First Commandment. (191: 31-192: 3) Using various words reminiscent of late medieval spirituality, he writes of trusting in the merits of Christ, [8] relying on and trusting wholly on God, [9] relying on the grace of God, [10] trusting in God, [11] and trusting in his word. [12] The word variations for faith and trust which he uses suggest the centering act of the personality, the relying on one's God for confidence, assurance, and comfort.

Of particular significance is the object of the confidence. True religion is determined by the direction of one's trust. Whether he speaks of the grace of God, or God, the word of God or of Christ, he is concerned with the Creator as the right object. The act of trusting, if directed toward the right end, is derived not from human capacity, but from the divine. It is the work of the Spirit of God and although Zwingli alludes to the word of God, it is all but dissolved into the work of the Spirit.

> One need not have a visible person in order to believe; for one person never converts another unless the Spirit who draws heart and mind, does so. Though one may need a preacher, he still does not cause the heart to believe; the Spirit and the word of God do that. Whoever claims that he assures or decides, is a deceiver and an anti-Christ, for he attributes to himself what is exclusively God's. (111: 7-13)

Belief itself is the work of God. (75: 36-76: 4)

False religion for Zwingli is living according to the flesh, whereas true, is living according to the Spirit. In **The Exposition of the Sixteenth Article** Zwingli has in effect produced a small treatise on Christian spirituality. In it he sets the law of the flesh over against the law of the spirit.

> To live according to the Spirit means to extricate oneself from the reason and power of the flesh, i.e. human nature, and to trust in the Spirit of God alone. Those who trust in the Lord Jesus Christ with all confidence will no longer

be damned by any law . . . For the law of the Spirit
which gives life, namely the teaching and directions of
the divine Spirit who quickens all living things, has set
me free in Christ Jesus. (81: 3-10)

To walk spiritually is to have confidence in Christ. (82: 7) Zwingli
links trust and confidence in Christ with the work of the Spirit.
Where Luther would contrast law and Gospel, in this treatise
he effectually contrasts law and Spirit. (cf. 83: 33-84: 2) This
is to say that he turns the true believer away from trusting in
human institutions, whether it is one's own aspirations or the
teaching magisterium of the Roman Church.

By contrast, the spirituality of his day misses the point.
It is empty and based on human capacity rather than the divine.
"Humanly invented statutes and commandments appear to be
beautiful to human eyes, but inwardly they are empty, vain, barren,
and useless; for where the Spirit of God is not, there nothing
other than falseness, hypocrisy, despair and a condemned and
terrible conscience are to be found." (95: 1-5) The reason they
are empty and vain is because they are not directed toward or
founded on the Spirit of God.

Integral to an understanding of spirituality is prayer
and worship. Zwingli's reflections in this area are consistent
with his affirmation on the centrality of faith and the assertion
of the prominence of the Creator. He addresses himself to prayer
in **The Exposition of the Twenty-first Article.** In the first place,
"there can be no prayer unless one first accepts that God is and
unless one goes to him in the sure confidence of going to one's
own gracious father." (224: 18-20) What is absolutely necessary
is faith. (223: 28) In fact, acting in faith is a kind of prayer.
"Thus it follows that when a person practices faith, he actually
prays when he thinks, 'God is creator of all things; he is the
highest good from whom all good things come. He never promises
anything to humankind unless he will keep his promise'." (224:
6-9) If prayer is praise, (223: 27) then what higher praise can
one offer than holding to him firmly in our hearts as the highest
good? (224: 10-13)

At this point Zwingli brings together theology, practice
and worship. Prayer is not an external act solely; it is setting
God at the center of one's life. It is living with God as the highest
good. This affects belief and it determines how one will live.
Prayer is "constant dependence on God." (227: 22) Zwingli illustrates this in a passage which concludes the first part of this
article. In it he opens true spirituality to the workaday world
of the layperson:

> That is true prayer which takes place in truth and in
> Spirit, but worship which uses parroted words does not
> last long . . . Thus a farmer may pray while plowing
> if he patiently carries out his work in God's name, asking
> God for the increase of the seed in faith, and frequently
> recalling that our present life is merely hardship and misery;
> but that yonder our gracious God shall give us rest and
> peace and joy. Thus he prays, though he may never move
> his mouth. Likewise the smith at the anvil; if he looks
> upon God in everything he does, he prays without ceasing.
> (228: 26-229: 5)

It is a striking affirmation of the priesthood of the believer. [13]

In the **Exposition** Zwingli interjects considerable reflection concerning human activity. He is concerned about good works, but they are predicated on the prior initiative of the Spirit in bringing them about. Certain works are clearly indicative of depending on God, while others are idolatrous. (cf. 93: 29-94: 9) The dependence on God will not cause the diminishing of good works. In fact, "every good work shall grow all the more, the more one trusts in God." (93: 31)

In regard to human activity Zwingli raises the issue of divine and human righteousness. The issue comes to be of great significance for Zwingli at this time, causing him even to publish his sermon **Divine and Human Righteousness** only a short time after the publication of **Exposition.** [14] In **The Exposition of the Thirty-ninth Article** Zwingli describes the "law of nature" which "comes solely from God and is nothing other really than the pure Spirit of God who inwardly draws and illumines." (327: 3-5) The "law of nature" was known also to the Gentiles because of the work of the "illuminating Spirit of God," who was himself unknown to them. (327: 5-7) This law of nature is "nothing other than the will of God." (328: 2-3) As such it is truly concerned with the inner person. "One cannot live better and more peacefully than when living by the law of nature." (327: 20-22) Unfortunately, the law of nature is not kept. Thus the government becomes necessary due to our "broken nature" and our "lame and half-righteousness." (327: 23-25) It is then the function of the rulers to govern in such a way as to "bring to their people the right and true knowledge of God." (330: 22-23) One should read in connection with these passages, Zwingli's sermon. He points to divine righteousness as that inward righteousness of God which is demanded of humanity, but which is beyond human capacity to fulfill. Human righteousness, on the other hand, "looks to the outward person." (484: 22) This latter righteousness may be fulfilled outwardly while the inner person is impious. "Note that I call this human righteousness a poor and feeble righteousness, simply because a person may be found to be righteous in human eyes when he is, nonetheless, not righteous in God's sight; for no one is righteous before God." (485: 26-29) [15]

Were people truly able to live the lives that are demanded of them by the righteousness of God, there would be no need for government. It is not possible, however, and thus the necessity of the civil authorities. Zwingli's acquiescence to the necessity of the magistrate hardly means that he begrudges its existence. He is ultimately favorably inclined to the possibility of a government's working in accordance with the divine teaching. [16] Büsser summarizes the matter succinctly: "Weil für Zwingli das Gesetz als der ewig gleichbleibende Wille Gottes auch Evangelium ist, anerkannte Zwingli die göttliche Gerechtigkeit auch als Richtschnur für das gesamte private, öffentliche, gesellschaftliche Leben." [17]

II

The publications of Summer 1523 did not stifle the growing unrest in Zurich and its environs. Several issues were at stake, including the matter of the paying of tithes, an issue with social, economic, and religious overtones. The matter of the reform of worship in Zurich came more into the forefront as fall approached. Leo Jud, Zwingli's associate now at St. Peter's in Zurich, preached against the use of images in the churches on 1 September. [18] It was a turning point. One week later there was a minor case of iconoclasm at St. Peter's, a more serious outbreak at the Fraumünster a week after that. The growing ferment was further fueled by the appearance of the small book of Ludwig Haetzer, "A Judgment of God Our Spouse Concerning How One Should Regard All Idols and Images." [19] Continuing unrest through the month finally brought the Council on September 29 to call for another disputation to settle the question of the Mass and of images.

The Second Disputation took place 26-28 October. It was a larger gathering than the first with a total of nine hundred including laypersons. The outcome of this disputation was never much in doubt. The issue at stake was not whether an evangelical, Zwinglian Reformation would take place, but what the nature of that reform was to be. It was the First Disputation that brought about the victory of the Protestant Reformation in Zurich. The Second Disputation assured a definitive spirituality of that reform. A fundamental question as to the nature of God and how God is to be worshipped was being raised. [20] The conclusions of the disputation, that images were not warranted, that the Mass was not a sacrifice and that there would be certain reform of these abuses in due time, found their way into the first of two treatises associated with the disputation, Zwingli's **Short Christian Instruction** which the City Council published in November. [21]

The **Instruction** contained a theological basis for the reform which was yet to be carried out; it likewise contained important clues to the understanding of Zwingli's spirituality.

Fundamental to the Zwinglian understanding is the authority of Scripture and the illuminating work of the Holy Spirit. Since the goal for which Zwingli was striving throughout his writings was scriptural Christianity, it was not surprising to encounter consistent affirmations of the importance of Scripture. True religion was biblical religion because it relied on God and not upon the human being:

> First, since anyone may well observe that the controversies of today arise solely out of some people's misunderstandings, and since all human teaching is in vain unless God enlightens and draws people inwardly, so every Christian, as an individual and when one prays in community, should call anxiously upon God to let the light of his word shine forth and draw us poor ignorant ones by his grace, so that we may learn to know him truly. And, as we know him, to acquire true love and to order all our actions out of love to him according to his pleasure--after this time eternally to receive, enjoy and possess him. (630: 2-11)

This brief passage contains the essence of Zwinglian spirituality. Error comes from depending on human teachings rather than on God. One ought rather to depend on God who draws inwardly according to his grace. After the believer has received illumination, then one orders one's life according to God and, in terms reminiscent of the best of medieval spirituality will eternally "receive, enjoy and possess" God.

In the course of the treatise Zwingli lays a theological basis for his perspective. [22] He begins with anthropology. Contrary to what is sometimes suggested concerning the Zurich reformer, he had a highly developed sense of sin and its implications for human activity. [23] The controversy centers about the distinctive word he used: prest. One often translates this term today as weakness, but care should be exercised in reading too much into that understanding. When Zwingli uses prest as weakness, he is not thinking of mere human frailty. Rather, he is thinking of impotence, the lack of the capacity to will or do good. Nor does he limit his understanding to this one word: "this is the right understanding of original sin: the fall, transgression, powerlessness, loss of God, weakness, sin or whatever you want to call it." (632: 25-27) [24] The point is, the human being is completely incapable on his own of coming to God. (636: 25-29) As human beings, however, we do not need to come to God on our own, for whatever is lacking in us, God has graciously supplied in Christ Jesus. [25]

In determining the theological groundings of Zwingli's spirituality one sees his emphasis on the human condition and the need for grace that is supplied in Christ. Zwingli's next concern is the implication of this grace experience for the Christian life. He calls those "false or weak Christians" who believe that grace has freed them from any obligation to do good. (640: 3)

> If they are now the children of God then they will act like sons. They devote themselves to the will of their father, after they have come again out of disfavor into grace. (640: 16-19)

That which makes the difference is faith. Faith is the watchman who struggles against the sin that constantly attacks the believer. (643: 24-27) Over against the person of faith is set the self-righteous one whom Zwingli calls "a completely godless person." (644: 4) True sin is defined as eygenschatz, the overweening opinion of one's self. (643: 1-2) Over against this Zwingli sets "the righteousness of faith . . . [which] rejects no one but itself, humbles itself, trusts in the mercy of God alone and builds on the rock." (643: 2-5) These antitheses, self-righteousness and faith, form the basis of Zwingli's understanding of false and true religion and are the foundational elements of his search for a Christian spirituality.

The one is characterized by turning to the creature; the other by turning to and depending on the Creator. The one is false religion; the other true.

> These are the real, true anti-Christs. Everything they should ascribe to and attribute to Jesus Christ, our savior, they take away from him and give it wrongly and falsely to another creature—without any scriptural foundation, against the clear word of God.
> In short, here no one should let himself be misled so as to seek grace from anyone but God himself. (646: 1-7) [26]

There are many "false Christians" who pretend to be followers of God, but are in reality only pretending to be so. (650: 9-15)

Zwingli encourages his followers to follow "the law of the living spirit," which is "the leading and instructing which God offers to us out of a true understanding of his word if we have depended on him." (649: 19-21) If we follow this law, we are freed from any external law that would make us pious or good. (651: 5-6) Thus are all believers freed from external laws that would presume to make one righteous. It is very specifically a concern of spirituality. These expressions of corporate and personal faith are rejected because they are humanly devised teachings and are not based on the word of God. (651: 9-12) Such is the basis for the rejection of images in worship and the Mass as sacrifice. [27]

Finally one should take note of the concern for the community that manifests itself in the writing and publication of the **Short Christian Instruction.** The treatise is designed to bring about unanimity of belief and practice in Zurich, not so much by coercion--though this element is not lacking--as by education. Clearly the government has the responsibility for enacting the reforms, but this is not affirmed by Zwingli because he is more political than religious. The magistracy has the responsibility from God to care for the whole of the community. There is a Christian way to bring about reform, i.e. through caution, order and peaceful change. There are, however, in Zurich those willful ones who sin against the priests. To act violently against the old guard is unchristian. "They are to be advised of their errors and are to do away with them. Let them die in peace as they have come." (652: 26-28) Zwingli wants to find "good ways to abolish the abuses." (663: 9)

The reformer is concerned also not only for the welfare of the city, but for the actual instruction of the people. In commenting on the images, he observed,

> at the same time, however, one is to proceed carefully so that evil does not result. For until Christian people are instructed rightly, that one should not pay the images any honor, one may still have patience until the weak are also able to follow--so that the matter may be brought to a conclusion with unanimity. (655: 4-8)

This concern for the weak, and the corresponding concentration on educating them, Zwingli developed later into his doctrine of offense. [28] It is clearly the pastor of a people who is writing and ministering daily in the midst of his people. It is not that Zwingli doesn't take the Gospel seriously, as later radical critics will charge, but that the pastoral concern for his people and the realization of the reality of the essential conservatism of people allows him to proceed cautiously. Such a commitment to the community became an integral part of the spirituality of Zwingli.

III

During the Second Disputation Zwingli had occasion to preach to the assembled gathering. He chose as his theme a topic particularly suited for the occasion and one that addresses directly the issue of a Christian piety: The Shepherd. Although a written manuscript was produced only later, in the typical fashion of Zwingli's sermonic publications, and was not published until June 1524, the sermon stands in juxtaposition to the Second Disputation with the **Short Christian Instruction** as a model Zwinglian statement of Christian spirituality. [29]

Zwingli is concerned first of all in the sermon for the spirituality of the pastor, the spiritual guardian of the people, but not exclusively so, for "these commands are not only for shepherds, but are for all people." [30] (15: 20) He draws a picture of two kinds of shepherds, and thus of two kinds of Christian: the false and the true. It is a continuation of the theme that runs through the whole of Zwingli's thought and it has implications for understanding Zwingli's spirituality.

The false shepherd is distinuished in various ways, but most of all one can see the false shepherd as the one whose life and actions are characterized by misdirected aim. The touchstone by which one may judge a true or false shepherd is whether one worships the true God who is Creator or whether one turns toward a false god and worships that which is a creature. "For that is one's God in which one trusts and in whom one takes refuge." (61: 28-29) To turn to anything less than the one, true God is to turn to foreign gods. This is wrong, for "no one may concoct anything that would improve or replace the divine." (21: 2-3)

In Zwingli's understanding the false shepherd is such precisely because he lives a life of pretence and sham. He appears to be one kind of person, but, in fact, is another. "They come in an unarmed, innocent form, just as if they, like the little sheep, could not injure," (45: 14-15) but, says Zwingli, "they also show by their bite that they are wolves." (45: 18-19) If one truly considers the actions of the false shepherds, it will be discovered that "they hypocritically cover their desires with the gracious activity of Jesus Christ, our Lord." (47: 2-4) They appear to be concerned about their flock of sheep, but "all they care about is the wool." (48: 28) The false shepherds only pretend to believe in Christ so that they may be thought to be his shepherds. "Truly, however, if you inspect the false shepherds down to their feet, you will find their wolf's claws always sticking out." (50: 14-16)

Clearly Zwingli understands false spirituality to be characterized by hypocrisy. He looks first of all to the manifestations of faith as they emerge in the behavior of the false shepherds. They ought to be judged on the basis of their works, but "by those works which God has commanded." (51: 21) Indeed, concludes Zwingli at this point,

> if the instructed would truly know what Christian works
> are, then they also would learn to recognize the shepherds

> by the works alone. Otherwise if the shepherd is avaricious, unchaste, a drunkard and a playactor, and at the same time passes himself off as God-fearing with much mass saying and external appearance of clothing and customs, then the simple sheep will think he is a shepherd, even though he is nothing other than a rapacious wolf. (52: 14-21)

It is a concern reminiscent of the humanist, but it is not only morals that is the concern, but also doctrine. Zwingli understands the unethical activity of the false shepherd to be idolatry. It is idolatry because one has turned to one's own reason, rather than being dependent on God and his word. (29: 28-30; 57: 14-18) In a summary statement at the end of his sermon, Zwingli points to the theological basis of his judgment. The false shepherds are all those "who lead from the Creator to the creature." (60: 4) The essence, then, of false religion is misdirected aim, the turning to and relying on that which is human and not to the true source of religion, God himself.

How, then, does Zwingli understand true religion to manifest itself? To portray now a positive view of Zwingli's spirituality, we look to the proper source of religion and then to its manifestations.

If a false piety is that directed to the creatures, then true spirituality is that turned to the Creator. The faithful person "knows to run to no one but God and his word, to take counsel therefrom and to trust faithfully in the same." (25: 13-15) It is a familiar theme in Zwingli and one that emerges consistently in his writing. [31] It is a life lived according to God's word and with no additions to it, the life characterized by the early Christians. [32]

In contrast to the misdirection of the false shepherds, the true shepherd turns to Christ, not as pretence for achieving one's own goals, but as the true source of the knowledge and love of God.

> Now if we trust that God is so faithful that he wants to compensate for our needs, and that he is so strong that he is capable of such response, then God is already in us; for our flesh does not recognize God in such a way. Now if such knowledge and trust of God is in us, then it does not come from us but from God. It is through his Son, Jesus Christ, that he instructs and makes certain in us these two things, that he can and wants to. (42: 8-14)

The imitatio Christi theme is not absent in Zwingli's thinking. "Since Christ is a perfect model, the shepherd must see that he relies only on his example." (20: 26-28) No one can find a better example. To seek another model would be to be guilty of the besetting sin of the false shepherds, i.e. trying to replace or improve the divine with the human. [33]

As the false shepherds can be distinguished by their actions, so also do ethical judgments function in determining a true spirituality.

> Therein we see that it is not enough only to take possession of salvation, it is also necessary to take care so that one does not lose or despise it.
> Most helpful toward that end is the shepherd's doing in practice what he teaches in words. (19: 27-31)

In his spirituality, then, Zwingli strives for a uniting of his theological perspective with the practical expression of it.

Where does this practical expression of faith begin? In terms reminiscent of late medieval ascetic spirituality, Zwingli insists that the Christian

> in the first place must deny himself, for he wants always and everywhere to be something, to be capable and to be able. He must be pawned and spurned in himself like a serf or menial servant; he must look up only to what God commands him doing nothing on his own power or knowledge, but considering the only guide, God, and his word. (16: 3-7)

After the true Christian empties himself, then "the next thing is to be filled again with God, that is, he has all his confidence and consolation in God." (17: 22-23) At the basis of this relationship is faith and the holding to God as the gracious and highest good. The motivation for living is love, which is closely allied with faith.

There are lengthy passages on love in **The Shepherd** that are lyrical in their expression and mystical in their devotion. This is neither the rationalist nor cool humanist scholar, but a pastor and serious Christian, concerned about the relationship to God of himself and his people.

> Love is therefore necessary so that all things be judged and measured by it. For the carpenter is not so certain with his eye; for him, a ruler is also necessary. All courage, skill and faith are nothing, if they are not judged according to love. (41: 3-7)

The two are united: first, faith and then follows love, and these form the basis of the Christian's piety. (54: 5)

One last feature of the piety of **The Shepherd** needs to be considered. Often in his early writings, but especially toward the end of this sermon Zwingli's frequent reference to the poor gives a decided social dimension to his concern. In the first place, the false shepherds have designed a spirituality that takes advantage of the poor and had profound implications for the health of the society.

> If they only knew that bought-masses are a horror to God and that for the honoring of God one should clothe the living images of God--poor Christians--and not wooden and stone idols, and that to worship God in the spirit and the truth--not senseless yelling--is the most God-pleasing song; that their indulgences have been nothing more than a permit for all vices, for with them they have robbed, stolen, practiced usury, fought, betrayed, indeed, begun all great evils. (51: 27-52: 4)

Those who do not care for the poor are false shepherds. (55: 9-11) The riches which they gather for themselves belong not to themselves, but to the poor (52: 13-14) and the poverty in which they are left is dangerous. [35]

IV

It now remains to draw several conclusions regarding Zwingli's spirituality as it appears in the writings studied here. The tentativeness of these conclusions is recognized in that only a portion of his writings have been examined, but it has been intentionally suggested here that these writings form the basis of the spirituality of the Zurich Reformation as such and that what follows after contains variations on these themes, but that they are nowhere substantially altered.

1. It is Zwingli's understanding of God that determines his spirituality. This in itself is not surprising, but the point is that it is his understanding of the spiritual nature of Divine Reality that shapes his understanding. It is a theocentric emphasis that governs his thinking rather than an institutional, political or even a Christocentric emphasis. When he speaks of the Spirit, he more often than not speaks of the Spirit of God rather than the Holy Spirit. This does not mean he is not trinitarian, but that one might well call his emphasis a spiritual theocentrism. [36] True spirituality is that directed toward the spiritual reality which is God. False spirituality is guilty of misdirected aim and is directed toward creatures rather than the Creator. This antithesis of false

and true religion runs through the whole of Zwingli's thinking. [37]

2. Scripture plays an understandable role near the center of his theology. In one sense Zwingli is a biblicist, but of a particular sort. The role of the Spirit in providing the necessary illumination and understanding of Scripture is crucial. It is not enough to point to Scripture, but one must ask after his hermeneutic and seek to understand the role of illumination in his use of Scripture. This does not depreciate Scripture in Zwingli's understanding but finds its true value. The centrality of Scripture and its significance in Zwingli's spirituality is nowhere better illustrated than by the fact that the Prophezei, Zwingli's bible school for educating pastors in Zurich, met in the choir of the Grossmünster. This daily study of the Scripture in the place of the recitation of the daily office suggests graphically what the center of the Zurich Reformation was understood to be. [38]

3. Faith and love are central elements of his spirituality and it is tempting to see elements of a mysticism of faith and love, not unlike Augustine's, in his thinking. To have faith itself is to worship God truly. Following on that faith is love which involves the believer in society. In one sense, faith and love are cardinal elements of true religion. The imitatio Christi motif is related to the understanding of these virtues. Action is a significant dimension of the piety of the Zurich reform. [39]

4. The notion of community is central. Zwingli is still a medieval person with appreciation for the whole community. The effort is to reform the whole community and this governs his methodology of reform. It also is seen in his effort to relate the Gospel to the whole life of the community. It is true that he becomes increasingly involved in politics, but in no sense is this separated from his activity as prophet and guardian. Indeed, it is but a continuing sign of his understanding of the comprehensiveness of the Gospel as it is related to the life of the people.

5. The sources of his spirituality have not been dealt with here, but a comment is in order, for he did not come to exist in a vacuum. Much too much is made of Zwingli's humanistic training as an intellectual program. Certainly it was that, but it was more. He gathers into himself many elements of that renaissance movement, not the least of which is neo-platonism, but certainly neo-stoic and other renaissance elements are not missing. It is clear that Erasmus was a major mediator of this tradition, but the Erasmian influence was not primarily intellectual, as it is usually described. Rather, it was religious in nature. [40] When Zwingli came to Erasmus he had spent years in study and was well grounded in the Fathers, notable Augustine, Origen, Jerome, Chrysostom and others. It is the spirit of Origen and Augustine that emerges so often in Zwingli's spirituality. Recognition of these elements is too often neglected. [41]

6. Finally, it must be noted that not everything was resolved in 1523. The question of laxity had not yet been fully dealt with and one can suggest that it never fully was. Not long after, Zwingli would encounter opponents who would find his alliance with the magistracy as no more productive of authentic Christian spirituality than he had found the "false shepherds" to be. Zwingli did continue to wrestle with this issue and sought ways to develop as much as possible his own brand of "believer's church" in Zurich. That was, after all, the goal of a true spirituality.

By the close of 1523 there were serious issues related to the matters of the sacraments which had not yet been raised, much less resolved. This was yet to come, but Zwingli would seek to resolve those issues with every confidence that "it is the Spirit which enlivens; the flesh profits nothing."

NOTES

1. Although many speak about and allude to the spirituality or piety of Zwingli, there is little as such to recommend. Various books and articles in addition to the writings of Zwingli would be helpful including the following: F. Schmidt-Clausing, **Zwingli** (Berlin, 1965); Abel E. Burckhardt, **Das Geistproblem bei Huldrych Zwingli** (Leipzig, 1932); Gottfried Locher, **Zwingli's Thought** (Leiden, 1981); Christof Gestrich, **Zwingli als Theologe** (Zurich, 1967); Erich Seeberg, "Der Gegensatz zwischen Zwingli, Schwenckfeld und Luther," **Reinhold Seeberg Festschrift** (Leipzig, 1929, 43-80); Francesco Erasmo Sciuto, "Lo spiritualismo di Zwingli nell 'opera 'Sulla chiarezza e certezza della parola di Dio'," **Humanität und Glaube. Gedenkschrift für Kurt Guggisberg** (Bern, 1973, 43-70); Christof Windhorst, "Wort und Geist. Zur Frage des Spiritualismus bei Balthasar Hubmaier im Vergleich zu Zwingli und Luther," **Mennonitische Geschichtsblätter**, 31, (1974):7-24; Walter Klaasen, "Spiritualization in the Reformation," MQR, 37, (April, 1963):67-77. Of older vintage, but still stimulating in regard to this topic is Christof Sigwart, **Ulrich Zwingli** (Stuttgart, 1855). Also useful in gaining some insight into the spirituality of the Reformed tradition are the following on John Calvin: Otto Gründler, "John Calvin: Ingrafting into Christ," **The Spirituality of Western Christendom** (Kalamazoo, 1976), 169-187; Lucien Richard, **The Spirituality of John Calvin** (Atlanta, 1974); F. L. Battles, **The Piety of John Calvin** (Grand Rapids, 1978).

For the working definition of "spirituality" which I employ here I am indebted to Gründler, 170-171: "Spirituality, then, may be defined as that specific mode of existence characteristic of homo religiosus by which he participates in the Sacred and conforms himself to it."

2. "Auslegen und Gründe des Schlussreden," Z II: 1-457. For any translations of this work throughout this paper I utilize the translation into English of Edward J. Furcha which will appear as Volume I of Furcha/Pipkin.

3. "Eine kurze christliche Einleitung," Z II: 626-663. I use my translation which appears as Volume II of Furcha/Pipkin.

4. "Der Hirt," Z III: 1-68. I use my translation which will appear in Volume II of Furcha/Pipkin.

5. There is as yet no consensus on the significance of the various disputations in Zurich. I find to be helpful the assertion of B. Moeller, "Zwinglis Disputationen. Studien zu den Anfängen der Kirchenbildung und des Synodalwesens im Protestantismus," **Zeitschrift der Savigny-Stiftung für Rechtsgeschichte, Kanonistische Abteilung,** 56 (1970): 275-324; 60 (1974): 213-364: "Dies aber war nun der Zweck der I. Disputation: Es handelte sich gewissermassen um die Gründungsversammlung der evangelischen Kirche von Zürich," 319. See also Potter, 100-104 for a good brief overview of the disputation. Further issues are discussed as well in H. A. Obermann, **Masters of the Reformation** (New York, 1981), 210ff. The standard view of the First Disputation is challenged by Locher, 110-115. He sees the Second Disputation as "Der Durchbruch." See Locher, 129-136.

6. The Latin poem is contained in Desiderius Erasmus, **Opera Omnia,** Joannes Clericus (ed.), V: 1319e-1320c. The poem was translated by Leo Jud into German and published by Froschauer in 1522 as "Ein expostulation oder klag Jhesu zu dem menschen der uss eygnem mutwill verdampt würt."

7. Unless noted otherwise the quotations are from Z II.

8. "verlasst in den verdienst Christi," 182: 5.

9. "gar in got gelassen und vertruwt," 182: 17-18.

10. "hynlassen uff die gnad gottes," 95: 14; "an die gnad gottes sich gelassen hat," 92: 256.

11. "an got gelasset," 93: 31.

12. "verlassen sind uff sin wort," 44: 13-14.

13. See also the expositions of articles 44-46, 348: 1-354: 3.

14. "Von göttlicher und menschlicher Gerechtigkeit," 30 July 1523, Z II: 458-525.

15. For a longer treatment of the issue of divine and human righteousness in Zwingli, see R. C. Walton, **Zwingli's Theocracy** (Toronto, 1967); Heinrich Schmid, **Zwinglis Lehre von der göttlichen und menschlichen Gerechtigkeit** (Zurich, 1959); F. Büsser, **Huldrych Zwingli** (Zurich, 1973).

16. Cf. Z II: 346: 15-347: 4.

17. Büsser, **Huldrych Zwingli**, 78-79.

18. On the matter of images and iconoclasm in Zurich see C. M. N. Eire, Idolatry and the Reformation: A Study of the Protestant Attack on Catholic Worship in Germany, Switzerland and France, 1500-1580. Yale dissertation, 1979; Margarete Stirm, **Die Bilderfrage in der Reformation** (Gütersloh, 1977); C. Garside, Jr., **Zwingli and the Arts** (New Haven, 1966).

19. Cf. Charles Garside, Jr., "Ludwig Haetzer's Pamphlet Against Images: A Critical Study," MQR, 24 (1960): 20-36.

20. I note again that Locher sees the Second Disputation as the Breakthrough. See above, note 5.

21. The semi-official nature of the **Instruction** has been recognized. It was included in two important collections of Reformed confessions: E. G. A. Böckel, **Die Bekenntnisschriften der evangelishch-reformierten Kirche**, (Leipzig, 1846) and E. F. Karl Müller, **Die Bekenntnisschriften der reformierten Kirche** (Leipzig, 1903). A new High German rendering is also currently available: G. G. Muras (ed.), **Huldrych Zwingli, Christliche Anleitung**, (Gütersloh, 1978). See also Bullinger I: 135-137 for a contemporary analysis of the significance of this treatise.

22. It must be observed that the theological ideas contained in the **Instruction** are found in greater detail in the **Exposition**. It is the ordering of the ideas and their inclusion here that makes them significant for his spirituality.

23. The recent description of Zwingli's doctrine of sin by K. Aland is a typical misreading of Zwingli: "Die Erbsünde verflüchtigt sich, sie wird mehr zur Krankheit, als dass sie als Schuld aufgefasst wird." **Geschichte der Christenheit**, II, (Gütersloh, 1982), 150.

24. Elsewhere Zwingli describes Adam's death in the Fall as "the loss of the grace and friendship of God, the loss of the indwelling, ruling or leading of the spirit of God, the loss of the perfect order of human nature, and the fall into sin.." 631: 17-20.

25. This is a fundamental expression of the Zwinglian understanding of the Gospel. See 637: 18-638: 26.

26. Indeed, in a typical reformed fashion, Zwingli affirms that even faith comes from God: "Faith is not the result of human reason nor power, but of the hand and power of God." 638: 32-33.

27. The last two sections of the treatise deal with the questions of the use of images and the Mass as sacrifice, both of which are rejected because they conflict with a true spirituality. See 654: 10-663: 22.

28. Zwingli treats the doctrine of offense systematically in the "De vera et falsa religione commentarius," Z III: 888: 32–899: 39.

29. The treatise was translated into Latin by Rudolph Gwalter in his sixteenth century edition of Zwingli's works. An English translation by John Wernon Synonoys appeared in 1550 and circulated widely throughout England and Scotland.

30. From this point the citations will refer to Z III unless otherwise noted.

31. For example: Z I 373: 30–31; Z I: 289: 3–6; Z I: 300:13–15; Z I: 317: 11–14 among many others.

32. "The Christian people never lived godlier and more innocently than when no human additions or obligations were added to the simple word of God." 49: 13–16.

33. "This is certain: it is only hypocrisy when one speaks beautifully of God but does not form one's life according to him." 19: 35–20: 2. "Not doing what God has commanded is idolatry, damaging and deceptive." 29: 25–27.

34. "If faith is there then along with it follows love. Now if love and faith are already there then it is out of these that work is done and not with a view to payment." 44:16–19. "It is apparent that nothing other than divine love can bring the shepherd to deny himself, to leave father and mother, to go forth without purse, knapsack and staff, to be dragged before the princes, beaten, falsely accused and killed, and that love may not exist without the fundamental of undoubting trust." 43: 1–5.

35. Further statements on the poor are found in the following: 46: 8–12; 55: 26–28; 58: 13–15; 59: 25–26; 66: 31–67: 6.

36. I choose this term deliberately rather than, say, "theocentric spiritualism" or "pneumatology," a term favored by Schmidt-Clausing. A number of scholars are adopting the latter term (e.g. Locher) but others (e.g. Gestrich) prefer spiritual to pneumatological. It will be some time before this issue is sufficiently resolved. Much more is at stake, of course, than one label.

37. The observation of Gottfried Locher is appropos: "Damit verläuft die Grenze zwischen wahrer und falscher Religion nicht zwischen Christentum und Heidentum, sondern primär mitten durch das Christentum, ja durch jedes menschliche Herz." Locher, 1956.

38. Bullinger's comment in which he links the study of the Bible with the monastic hours of prayer is important: "Wie nun under dem Bapsthumm prim, tertz, Sept und non im Chor gelaesen und gesungen, nam man fuer, an deren statt umm die 8 im Chor (dann anfangs was noch kein Lectorium gepuwen, dahim hernach, und imm wynter uff die Stuben der Chorherren, dise Lection gelegen und gelegt ist) die heiligen biblischen geschrifft zuo raechtem quotem christlichem

verstand, uss den urspruenglichen sprachen, zuo laesen. Das alles ordnet der zwingli gar ordentlich." Bullinger I: 290. The opening prayer, which Bullinger gives in its entirety in the same place, is also significant for understanding the biblical spirituality of Zwingli. See F. Schmidt-Clausing, "Das Prophezeigebet," ZWA 12 (1964): 10-34. For Zwingli the educator see O. Rückert, **Ulrich Zwinglis Ideen zur Erziehung und Bildung** (Gotha, 1900), and my article on Zwingli the educator in E. Towns (ed.), **A History of Religious Educators** (Grand Rapids, 1975), 124-135.

39. A study of the word "fromm" and "Frommigkeit" which, according to context and person writing, means variously "pious," "godly" or "righteous" had varying meanings in the sixteenth century, not all of which were religious. Indeed it is true that the word often had ethical implications and was related to the various spheres of human activity. See V. Günter, "Fromm" in der Zürcher Reformation, Diss. Basel, Aarau, 1955 and E. E. Müller, "Das mittelalterliche und das reformatorische 'Fromm'," **Beiträge zur Geschichte der deutschen Sprache und Literatur**, 95 (1973): 333-357. A study of various sixteenth century lexicons reveals this ethical emphasis as well as a growing religious usage of the term. See, for example, Josua Maaler, **Die Teütsch spraach. Dictionarium Germanicolatinum novum** (Zurich, 1561), 144b for a listing of variations on "fromm."

40. This point is further developed in H. Wayne Pipkin, "The Making of a Pastor: Huldrych Zwingli's Path from Humanism to Reformation," Reformed Review, 37 (1984). Not only is it helpful to read Erasmus as such, but it is most instructful to read the translations of Erasmus done by Leo Jud. One finds, for example, the German translations of Erasmus' paraphrases of the Pauline epistles (1521), Jud's translation of the Enchiridion (1521) and the full New Testament, excepting Revelation (1523). This latter translation contains some very illuminating passages in the paraphrases of Timothy and Titus. When reading these translations one must keep reminding oneself that one is reading Erasmus and not Zwingli: the similarities are striking.

41. See Alfred Schindler, **Zwingli und die Kirchenväter**, (Zürich, 1984) for a helpful study of the patristic dependence of Zwingli. Schindler is a patristics scholar and therefore brings to this study a dimension that is often missing in Zwingli scholarship. One must respect his observations on the significance of Augustine, and of course of other fathers as well, in the thought of Zwingli. An anecdote related in note 99 should stimulate further research in the area: "Hier erinnere ich mich an eine persönliche Aeusserung Blankes, nachdem er meine Dissertation gelesen hatte: 'Jetzt sehe ich, woher Zwingli seinen Spiritualismus hatte, nämlich von Augustin'. Die Aeusserung muss sich auf das Verständnis von 'Wort' als einem äusseren Zeichen, welches grundsätlich von 'inneren Wort' geschieden ist, bezogen haben." (84) This is more than an anecdotal study, however, and Schindler's analyses suggest a considerable influence of Augustine.

ZWINGLI AND THE "VIRI MULTI ET EXCELLENTES"
THE CHRISTIAN RENAISSANCE'S REPUDIATION OF NEOTERICI
AND THE BEGINNINGS OF REFORMED PROTESTANTISM

James M. Stayer

The beginnings of the Reformation in Zurich have often been examined by weighing the theological influence of Martin Luther upon Ulrich Zwingli. Most recently and productively this has been done by Wilhelm H. Neuser, in his book, **Die reformatorische Wende bei Zwingli.** [1] Neuser has shown that there was a significant theological influence of Luther on Zwingli in the early fifteen-twenties. He has also made a good case that, in his reminiscences as Zurich Reformer, [2] Zwingli defensively minimized his debts both to Luther and to Erasmus of Rotterdam.

The object of this essay is not to deny either Luther's theological impact on Zwingli or the apologetic content of Zwingli's autobiographical reminiscences. Luther had an influence on all the other Reformers, both his disciples and his rivals, and all Reformers, including Luther, remembered their past in a way calculated to enhance, rather than to diminish, their teaching authority. The object here is rather to examine another fruitful finding of Neuser's, namely that Zwingli believed that, rather than being a disciple of either Erasmus or Luther, he had emerged from a brotherhood of Christian humanists, "viri multi et excellentes," [3] intent on achieving the Christian Renaissance through the rediscovery of the Gospel.

At first glance this notion seems to be what Walther Köhler called it on the occasion of the 1919 anniversary of the Zurich Reformation--an incapacity to distinguish between humanism and the Reformation. [4] Moreover, to the moment of his call to be a public preacher in Zurich at the beginning of 1519, Zwingli's Christian humanism was that of a papal partisan rather than an anti-papalist. At the time the humanist reformers had seemed to Zurich's ruling elite, who were papal partisans in the political sense of being anti-French in the military struggles over Italy, to be at once learned and useful, progressive but not dangerous, thus the very pinnacle of respectability. Yet by 1522 and 1523 this same ruling group found itself turned against its strategic intention from being papalist to becoming anti-papalist. Without quite knowing what had happened, it had allowed itself to become committed to harboring and protecting the most radically anti-Roman religious establishment of the early Reformation. By this time Erasmus wanted nothing further to do with Zwingli, his erstwhile humanist protégé, and some at least of the "viri multi et excellentes" were busy destroying Zwingli's humanist letters to them--creating lamentable gaps in our picture of the early Reformation in Zurich. Superficially the case for historical discontinuity between Christian humanism and the Reformation could hardly be stronger.

But Ulrich Zwingli, living out the early Reformation in Zurich, saw things differently. In August 1522, when he replied publicly in the **Apologeticus Archeteles** to an attack on him penned by Johannes Fabri, an erstwhile humanist comrade newly returned from Rome, he placed himself among "tantum numerum doctissimorum hominum" straining every nerve to restore the languages and literary text of the Scriptures. He urged his adversary to cease his obstinate opposition to the Christian Renaissance. [6] Unlike Luther, who believed he was the father of the Reformation, Zwingli saw himself as part of a fraternity of Reformers. Unlike many of today's church historians and theologians, Zwingli made no distinction between Christian Renaissance and Reformation, even at the moment of his break with Rome.

It is possible to judge that Zwingli was mistaken, but it is at least necessary first to try to understand why he saw things as he did. This is all the more important because his perception of how the Reformation began was the general one in Reformed churches, in Geneva, the Netherlands and England as well as Zurich. Here Erasmus' 1516 edition of the New Testament and his **Paraphrases**, rather than Luther's Ninety-Five Theses, were seen as the beginning of the Reformation. [7] A popular poem circulating in Zurich in the thirties, quite possibly by Leo Jud, described the succession of Biblical Reformers as beginning even with John Reuchlin. [8] This should alert us to the fact that there is more substance in the three-sided relation of scholasticism, humanism and Reformation than a "productive misunderstanding" of Luther.

This essay will propose that the previously mentioned **Apologeticus Archeteles** [9] and the printed sermon, **Von clarheit und gwüsse oder krafft des worts gottes,** [10] which appeared within two weeks of each other in late August and early September 1522, marked Zwingli's public commitment to an anti-papalist

Reformation in Zurich. In them Zwingli took the offensive not only against local conservatives in Zurich but also against an episcopal admonition directly inspired from Rome. Likewise, in these writings he declared himself to stand upon the sole authority of the Scriptures against all extra-Scriptural authority, whether papal, scholastic or even patristic.

In the **Archeteles** Zwingli trumpeted the anticlerical rhetoric of the early Reformation. He characterized his adversary, Fabri, as saying:

> "We are the priests, you are the laymen: we are the learned, you are the ignorant: the keys are ours, the purses yours: it is for us to pass our days in leisure, for you to earn your bread by the sweat of your brow: you must be kept from adultery, we shall revel freely in every sort of lust: you shall pay tribute and taxes, we will soothe our leisure with your offerings . . . " [11]

The popes are accused of claiming infallibility. [12] Above all, Fabri is roasted for his acceptance of extra-Scriptural revelation and the authority of scholastic doctors:

> "You once said (you know where yourself) that Christ said [John 16], 'I have yet many things to say to you, but you cannot bear them now,' for the purpose of reserving some parts of his testament to be afterwards spread about by Thomases and Scotuses." [13]

Fabri had visited with Zwingli and his humanist friends in Zurich as late as the fall of 1520. [14] Indeed, he was counted as one of them and his choice for Rome was part of the "division of spirits" among the humanists going on under the impact of the Luther controversy. [15] When the fronts had hardened a year later Zwingli complained to another of his important humanist correspondents, Beatus Rhenanus, that Fabri "will not budge an inch from the darkness of Scotus." [16] Fabri's combination of the scholastic via antiqua (his "Thomism" and "Scotism"), humanism and papalism had once not seemed so monstrous to Zwingli, because Zwingli had earlier shared precisely these same allegiances.

In this essay we will address ourselves to two important issues concerning Zwingli's development into a Reformer from among the "viri multi et excellentes" in the humanist brotherhood. The first is his abandonment of the via antiqua (never a complete one, as his controversial writings against Luther would show) in the pre-Zurich years. The second is his shift of fronts from papalist to anti-papalist in Zurich. It will be proposed that the first change, the abandonment of scholasticism, established important foundations for the later rejection of papalism, and that

Zwingli's affirmation of the sole authority of the Scriptures was part of the humanist battle to establish a new exegetical theology different from the dialectical theology of the scholastics. Of course important parts of Zwingli's intellectual and religious development cannot be investigated from this particular focus. Nevertheless, clearing away some inadequate stereotypes about the relations of scholasticism, humanism and Reformation does shed light on Zwingli as Reformer, and perhaps can contribute to understanding other Reformers as well.

Zwingli's intellectual and religious education before his encounter with Erasmian humanism and its sacred philology was eclectic, perhaps indigestibly eclectic. His schooling in the via antiqua at the university in Basel (1502-1506) does not make him "Scotist," in the sense that his beliefs can be understood from careful study of Duns Scotus. [17] Moreover he was not a scholastic before he became a humanist. He and his teachers and early associates, Lupulus, Thomas Wittenbach, Leo Jud, Glarean, were humanists and scholastics at the same time, just as were the two Picos and Jacques Lefèvre d'Etaples, whom Zwingli read in his pre-Erasmian years at Glarus. Comments like Oswald Myconius's, that Zwingli studied scholastic theology only "because the regular course of things demanded it," and "continued in the enemy camp, like a spy" [18] are contradicted by what we have of Zwingli's early correspondence. Glarean, for instance, referred to Zwingli as an "Aristotelian" in a letter from the 1507-1510 period, while he was a student at Cologne and Zwingli was beginning the pastorate at Glarus. [19] Zwingli possessed a heavily annotated edition of Scotus' commentary on the **Sentences** in a Venetian edition of 1503 and purchased the Basel edition of a reference work on Scotist theology by Johannes de Colonia. [20]

In 1510, Glarean, finishing at Cologne, asked Zwingli to help him to get a teaching post as a Scotist at Basel, because the "via seu secta Scoti" had an approach he much preferred to "the figments and nonsense about terminist logic of the innovators (neotericorum)." [21] Glarean assumed rightly, at this time, that Zwingli shared his distaste for the neoterici, in this case the via moderna of William of Ockham. The phrase would recur in their later polemics, extended from the Oakhamist terminists to scholastic teachers in general. At this point, however, Glarean and Zwingli, to judge from their correspondence and the books they read, were sympathetic to the scholastic via antiqua. It has sometimes been assumed that Ockhamism or "nominalism" as it was dubbed by its enemies, was the last impulse of scholasticism before Christian humanism and the Reformation. In fact the emergence of the via antiqua, as a conscious revival of the study of Aristotle through his classical scholastic commentators, who were less technical and less narrowly logical than the Ockhamists, began in Paris in the late fifteenth century and established itself in most South German universities (including Basel). It was intended as a return to a more "realistic," less "sophistical" approach to Aristotle, based on Averroes, Albertus Magnus, Thomas Aquinas, Aegidius Romanus, Alexander of Hales, Scotus and Bonaventura, according to its Parisian manifesto of 1493. In the battle against the Ockhamists in the discipline of logic Scotist techniques were applied: Scotist formalizantes challenged Ockhamist terministae in most of the teaching bodies. But in its broader philosophical and theological approach the via antiqua was a self-consciously eclectic revival of pre-Ockhamist scholasticism. [22] This eclecticism would have been compounded in Zwingli's case because the competition between the two "ways" was compromised at Basel by a university statute of 1494, with the result that his earlier, logical studies were guided by the terministae rather than the formalizantes. [23] The evidence is clear that the via antiqua of his university studies left a strong mark on Zwingli's later development; but, because of its inherent eclecticism it is idle to dispute, as has been done recently, whether this influence was Scotist or Thomist. [24] Again Zwingli himself is a very reliable witness, as when he wrote later: "Revocavit nos Luterus ad Scotica et Thomistica." [25]

In this connection his reminiscence about scholastic influence on his early beliefs on providence and predestination is worth a glance, all the more so since a change in attitudes on free will and predestination has frequently been regarded as Zwingli's real departure from Christian humanism into the Reformation camp:

> The view of Thomas Aquinas upon predestination, if only I remember his doctrine correctly, was this: God, seeing all things before they take place, predestined man's fate at the time when by his wisdom he saw what he was going to be like. This opinion pleased me once, when I cultivated scholasticism, but when I abandoned that and adhered to the purity of the divine oracles, it displeased me greatly. For St. Thomas believes that God's disposition in regard to us follows our own disposition. [26]

This interpretation of St. Thomas on predestination now seems incorrect, judged by the standard of his mature views in the **Summa Theologica**. However, it was held by such late medieval theologians as Gabriel Biel, based on Thomas's commentary on the **Sentences,** and it was still current in Zwingli's time. [27]

Suffice it to say that the via antiqua, which was less narrowly focused on logic than the via moderna, was receptive to the literary and rhetorical objectives of early humanism--and involved such outstanding humanists as Conrad Celtis, Rudolf Agricola and Lefèvre d'Etaples. [28] The Reuchlin controversy in which the Thomists at Cologne began to attack humanist study of sacred literature was one of the catalysts of the new division between scholastic realist and humanist. It began in 1510 and reached a boil with the publication of **The Letters of Obscure Men** in 1515-1517. The case is clear with Zwingli's friend and correspondent, Glarean. In 1512 he was still a friend of the Cologne scholastic, Ortvinus Gratius. Their works appeared in print together. The next year he vainly tried to dissuade Gratius from siding against Reuchlin. Gratius became the chief scholastic "villain" of **The Letters of Obscure Men** and Glarean one of the humanist "heroes." [29] Glarean moved to Basel shortly before Erasmus first came there to use Froben's press in August 1514. He and Erasmus soon became fast friends and he served as an intermediary between Erasmus and Zwingli.

Zwingli was ever a "spiritual Basler" in his pre-Zurich years, first attracted by the scholastic culture of the university, then by humanist scholars who worked for and used Basel's famous printing presses. He made his first trip to Basel to visit the great Erasmus in 1516, just after the publication there of the **Novum Instrumentum**, Erasmus' edition of the Greek New Testament, together with a fresh Latin translation and critical annotations. [30]

Zwingli's letters to humanist friends continued full of projects "to go down to Basel" and visit Erasmus and he actually made a visit as late as January 1522. [31] However coy Zwingli later became about his original allegiance to Erasmus, the evidence for it is overwhelming, and nowhere stronger and more explicit than in a devoted letter to Erasmus that he wrote after his introductory visit, dated 29 April 1516.

Zwingli's numerous reminiscences place the beginning of his preaching the Gospel between 1515 and 1517--before he heard of Luther, as he often said, and at the time of the appearance of the **Novum Instrumentum**. He almost immediately began to study Erasmus' New Testament, indeed to copy and memorize it in Greek at the beginning of his period as preacher at Einsiedeln [32] Zwingli seems to have been one of the inspirers of the later Reformed standpoint that Erasmus' Scriptural scholarship began the Reformation.

Because of the break which later occurred between them, it has been argued that Zwingli's allegiance was to the Scriptures rather than to the person of Erasmus. That is a viewpoint that lends itself easily to unverifiable psychological speculation. [33] There is no evidence that there was a difference of approach to Biblical scholarship between Zwingli and Erasmus in the Einsiedeln years. On the contrary, Zwingli absorbed many of Erasmus' most characteristic themes--spiritualism, imitatio Christi and an exegetical method patterned on the Greek fathers. [34] He kept these stresses throughout his career as a Reformer.

Two areas, however, where Zwingli and Erasmus are seen to have differed sooner or later are Zwingli's predestinarianism as opposed to Erasmus' defense of free will, [35] and Zwingli's radical formulation of the principle of Scriptural authority as scriptura sui ipsius interpres (the Scripture interprets itself) in contrast to Erasmus' view that the Church Fathers were the traditionally approved and legitimate interpreters of Scripture. [36] Here, if anywhere, it should be possible to identify the turn from Christian Renaissance to Reformation, a turn about which Zwingli, it must be remembered, gives us no direct information.

The matter of when Zwingli adopted the Reformation's doctrine of predestination may be one of the bigger straw men in the discussion of his reformatorischer Wende. If we are to accept his statement from **De Providentia Dei**, he abandoned the subordination of predestination to foreknowledge (which allowed for the freedom of the will) at the same time he turned away from scholasticism. [37] There is nothing inherently improbable about this--the delicate balance of divine predestination with human free will, both of which had to be affirmed, was a preoccupation of scholastics not humanists. The most prominent humanist statement on the subject, before Erasmus took it up, was not Pico's lyrical **Oration** (which had the odor of heresy about it) but Lorenzo Valla's **De libero arbitrio**, which had a standpoint exactly opposite to the later one of Erasmus. Valla made a firm statement that God's predestination rested not on his foreknowledge but on his eternal will; this work was edited by Zwingli's correspondent, and fellow humanist Reformer, Vadian, in 1516 and 1518. [38]

A close study of Zwingli's marginalia in the books and manuscripts in his personal library from the period before he came to Zurich yields an equivocal result. Zwingli's famous transcription of Paul to the Romans at Einsiedeln in 1517 contains many patristic marginal notations. Origen's voluntarist standpoint, preferred by Erasmus, is registered there; [39] but Origen was criticized: "I defer to the strait way of the cross of Christ, Origen to the broad one of the knowledge and wisdom of God." [40] A note to Lefèvre's **Psalterium quintuplex** from the same period seems to acknowledge the metaphysical contingency of some future events. [41] When Zwingli worked through a book on predestination by John Eck, his marginalia showed irritation both with Eck's scholastic method of exposition and his stress on merit and reward. [42]

An important preoccupation of Zwingli's providential piety from his scholastic period in Glarus onward was God's all-directing hand. In a tract on the subject by Giovanni Francesco Pico he underscored the allusion to Romans 9:20-22: "The earthen pot cannot properly complain about the skill of the potter." [43] The poem celebrating his recovery from the plague in Zurich in 1519 struck the same note: "Din haf bin ich--mach gantz ald brich." [44] The correspondence of the period when Zwingli was nerving himself for the break with Rome contains more of the same. Thus, the famous letter to Oswald Myconius of 24 July 1520, in which Zwingli brought himself to recognize the probability of a bull of excommunication against Luther: "I ask only that Christ permit me to endure everything with a manly heart and that he handle me as his clay vessel just as it pleases him--either to make me firm or shatter me." [45] At the end of 1521 he told Berchtold Haller in Berne that everything happens at God's command. [46] Finally, to Myconius on the eve of the publication of **Archeteles:** "We are God's vessels; he can use us to honor or disgrace." [47] This theme in Zwingli's thought is well known. There have been attempts to identify forceful expressions of it, whether the plague poem or the Myconius letter of July 1520, as the moment when Zwingli abandoned the humanist belief in free will for the Reformation belief in predestination. However, throughout the period, at least to March 1522 when he was still working on projects to avoid a public rupture between Luther and Erasmus, [48] Zwingli continued to regard Erasmus as part of his Reformation. Origen he cited respectfully both before and after his break with the papacy. [49] There is no good evidence that he valued either Erasmus or Origen as advocates of free will against predestination. Erasmus identified himself with that issue only when he took it up against Luther. Freedom of the will was rather a scholastic than a humanist position, since the majority of humanists inclined themselves to accepting some sort of necessity--whether the language was antique pagan or Christian or a combination of both. To summarize, the evidence suggests that Zwingli had abandoned notions of the subordination of divine predestination to divine foreknowledge (i.e., free will) well before he worked out a Reformed theology, and quite possibly when he turned away from scholastic theology to the Christian Renaissance, ca. 1516.

The more pregnant hypothesis about a possible disjuncture between Zwingli's humanist period and his period as a Reformer concerns his radical reliance on sola scriptura, the formal principle of the Reformation. This time Zwingli himself seems to supply the confirming evidence. As he remembered in **Von clarheit und gwüsse oder krafft des worts gottes:**

> When I began to rely entirely upon the Holy Scriptures
> seven or eight years ago, the philosophy and theology
> of the disputers was always getting in the way. So I
> finally got to the point that I thought--by the leading
> of the Scriptures and the Word of God--"You have to
> put all that aside and learn the meaning of God purely
> from his own simple Word". [50]

A comment in **Archeteles** seems explicitly to exclude patristic as well as scholastic authority:

> Thus you will find that in Augustine's opinion you ought to have unhesitating confidence in those only who are the authors of those Scriptures which are called Canonical (and these are those which are contained in the Bible) . . . Hence you have the Scripture as master and teacher and guide, not the Fathers, not this misunderstood Church of certain people. [51]

Later on in Zwingli's most systematic theological work, the **De vera et falsa religione commentarius** of 1525, his position was that:

> I have quoted these things from the weightiest of the Fathers, not because I wish to support by human authority a thing plain in itself and confirmed by the Word of God, but that it might become manifest to the feebler brethren that I am not the first to put forth this view, and that it does not lack very strong support. [52]

In fact, the Einsiedeln period was a period of intense patristic study for Zwingli, particularly of the Greek Fathers. His study then of the Froben edition of Chrysostom, with its series of sermons on Matthew, undoubtedly inspired his decision, upon the beginning of his Zurich ministry, to abandon the traditional order of daily Scripture lessons and preach on Matthew from beginning to end. Caspar Hedio, the future Strasbourg Reformer, described Zwingli's preaching at Einsiedeln, after a visit there, as "elegant, learned, weighty, substantial, penetrating, indeed such as to restore to us the power of the Fathers (veterum theologorum)." [53] Beatus Rhenanus also saw the significance of the Einsiedeln period as an abandonment of the neoterici for the veteres theologi, when he wrote Zwingli:

> I well know that you and your comrades present the purest philosophy of Christ to the people from the very sources--that is, not distorted by the Scotists and the Gabrielists, but elucidated genuinely and purely from Augustine, Ambrose, Cyprian, Jerome. [54]

There are good reasons to think that the anti-scholastic patristic stress continued in the preaching of Zwingli's early Zurich years leading up to the publication of the **Archeteles.** At least this was how Zwingli's preaching was perceived by Konrad Hofmann, one of Zwingli's predecessors at the Grossmünster and his conservative critic. In a long attack dating from the end of 1521 he complained that Zwingli publicly repudiated all the theologians and canonists "whom he calls new," that is, all who have taught in the last 380 years. Hofmann mentions by name a long list of scholastics whom Zwingli subjected to public scorn before the laity; and what is striking is that it is the eclectic honor roll of the via antiqua that is mentioned--Alexander of Hales, Bonaventura, Albertus Magnus, Aegidius Romanus, Thomas and Scotus. The Ockhamists were not worth mentioning, whether for Hofmann or Zwingli; in any case the figures Zwingli had once revered as approved theologians of the via antiqua were now classed with the Ockhamists as neoterici. [55] But Hofmann did not complain about Zwingli's disrespect for the Fathers. On the contrary, he objected to Zwingli's heavy reliance on Origen; and one of his demands was that Zwingli henceforth "present no odd teachings to the people, which he has gotten from some Greek books that have not yet been translated into Latin and are opposed to the Latin teachers." [56]

In a letter to Beatus Rhenanus, written in June 1520, just as the break between Luther and the papacy was becoming too clear to be ignored, Zwingli gave special praise to his fellow preacher Konrad Schmid of Küsnacht, a former student of Beatus Rhenanus. He described how Schmid had been weaned from scholasticism to the point where he was preaching the Gospel just as Zwingli did: "The man occupies himself with the Holy Scriptures and besides with Origen, Cyprian, Chrysostom, Jerome, Ambrose and the others." (my emphasis) Citing Origen on the behavior of a true bishop in this same letter, Zwingli enumerated the true bishops of his day: Reuchlin, Zasius, Pirkheimer, Rhenanus himself, Vadian, Melanchthon, Glarean, Petrus Mosellanus, Myconius, Sapidus. [57] This is one of the places where Zwingli got most specific in naming the "viri multi et excellentes" whom he was later to tell Luther were the real progenitors of the Reformation. These were not persons who abandoned the Fathers to allow the Scriptures to interpret themselves; that was never the practice of the Reformed churches, at most of some Anabaptists on their fringes; and, whatever he theorized in his writings of August and September 1522, it does not appear to have been Zwingli's own practice.

In his treatise **On the Clarity and Certainty or Power of the Word of God** in September 1522 Zwingli did indeed take up an absolutist position, basing his version of the Gospel on the inspiration of the Holy Spirit as opposed to all human authorities. It was an effective retort to his papalist enemies at the moment he broke with their traditions. It did not mean that the obvious interpretation was the best one. For instance, Zwingli mentioned Abraham's acceptance of God's command to sacrifice Isaac as a moment when the Spirit must have inspired, because otherwise the command would have lacked all reason and consistency. [58] He dealt with the objections of traditionalists that they, too called on the Spirit and came to a different result than he--and that therefore a traditional arbitrator must choose among conflicting interpretations--as proof that they preferred human to divine authority and therefore were bereft of the Spirit. [59] It was an absolutely dogmatic stance secured in its circularity. Because of its very arbitrariness, however, it became necessary for Zwingli and the other Reformed to invoke the Fathers, as they afterwards did, to show that they were not the first to hold their views and that they did "not lack very strong support." The claims to rely upon scriptura sola (or scriptura sui ipsius interpres) of Lutheran, Reformed and Anabaptist referred in practice to different ways of interpreting the Scriptures. De facto patristic authority was strongest among the Reformed because of their humanist antecedents.

From April to June 1520 Zwingli was involved in a humanist campaign organized by Erasmus himself to collect letters of support for Martin Dorp, a professor of theology at Louvain who was resisting the consensus of his colleagues against Luther. Dorp also took the stand that it was necessary for a theologian to learn Greek and Hebrew in order to study the Scriptures properly. [60] This was a vital issue for Erasmus, who had in 1519 engaged in controversy with the Louvain theologian, Latomus, on the necessity of languages for the theologian. According to Latomus the true theologian had no real need of the Scriptures, as he could take the Scriptural truths delivered to him by mere exegetes and arrange them in a timeless logical system. This view horrified Erasmus for whom the true theologian was the exegete, the tractator divinorum Voluminum. He insisted against Latomus that that was precisely what the Fathers had been, and that only through their careful and precise exegesis of the literal, historical meaning of Scripture could they ascend to a higher, spiritual sense. [61] Erasmus' definition of a humanist method in theology, that was an attempted revival of the patristic method, remained in force in the Reformed churches in Zurich, Basel and Geneva, in a what that it certainly did not among Lutherans or Anabaptists.

The argument has been, then, that in the areas of predestinarian beliefs and use of Scriptures, previously taken to mark the divide between Zwingli's Christian humanist and Reformed careers, there is no evidence of a turning point in the early Zurich years. Hence his claim that the Gospel continued to mean the same thing to him from 1516 onward becomes a lot more credible. However, if as we argued in an earlier article, Zwingli was called to Zurich as a protégé of Cardinal Mathias Shiner and as a papal partisan, there was indeed a point or a process by which Zwingli's Christian humanism turned against Rome--and soon afterwards against the considerable number of the "viri multi et excellentes," led by Erasmus himself, who maintained their allegiance to Rome. We can only suggest the outlines of what occurred, a process well studied elsewhere.

In the first year of his Zurich pastorate, before it was necessary to make some kind of public choice between the papacy and Luther, Zwingli maintained his connection with Schiner. He even used it to protect him against the enemies of the Christian Renaissance. In 1519 Schiner, staying in Zurich, was Zwingli's table companion and almost part of his humanist fraternity. Glarean and Beatus Rhenanus used their correspondence with Zwingli to communicate with the Cardinal. All sympathized with his political moves to block the election of Francis I of France as Holy Roman Emperor. [62] When one of Zwingli's traditionalist opponents wrote against him, Schiner used his influence with the bishop and council at Basel to see that the work was not published. [63] The anti-French partisanship that brought Zwingli to Zurich continued to bind him to the Cardinal. [64] Schiner, however, was for the time-being more papalist than the pope, since Leo X had to temporize with the French who then dominated northern Italy. In those years Schiner was somewhat out of favor in Rome and not averse to the anticlerical mood of the Christian humanist reformers. [65]

In 1520 when it became necessary to take a stand on the Luther issue, Schiner automatically accepted the excommunication bull. Zwingli, on the other hand, still on friendly terms with the papal representative in Switzerland, warned him that to act against Luther would lead to an undermining of the papal authority throughout the German-speaking countries. [66] Zwingli and his correspondents, including Erasmus, regarded the attacks against Luther as a threat to the whole anti-scholastic renewal of theology carried on by the Christian Renaissance.

Zwingli's sallies against the Zurich patricians who received French money were of a piece with a preaching that was unusually forceful and down to earth, named names and interested itself in the day-to-day incidents of civic life. His conservative predecessor, Konrad Hofmann, noted all this and found it deplorable. Zwingli quickly attracted a personal following. [67] Already at the end of 1519 he could write to Myconius: "We do not stand alone. In Zurich there are already more than two thousand more or less enlightened people who have up to now drunk spiritual milk and can soon digest solid food." [68] Zurich had five thousand inhabitants. In other words, while Schiner and his original patrons in the city government were still firmly behind him, Zwingli himself became a political factor in the life of the community. In these early modern towns with their negligible coercive powers, such a pastor's capacity to disturb public order, if necessary for the protection of his person and his mission, could not be taken lightly.

In 1520 the council published a mandate calling for the preaching of the Gospel. This was probably a gesture of support for Zwingli, but not a code word even for the support of the Christian Renaissance, much less for an anti-papal Reformation. [69] This is indicated by Hofmann's later indignant protest against Zwingli's trying to claim that he alone preached the Gospel properly:

> He claims that the Gospel was suppressed, hidden or not preached, or at least not rightly preached, or that someone forbade, prevented or dissuaded him from preaching and teaching the Holy Gospel and the old teachers . . . Now as long as I have had the capacity to understand I have always heard the preaching of the spiritual teaching, the Holy Gospel, and heard it and the other approved Holy writings to be esteemed, praised and obeyed. [70]

Nevertheless, when the quarrel between Zwingli and the religious orders heated up in the summer of 1522, the council referred back to this mandate as a justification for telling the monks not to base their teaching on Thomas and Scotus but on the Scriptures alone. [71]

Meanwhile 1521 was the year that Zwingli strengthened his hold on public policy in Zurich by radicalizing his opposition to mercenary warfare and abandoning all remnants of his erstwhile political papalism (he had given up his papal pension of fifty gulden in the previous year). In May Zurich alone of the Swiss Confederacy declined to participate in a mercenary alliance with Francis I. Zwingli was true to his traditional partisan loyalties in making a major contribution to this outcome. When in the summer Cardinal Schiner, now restored to favor in Rome, called on standing treaties to get a force of Zurichers to do some fighting for the pope in central Italy, Zwingli broke openly with his former patron. He warned from the pulpit against people who "quite appropriately wear red hats and cloaks; for if you shake them crowns and ducats fall out, and if you wring them out, the blood of your son, brother, father or good friend will run out." [72] The ruling group decided to honor the treaty, which Zwingli suggested should be sent back to Rome with a dagger stuck through it. But on 11 January 1522 the council met Zwingli's Erasmian pacifist program with a general prohibition of mercenary fighting by Zurichers, "whether for the pope, the Emperor, the King of France or any other princes and lords." [73]

Zwingli did not yet have a council committed to his religious views. That did not occur until 1526. But in his first three years in the pulpit in the Grossmünster he had established too strong a place in the civic and religious life of the town for anyone to challenge him effectively.

He never denied that the Luther affair had provided
the catalyst for the break with Rome, but he insisted that the
Gospel he preached in Zurich was the one he had preached since
1516, and that the Reformation was in divine terms the work
of the Holy Spirit, in human terms the work of a fraternity of
scholars of the Scripture, not the achievement of a single individual, however heroic. Is it out of place to suggest that Reformation
historians are only in the last twenty years catching up with
Zwingli's view of things? [74]

NOTES

1. (Neukirchen, 1977). See my review of Neuser in Zwa XV, 67-69.
The other most important contributions to the specific discussion of Zwingli's
development as a Reformer are Arthur Rich, **Die Anfänge der Theologie Huldrych
Zwinglis** (Zurich, 1949); J. F. Gerhard Goeters, "Zwinglis Werdegang als Erasmianer,"
in **Reformation and Humanismus. Robert Stupperich zum 65. Geburtstag** (Witten,
1949), 255-271; Gottfried W. Locher, **Die Zwinglische Reformation in Rahmen
der europäischen Kirchengeschichte** (Göttingen & Zurich, 1979), 55-122, esp. 115-
122.

2. Ulrich Gäbler, **Huldrych Zwingli im 20. Jahrhundert. Forschungsbericht
und annotierte Bibliographie 1897-1972** (Zurich, 1975), 41-44, has a valuable
comparison of Zwingli's autobiographical statements about the beginning of his
Reformation career.

3. Neuser, 65-70. Z V, 712-713: "Fuerunt multi atque excellentes
viri, qui, antequam Luteri nomen esset tam celebre, viderunt, unde penderet religio,
longe aliis praeceptoribus, quam tu putes, docti."

4. "Zwingli als Theologe," in **Ulrich Zwingli zum Gedächtnis der
Zürcher Reformation 1519-1919** (Zurich, 1919), 35.

5. See my "Zwingli before Zürich: Humanist Reformer and Papal
Partisan," ARG LXXII (1981), 55-68.

6. Z I, 273, 301. English citations from the **Archeteles** are from
Samuel Macauley Jackson (ed.), **The Latin Works and the Correspondence of Huldreich Zwingli** (New York & London, 1912), vol. I, here 222, 257.

7. Locher, **Zwinglische Reformation,** 121, n. 255.

8. Paul Boesch, "Zwingli-Gedichte (1539) des Andreas Zebedeus
und des Rudolph Gwalther," Zwa IX, 208-220; Gottfried W. Locher, "Eine alte
Deutung des Namens Zwingli" Zwa IX, 307-310.

9. Z I, 249-327.

10. Z I, 328-384.

11. Z I, 308; **Latin Works**, I, 267.

12. Z I, 309.

13. Z I, 303; **Latin Works**, I, 260.

14. Z VII, 354.

15. See Kurt Maeder, **Die Via Media in der Schweizerischen Reformation** (Zurich, 1970), <u>re</u> "die Scheidung der Geister," 54-88.

16. Z VII, 473.

17. See Oskar Farner, **Huldrych Zwingli**, I (Zurich, 1943), 213-226; Goeters, 256-262. The argument here varies significantly from both.

18. **Latin Works**, I, 4-5.

19. Z VII; <u>re</u> dating Goeters, 257-258, n. 15.

20. Goeters, 256-257; Walther Köhler, **Huldrych Zwinglis Bibliothek** (Zurich, 1921), 10-11, n. 74, 290.

21. Z VII, 3: "ut lectio mihi philosophica in via seu secta Scoti daretur, cuius doctrina luculentior et verior neotericorum de termino, figmentis atque nugaculis."

22. Hermann Hermelink, **Die theologische Fakultät in Tübingen vor der Reformation** (Tübingen, 1906), 133-145, 151.

23. J. V. Pollet, **Huldrych Zwingli et la Reforme en Suisse d'après les recherches recentes** (Paris, 1963), 15-16, 16. n. 1.

24. Locher, **Zwinglische Reformation**, 63, n. 49 vs. Goeters, 256-262.

25. Z IX, 537.

26. SS IV, 113; Clarence Nevin Heller (ed.) **The Latin Works of Huldreich Zwingli** (Philadelphia, 1929), vol. III, 184.

27. See the similar cases of Biel and John Eck in Heiko A. Oberman, **The Harvest of Medieval Theology** (Grand Rapids, 1967), 141-145. This seems to undermine the argument in Goeters, 259-260.

28. Hermelink, 152-154; Köhler, "Zwingli als Theologe," 15-16, 22.

29. O. F. Fritzsche, **Glarean, sein Leben und seine Schriften** (Frauenfeld, 1890), 10, 12, 18-20, 22, 85.

30. Z VII, 35-36; for the proper dating, see Goeters, 265, n. 59, 266, n. 62. Zwingli does not seem to have owned a copy of the 1516 **Novum Instrumentum;** he probably used the copy at the Cloister of Einsiedeln. He owned the 1519 edition (Köhler, **Zwinglis Bibliothek** n. 106).

31. Z VII, 329, 440, 494-495, 499-500.

32. Goeters 1969, 268-269; Walther Köhler, in Z XII, 1-2.

33. For instance in Gottfried W. Locher, "Zwingli and Erasmus," Zwa XIII, 37-61, esp. 46, 56-57.

34. Re imitatio Christi, Locher, **Zwinglische Reformation**, 116, n. 228; re spiritualism (which I use deliberately, rather than the euphemism "pneumatology") Christoph Gestrich, **Zwingli als Theologe. Glaube und Geist beim Züricher Reformator** (Zurich & Stuttgart, 1967), passim, esp. 25, n. 21.

35. The particular stress of Arthur Rich.

36. The particular stress of Gottfried W. Locher.

37. SS IV, 113; **Latin Works,** III, 184.

38. J. M. Usteri, "Initia Zwinglii," in **Theologische Studien und Kritiken** LIX (1886), 153-154.

39. Z XII, 27: to Rom. 8:30: "Or[igenes]: non propterea erit aliquid, quia id scit deus futurum, sed quia futurum scitur a deo, antequam fiat."

40. Z XII, 28.

41. Z XII, 281: "futura enim vel contingenter vel necessario deo tam sunt certa et praesentia quam nobis preterita quae mutari non possunt."

42. Usteri, "Initia Zwinglii" (1885), 647-652; Z XII, 246-253.

43. Ibid., 644: "Nec vas testaceum figuli artem culpare merito potest."

44. Z I, 67.

45. Z VII, 344: "hoc unum Christum obtestans, ut masculo omnia pectore ferre donet et me, figulinum suum, rumpat aut firmet, ut illi placitum sit."

46. Ibid., 486.

47. Ibid., "Eius enim vasculum sumus; nobis uti potest et ad honorem et ad ignominiam."

48. Ibid., 496-498.

49. E.g., Z III, 811-813; Z VII, 289, 325.

50. Z I, 379.

51. Ibid., 306-307; **Latin Works**, I, 264-265.

52. Z III, 816; **Latin Works**, III, 247-248.

53. Z VII, 106, 213; Z XII, 169-170, 172-186; Goeters, 269-271, n. 78.

54. Z VII, 115; an explicit reference to the neoterici in the new sense of referring not merely to the moderni but to all scholastics, on Z VII, 288; Z V, 925; to the veteres theologi on Z V 929.

55. Staatsarchiv Zürich E I 3.2a fasc. 11, 138ro.,vo: ". . . meister Vrich Zwingly vnsser lütpriester die summisten, lerer vnd prediger (die er nüw nempt) die da in achtzig vnd dryhundert iaren har, geschriben vnd gelert hand, als dann sind in der heiligen geschrifft der meister von den hochen sinnen, Alexander de Ales, Sctus Bonaventura, Albertus Magnus, Beatus Thomas, Petrus de Palude, Egdius Romanus . . . offenlich vff der kantzel vor dem gemeinen versamloten volck genempt hatt toll fantasten, vnd ire lere wüst pfutzen oder mistlachen . . . vnd Sant Thomas mit dez Scoto für ander geschulttet, verachttet vnd vernütet hatt . . . " (Erasmus, in the **Enchiridion**, anticipated this classification of all scholastic theologians as neoterici, LBV, 8 D.)

56. Ibid., 140ro.,vo.: ". . . das er ouch kein seltzamj lere dem volck fürgebe, die er nach sinen beduncken gezogen vs ettlichen krüchischen bücheren, die noch nit in die Latinisch sprach gewendt sind, die wider die latinschen lerer sye."

57. Z VII, 323-327.

58. Z I, 362-363.

59. Ibid., 374-376.

60. Z VII, 292-293, 308, 328, esp. 308: "Legisti praeterea orationem Dorpii de linguis discendis propter sacras literas."

61. G. Chantraine, "L'Apologia ad Latomum. Deux conceptions de la theologie," in J. Coppens (ed.), **Scrinium Erasmianum**, vol. II (Leyden, 1969), 51-75; J. Clericus (ed.), **Desiderii Erasmi Roterodami opera omnia** (Leyden, 1703-1706), IX, 79B-106E (**Apologia rejiciens quorundam suspiciones ac rumores, natos ex dialogo figurato, qui Jacobo Latomo Sacrae Theologiae licentiato inscribitur**).

154

62. Z VII, 128, 146-147, 150, 157-158, 162, 179, 187.

63. Ibid., 230-231.

64. Esp. ibid., 191-192.

65. Albert Büchi, **Kardinal Matthäus Schiner als Staatsmann und Kirchen-fürst,** II (Freibourg & Leipzig, 1937), 424-433.

66. Z VII, 344.

67. Staatsarchiv Zürich E I 3.2a fasc. 11, 130ro - 136vo.

68. Z VII, 245: "Non enim soli sumus: Tiguri plus duobus millibus parvulorum et rationalium, qui lac iam spiritale sugentes mox solidum cibum perficient . . . ".

69. Locher, **Zwinglische Reformation,** 94-95, where there is a clarifying and convincing discussion of the previously disputed issue of the mandate of 1520.

70. Staatsarchiv Zürich E I 3.2a fasc. 11, 140vo.: ". . . er fürgipt oder fürgeben hatt, das man das heilig Euangelium vnderschlagen, verborgen, oder nit geprediget hab, oder nit recht gepredigt hab, oder das im iemant verbotten, gewert, oder widerratten hab ze predigen vnd ze leren das heilig euangelium oder die altten lerer . . . dann ich hab allwegen, so lang ich ettwas verstands hab gehept, der geistlichen lere, das heilig euangelium hören predigen, vnd das selb vnd die ander bewert heilig gschrifft also hoch hören achtten, loben vnd haltten . . ."

71. Z VII, 549; Locher, **Zwinglische Reformation,** 100-101.

72. Z I, 73: "Sy tragind billich rote hut und mäntel; dann schütte man sy, so fallind duggaten und kronen herus; winde man sy, so rundt dines suns, bruders, vatters und guten fründts blut herus."

73. Oskar Farner, **Huldrych Zwingli,** III (Zurich, 1954), 222-236, esp. 234.

74. This essay was written in 1983 while I was enjoying the support of a Leave Fellowship from the Social Sciences and Humanities Research Council of Canada. An abridged version of it was read at the meeting of the American Society for Reformation Research, Kalamazoo, Michigan, May 10, 1984. Thanks are due to Prof. Ulrich Gäbler of the Free University of Amsterdam for corrections originating from his comment on the paper read at Kalamazoo.

ZWINGLI'S SACRAMENTAL VIEWS

Peter Stephens

The sacraments in Zwingli can be properly understood only in the context of his life and theology, for it is not this or that doctrine which impinges on the sacraments, but all of them in one way or another. The sovereignty of God, the person and work of Christ, the presence of the Spirit, all affect Zwingli's understanding of the sacraments, as does his doctrine of Scripture, salvation, humankind, and the church. Some have a more decisive role than others, but they all interpenetrate in the way he formulates his view of them. Moreover, the sacraments were at the heart of medieval religion and were therefore naturally at the heart of the conflict provoked by the reformation. Zwingli's view of them is expressed largely in controversial writings which gives a greater emphasis to the opinions he rejects than to those he holds. The constant controversy may also have been one of the factors preventing him from expressing a more positive view. [1]

The word sacrament itself is rejected by Zwingli, both because it is wrongly understood by people and because it groups together rites which are better understood individually. In the **Exposition of the Articles** in 1523 he points out that "sacrament" is derived from sacramentum, meaning an oath. It could therefore be used of those things which "God has instituted, commanded, and ordained with his word, which is as firm and sure as if he had sworn an oath thereto". That however would exclude things which we call sacraments of which God has not spoken, such as confirmation; and it would include what we do not, such as alms and excommunication. Nevertheless Zwingli can accept the use of the term sacrament for the body and blood of Christ, if it means "a sure sign or seal". The sacrament can also be an assurance of the forgiveness of sins by Christ to believers who are weak. The sacraments are called pledges. But we should not use the same term to cover both things instituted by God and things instituted by human beings. In any case the term sacrament is a Latin word which Germans do not understand and do not need, as each of those rites called a sacrament has its own name. Moreover, it is a word that Christ did not use. [2]

Between the **Exposition of the Articles** and the discussion of the sacraments in his **Commentary** of 1525 some important changes take place in Zwingli's presentation of the sacraments. The term oath is seen as referring to our oath or pledge rather than to God's oath, and the idea of the sacraments as an assurance of forgiveness disappears. The changes take place in discussions primarily of the Lord's Supper, the first one particularly in reflection on 1 Corinthians 10. In his discussion of 1 Corinthians 10:16-17 in **Proposal** (May 1524) Zwingli refers to the sacrament as "an inward and outward union of Christian people". We eat and drink "so that we may testify to all men that we are one body and one brotherhood". We are moveover obliged to give ourselves for one another just as Christ gave himself for us. Alongside this new view the old view is present that the sacrament is "a sign and assurance of the testament", the testament being the forgiveness of sins. We take the sign and assurance of the testament both for the hunger of the soul and for the renewal of the brotherhood. However by sharing in the sacrament no one can strengthen or testify to the faith of someone else. [3]

The **Christian Reply to Bishop Hugo** of August 1524 gives further expression to this new position. We publicly bind ourselves to our brethren in the pledge or covenant (Pflicht) which Christ has instituted. He indeed gave us before his death a will or sacrament with which we pledge ourselves eternally to each other, just as Christ has bound us to God. [4] In his **Reply to Emser** written at the same time he speaks of the eucharist as being given so that "by this sacred pledge (initiation) as it were" we may be united into the one army and people of God. [5] Zwingli also begins to relate the oath of allegiance which Christians make to the meaning of the word sacrament, as an oath. [6] This illustrates in part the way in which the accent has shifted from God to Christians as the subject of the Sacraments. The covenant or oath that Christians make to each other is illustrated by analogies from Swiss national life, although its origin is not to be found there, but rather in the interpretation of 1 Corinthians 10. [7]

A change also takes place in what is said about the sacraments as strengthening faith. In this the dualism in Zwingli's anthropology plays a part. The letter to Thomas Wyttenbach (June 1523) speaks of those who are weak in faith as strengthened by the sacraments. The sacraments strengthen faith, but do not give it where it does not exist. The spirit which is inwardly taught by the Holy Spirit is made more sure and joyful by a visible sign. In this context Zwingli refers to the body as weighing down the soul, and blinding the spirit with its mists. However, the later strong contrast and separation in which the body has no effect on the spirit is not explicit here. Although the strong in faith do not need the sacrament for the strengthening of faith, yet they come to it for spiritual enjoyment and to delight (amoe-nare) their faith. [8]

Zwingli's letter to Fridolin Lindauer (October 1524) contrasts the outward and the inward person rather than the weak and strong in faith. The sacraments are said to be given for the instruction of the outward person which grasps matters through the senses, whereas the inward person cannot learn or become a believer through outward things. So that God may satisfy the whole being, that is the inward as well as the outward, he commands that the person who already believes should be baptized. He does not do this because he wants the spirit to be purified in this way, for a substance that is incorporeal cannot be purified by a corporeal element, but so that the outward person may be initiated by the visible sign and become certain of the thing which happens with the inward person by the light of faith or the manifest word of the grace of God. [9]

The sacraments are now no longer called assurances of salvation, though they are in some sense an assurance for the outward person. Whereas before this, the man who was strong in faith, probably by virtue of the clear word of God's grace, did not need the sacraments to strengthen his faith, although the man weak in faith did, now it is man as a person with senses for whom the sacraments are useful, for it is the senses to which the sacraments appeal, not the spirit. As Zwingli is to put it in **Those Who Give Cause for Sedition** in December 1524, "our eyes want also to see, otherwise Christ would not have instituted" baptism and the eucharist. [10]

In his second main discussion of the sacraments in the **Commentary**, the change of position from **Exposition of the Articles** is evident. Again Zwingli criticizes the use of the term sacrament as obscuring and confusing the meaning of the things to which it is applied. However because it has come into use he is prepared to accept it, but only for baptism and the Lord's Supper, since they are initiatory ceremonies or pledges. [11] This has now become the fundamental element in his understanding of the sacraments. He arrives at this by pointing out that the word sacrament meant for Varro "a pledge which litigants deposited at some altar, and the winner got back his pledge or money". It is also an oath, a use still current in France and Italy; and finally it is a "military sacrament by which soldiers are bound to obey their general according to the rights or laws of war". The word was not used "among the ancients to mean a sacred and secret thing", nor does it properly represent the Greek word mystery in Ephesians 5:32. In the light of all this Zwingli states that "a sacrament is nothing else than an initiatory ceremony or a pledging. For just as those who were about to enter upon litigation deposited a certain amount of money, which could not be taken away except by the winner, so those who are initiated by sacraments bind and pledge themselves, and, as it were, seal a contract not to draw back". [12]

From this standpoint he attacks three other positions: Catholic, Lutheran, and Anabaptist. The first is expressed in the way ordinary people understand the word sacrament; hence Zwingli's desire not to use the term. "For when they hear the word sacrament they think of something great and holy which by its own power can free the conscience from sin." However a sacrament "cannot have any power to free the conscience, if it is simply an initiation or public inauguration". Underlying Zwingli's attack on this position is his understanding of God and salvation. God alone is able to free his conscience, "for it is known to him alone, for he alone can penetrate to it". He supports this by referenced to the words of Solomon, "For you alone know the hearts of the children of men" (2 Chronicles 6:30) and those of the Pharisees, "Who can forgive sins, but God alone?" (Luke 5:21). An implication of all this is that no created thing can know a person inwardly or cleanse his mind or conscience. [13]

Zwingli can accept the Lutheran view when it speaks of a sacrament as "the sign of a holy thing", but not when it insists "that when you perform the sacrament outwardly a purification is certainly performed inwardly". His opposition to this view springs from his understanding of faith and of the freedom of the Spirit, and from the testimony of what happened with baptism in the New Testament. Faith "is born only when a man begins to despair of himself, and to see that he must trust in God alone". The change that happens in the believer as he becomes a new person through the work of the Spirit is something of which he is aware. Water does not contribute to this, for you could cover people with the River Jordan and say the baptismal words a thousand times, but people would not feel a change of mind. However, because of superstitious views of the sacraments, people may of course think "they have found, nay, actually felt, salvation, when they have not felt anything at all within, as is shown by their subsequent lives". Acts 19 gives an example of this, while in Acts 10 Cornelius received the Spirit and was sure of the grace of God before baptism. Then Zwingli presents a more fundamental objection to the view that, at the same time as we administer the sacraments outwardly, what they signify happens inwardly. With such a view "the freedom of the divine Spirit would be bound, who distributes to each, as he wills, that is: to whom, when, and where he will". However, the examples given from the New Testament show that the Spirit is not bound by signs. [14]

The Anabaptists rightly reject the Catholic and Lutheran positions. However they hold that "a sacrament is a sign which is given only when atonement has been made in the mind, but is given for the purpose of rendering the recipient sure that what is signified by the sacrament has now been accomplished". But, Zwingli asks, what is the need of baptism to make someone sure, when if he believes he is already sure of God's forgiveness? [15]

Zwingli's view differs from all these. For him sacraments are signs "by which a man proves to the church that he either aims to be, or is, a soldier of Christ, and which inform the whole church rather than yourself of your faith". By baptism and the Lord's Supper we are initiated, that by the first we give in our name, that is, enter the church, and by the second, remembering Christ's victory, we show ourselves members of his church. "In baptism we receive a token (symbolum) that we are to fashion our lives according to the rule of Christ; by the Lord's Supper we give proof that we trust in the death of Christ . . . " This faith in Christ involves the living of a new life in accordance with Christ's commands.

Baptism, Rebaptism and Infant Baptism, published two months after the **Commentary,** offers a positive as well as a negative view of the sacraments. Christ is seen as one who has done away with outward things so that we are not to look for justification in them. (In Christ it is the Spirit who gives life, not outward things.) However, Christ has given us two outward signs "as a concession to our frailty". Zwingli uses the word sacrament of these, but only after stating that no outward thing can take away sin. Sacrament is rather equivalent to a pledge of allegiance (Pflichtszeichen).

> If a man sews on a white cross, he proclaims that he wishes to be a confederate. And if he makes the pilgrimage to Nähenfels and gives God praise and thanksgiving for the victory vouchsafed to our forefathers, he testifies that he is a confederate indeed. Similarly the man who receives the mark of baptism is the one who is resolved to hear what God says to him, to learn the divine precepts and to live his life in accordance with them. And the man who in the remembrance or supper gives thanks to God in the congregation testifies to the fact that from the very heart he rejoices in the death of Christ and thanks him for it. [17]

Zwingli makes a sharp distinction between the sign and what it signifies, insisting that signs cannot be what they signify, or they are no longer signs. He also compares the two main signs of the Old Testament and of the New, a comparison that was to be influential in his sacramental teaching. These covenant signs he distinguishes from other signs. He allows that "some signs are given the better to confirm faith, or in some sort to reassure the flesh, which does not allow faith any rest", but they are miraculous signs not covenant signs. The fundamental reason Zwingli gives for this is that outward things cannot confirm faith, as faith does not come from them, but from God. This of course raises the question whether miraculous signs can confirm faith. He admits that they were given to confirm faith, "but even this does not mean that they add anything to faith or augment it, but that they satisfy the curiosity of the flesh which is constantly itching to see and to know". However if a person has no faith miraculous signs do not give him faith, as examples from the Bible show. Zwingli confesses that earlier he erroneously held the view that sacraments confirm faith. [18]

There is an important change in Zwingli's understanding of covenant signs in 1525, deriving from his understanding of the covenant. Zwingli had naturally used the term covenant of God's covenant with man, but in 1525 this view is developed and is related to the sacraments as signs of the covenant of grace made by God with man, that he will be their God and they will be his people. [19] Until this the sacraments have been seen as the covenant or pledge made between the Christian and his fellow Christians. This development takes place in terms of the eucharist but is of particular importance in Zwingli's controversy with the Anabaptists, as it gives greater coherence to his arguments for infant baptism. [20] This change gives a stronger theological and historical dimension to Zwingli's understanding of the sacraments.

Although there is a clear change of emphasis and expression in Zwingli's later writings there is not that fundamental change of position which some have asserted. The most obvious change is in **Exposition of the Faith** which merits separate attention. The other writings can be grouped together, especially **Two Replies to Luther's Book, Confession of the Faith, The Providence of God,** and to some extent **Letter to the Princes of Germany.** [21]

The fundamental role of the sovereignty of God in Zwingli's understanding of the sacraments is clear in **Confession of the Faith.** It dominates the first half of the article on the sacraments. The reason why they cannot enter grace is that grace is given by the Spirit. "Moreover, a channel or vehicle is not necessary to the Spirit, for he himself is the virtue and energy whereby all things are borne, and has no need of being borne." In his sovereign freedom the Spirit does not need outward means and is certainly not bound by them, either in the sense that he must work where they are present, "for if it were thus it would be known how, where, whence, and whither the Spirit is given", or in the sense that he cannot work apart from them, for the Spirit blows where he wills. Elsewhere the freedom of the Spirit in relation to outward means is put more positively, where Zwingli says, "And one and the same Spirit works all things, sometimes without, sometimes with the external instrument, and in inspiring draws where, as much, and whom he wills." [22] Although certain things are attributed to the sacraments in scripture, that is simply parallel to the way in which forgiveness of sins is ascribed to the apostles. If the sacraments were of themselves effective then Judas would have repented. However, repentance is the work of the Spirit, as is faith, which the Spirit effects before the sacraments take place. Zwingli regards as sacramentarians those who "attribute to the symbols what belongs only to the divine power and the Holy Spirit working immediately in our souls", and who thus lead people away from simple trust in God to trust in the power of symbols. [23] His concern is that glory shall be given to God and not to the sacraments. [24]

Zwingli's profound suspicion of outward things in religion is derived in part from Augustine's neo-platonism with its stress on the inward over against the outward, the Spirit over against the visible. He is constantly quoted in Zwingli's support, notably in **Letter to the Princes of Germany.** [25] However, the suspicion of outward things needs also to be set in the context of medieval religion, with its superstitious attachment to people, places, and things, not least to the sacraments, and the financial exploitation of this by the church. This attachment is for him a restoration of Judaism and puts man and his works in the place of God.

> For if we think overwise of the sacraments, as that when externally used they cleanse internally, Judaism is restored, which believed that crimes were expiated, and grace, as it were, purchased and obtained by various anointings, ointments, offerings, victims, and banquets. Nevertheless, the prophets, especially Isaiah and Jeremiah, always most steadfastly urged in their teaching that the promises and benefits of God are given by God's liberality, and not with respect to merits or external ceremonies. [26]

The sharp distinction between the sign and what it signifies fits this basic theological position. In this context he happily accepts in **Two Replies to Luther's Book** the traditional definitions of a sacrament as "a sign of a holy thing" or "a visible form or figure of an invisible grace". The sign is not the holy thing itself, although it takes the name of what it signifies. This is true of secular signs as it is of biblical signs. Moreover, it does not follow that what is signified is present with the sign, otherwise since baptism is the sacrament of the death of Christ, Christ would have to die wherever there was a baptism. It is rather a sacrament of something that has happened. Furthermore a sacrament does not make present what it signifies, but it shows and attests that what it signifies is there. Thus baptism does not make people God's children, but those who are already God's children receive the sign and testimony of God's children. [27] Zwingli can therefore speak of a sacrament as a sign of a grace that has been given. [28] The signs make their appeal to the senses, but what they signify must already be present to the mind or soul. [29]

The Bible is full of examples in which God makes use of what is outward to accomplish his purposes, and the commentaries naturally refer to this. It is allowed that God could act without means, but nevertheless he uses them. Thus in the story of the flood he used wind and rain, which he had created for this, although he could have filled the earth with water by his word alone. [30] Unlike us God does not need to use outward means; he uses them for our sake not for his own. [31] This does not alter the fact that the power is entirely of God and that it does not reside in the means that are used. It is God who for example heals the sick, which he does through the outward means that he has chosen. [32] This position is at one with Zwingli's view that God is the cause of all things. "And to put it briefly, the ground does not bring forth, nor the water nourish, nor the air fructify, nor the fire warm, nor the sun itself, but rather that power which is the origin of all things, their life and strength, uses the earth as the instrument wherewith to produce and create." [33]

This sense that it is God who is at work in all outward things could have led to a more positive view of the sacraments as means that God uses, although it would still have been qualified by Zwingli's sharp distinction between the outward and the inward. In such a view God's sovereignty could have been safeguarded, and the doctrine of election could have been used, as with Bucer, to indicate that the sacraments are effective only with the elect. The distinction of outward and inward could have been expressed by the use of the preposition with (rather than with Luther the prepositions in and under) to express the relationship between what is signified and the sign. But the opposition of outward and inward is so strong in Zwingli's thinking that this development does not seem possible for him. Nevertheless in **Exposition of the Faith,** and at some points in other writings, he does speak more positively of the outward signs, and seems to allow that things happen together on two levels.

Indeed the whole presentation of the sacraments in **Exposition of the Faith** is essentially positive. Earlier, in the opening section on God and the worship of God, Zwingli makes it clear that we are not to trust in the sacraments for that would be to make them God, whereas they are creatures not creator. They are signs of holy things, but they are not more what they signify than the word 'ape' when written down is an ape. Zwingli asserts that they do not have the power that belongs to God alone, but he heads his section on sacraments the power (or virtue) of the sacraments. [34]

The first two virtues are historical. First, the sacraments were instituted by Christ and what is more he received the one and was the first to celebrate the other. Second, they testify to actual historical events. The next three, perhaps four, virtues involve the relationship between the sign and what it signifies, of which one, the third virtue, is already familiar: they take the place and name of what they signify. [35]

The fourth virtue is that they signify high things. Here Zwingli uses the analogy of the ring which was used earlier in **The Lord's Supper.** [36] The value of the Queen's ring comes less from the value of the gold than from the value of the person it represents, the king. "In the same way the bread and wine are the symbols of the friendship by which God is reconciled to the human race in and through his Son." The bread can therefore be spoken of as consecrated and not common, and it is called the body of Christ as well as bread. [37]

The analogy is expounded at much greater length in **Letter to the Princes of Germany** as a statement of his view of the eucharist. There is here a stronger sense of something happening at two levels. A husband, before going on a long journey, gives his wife a ring with his image cut upon it, saying, "Here am I, your husband, for you to keep and delight in in my absence". He is a type of Christ, who when going away left his spouse, the church, his own image in the sacrament of the supper. "As he is the strong foundation of our hope, so does the bread strengthen mankind, and as wine refreshes the heart of man, so does he raise up despairing consciences." It is as if Christ said, "I am wholly yours in all that I am. In witness of this I entrust to you a symbol of this my surrender and testament, to awaken in you the remembrance of me and of my goodness to you, that when you see this bread and this cup, held forth in this memorial supper, you may remember me as delivered up for you, just as if you saw me before you as you see me now, eating with you . . . "

> Thus I say we have the Lord's Supper distinguished by the presence of Christ. But in all this is not the presence of the body of Christ sacramentally and to the eye of faith, as I have always said, the gist of the whole matter? . . . The repast of the supper, though not Christ's material body, rises to high value because it was given and instituted as an everlasting sign of the love of Christ, and

> because as often as it is celebrated it so represents
> him who so loves us that we gaze upon him with the
> eye of the mind and adore and worship him . . . In the
> supper the body of Christ is the more present to the
> contemplation of the believing mind, the greater one's
> faith and love is towards Christ. [38]

All this is still only representing Christ rather than presenting him, but there is a clear relationship for the believer between what is happening outwardly and what is happening inwardly.

The fifth virtue is the twofold analogy between the signs and what they signify. There is an analogy to Christ, for the bread sustains human life as Christ sustains the soul, and to us, for the bread is made up of many grains as the body of the church is made up of many members. [39]

The next virtue is dealt with at greatest length, and with the fourth is the closest Zwingli comes to a traditional affirmation of what the sacraments do, when he says that they "augment faith and are an aid to it". They are a help in terms of the senses, for it is through them that we are so often led astray. The sacraments appeal powerfully to the senses. They are indeed "like bridles which serve to check the senses when they are on the point of dashing off in pursuit of their own desires, and to recall them to the obedience of the heart and of faith". "Therefore the sacraments assist the contemplation of faith . . . " [40]

In **Letter to the Princes of Germany** Zwingli makes it clear that the sacraments were instituted to make use of the senses. He grants that "all created things invite us to the contemplation of the deity, yet this invitation is an altogether dumb one. In the sacraments we have a living and speaking invitation. For the Lord himself speaks, the elements speak, and they speak and suggest (suadent) to the senses the same thing that the word and the Spirit do to the mind." Therefore the believer does not neglect or despise the sacraments. Indeed Zwingli's encouragement of their use is eager rather than defensive.

> For who can disdain the things of 'love? And is not the
> love of God and of one's neighbour eager to call to
> mind the goodness of God and to praise and magnify
> him with thanksgiving? Is it not eager to be united to
> its neighbour by the bond of the Spirit and to bear witness
> thereto openly? Does it not desire to have its faith propped
> up and restored, when it sees it wavering? And where
> in the world can he hope to find that better than in
> the celebration of the sacraments, as far as visible things
> are concerned?

However the appeal to the senses in the sacrament, powerful as it is, is ineffective unless the person has faith, unless the Spirit is present and active in him. "But when these things are contemplated the sacraments not only set them before our eyes, but even enable them to penetrate to the mind. But what leads the way? The Spirit." "Since, therefore, this presence amounts to nothing without the contemplation of faith, it belongs to faith that the things are or become present, and not to the sacraments. For, however much they lay hold on the senses and lead to reverence for the things that are done, these handmaidens can effect nothing unless their mistress, faith, first rules and commands on the throne of the heart." [41] At points throughout his writings Zwingli refers to the fact that the weak in faith need the sacraments or that they serve the senses, though particularly in his later works. However he does it in these two works more fully and positively than elsewhere. In the earlier writings it seems much more a matter of concession to the weak. [42]

The seventh virtue of the sacraments is that they act as an oath. Those who eat his body sacramentally are joined in one body, so that any one who enters it without faith betrays the body of Christ, both the head and the members of the body. [43]

There is a movement in Zwingli's understanding of the sacraments from the earlier writings where they are signs of the covenant with which God assures us, through a period where the emphasis is on them as signs with which we assure others that we are one with them in the church, to the later writings where something of both these emphases is present. The positive note of the later writings is developed largely in terms of an appeal to man outwardly through the senses. The appeal is always only to believers, so that a sacrament may confirm faith, but does not give it.

A number of factors combine to make Zwingli deny that the sacraments give faith or the Spirit. Fundamental among them is the understanding of the sovereignty of God and the freedom of the Spirit, together with his view of faith, but there is also the neo-platonic element in his view of man which denies that outward things can reach and affect the soul. This plays an important part from 1524, whether or not influenced by Hoen's letter, though it is somewhat modified in his last writings.

Zwingli's thinking about the sacraments is closely linked to the church and they are conceived corporately in terms of the church rather than individually in terms of salvation. This is true of both ways in which they are understood as covenant signs--as our pledges to our fellow believers that we are one with them in God's people and as God's pledge to us that he is our God and that we are his people. Both these elements are developed in the course of controversy, though neither is ultimately dependent on the controversy. Yet undoubtedly controversy heightened the negative elements in Zwingli's theology, the denial of what he held to be false views of the sacraments. The more positive notes in his later writings do not seem to depend on the absence of controversy, but they are in some ways confessional writings and this may have stimulated a more constructive formulation of sacramental doctrine, as did the influence of Bucer and Oecolampadius. [44]

NOTES

1. A comparison may be made with Bucer. Bucer's view of word and sacrament is more positively expressed in the thirties than in the twenties, and this happens in a way that is consistent with his theology as a whole and not by a change in his theology. The doctrine of election plays an important part in this. Interestingly in 1536, when his views are regarded by many as Lutheran, he could speak positively of Zwingli. "Christ alone effects the whole of salvation in us, and he does it not by some other power, but by his Spirit alone. However, for this he uses with us the word, both the visible word in the sacraments and the audible word in the gospel. By them he brings and offers remission of sins . . . Zwingli recognized this; hence, when he denied that the sacraments dispense grace, he meant that the sacraments, that is the outward action, are not of themselves effective, but that everything belonging to our salvation depends on the inward action of Christ, of whom the sacraments are, in their way, instruments." **In sacra qvatvor evangelia, Enarrationes perpetvae** (Basel, 1536), 485 B.

2. Z II: 120: 23-121: 2, 122: 5-7, 127: 22-28, 125: 6-7, 124: 13-15, 125: 19-25, 126: 33-127: 5. Zwingli also refers to the definition by Peter Lombard of a sacrament as a sign of a holy thing. Z II: 121: 3-4. Through the years Zwingli returns to this scholastic summary of Augustine; view, though in various forms, for example, "Credo igitur, O Caesar, sacramentum esse sacrae rei, hoc est: factae gratiae signum." Z VI/II: 805: 6-7. With Zwingli there is a clear distinction between the sign and what it signifies. Here he stands, like Erasmus in the Franciscan tradition. For the continued concern about the misunderstanding of the word sacrament, see for example Z III: 487: 3-7, 762: 32-35.

3. Z III: 124: 32-127: 27, especially 124: 32-125: 4. 10-14; 126: 9-11, 25-31; 127: 23-25. The great stress on unity as a function of the sacraments is expressed here and frequently elsewhere in Zwingli, for example in Z III: 226: 16-228: 28. It is an emphasis to be found in Augustine and Erasmus.

4.   Z III: 227: 11-228: 28, especially 227: 26-228: 11.

5.   Z III: 282: 29-32. The term is used of baptism, for example in Z VIII: 269: 19-21.

6.   Z III: 348: 6-22. Erasmus also speaks of the meaning of the word sacrament as an oath.

7.   Z III: 533: 4-534: 13, 28-535: 30. "Also in disem sacrament verbindt sich der mensch mit allen gloubigen offenlich . . . Nun ist diss sacrament ein offner eyd und pflicht, das sich der mensch für einen Christen hierinn usgibt und offnet." Z III: 535: 18-19, 27-29.

8.   Z VIII: 85: 13-26, 34-86: 21.

9.   Z VIII: 236: 3-13. He relates this to Augustine "qum dixit, etiam, qum verbum accedat ad elementum, fide tamen omnia confici". Z VIII: 236: 13-14.

10.   Z III: 411: 16-18.

11.   Z III: 762: 23-763: 5.

12.   Z III: 758: 15-759: 18; **Latin Works** III: 180-181.

13.   Z III: 757: 10-13. 759: 18-760: 4; **Latin Works** III: 179, 181.

14.   Z III: 757: 13-17, 760: 4-761: 8; **Latin Works** III: 179, 182.

15.   Z III: 757: 17-20, 761: 8-22; **Latin Works** III: 179. Note the reference to the increase of faith in Z IV 14: 8-15.

16.   Z III: 761: 22-38 (**Latin Works** III: 184), 775: 26-30, 807: 20-24.

17.   Z IV: 217: 6-218: 13; LCC XXIV: 131. From 1525 Zwingli uses Pflichtzeichen as the equivalent in German of sacramentum. Z IV: 218: 3-4.

18.   Z IV: 218: 13-17, 219: 1-25, 226: 29-229: 7 (LCC XXIV: 138-139), 292: 4-6. See also Z VI/II 206: 31-207: 4. The comparison between Old Testament and New Testament signs is made even more strongly in **Refutation** where Zwingli points out that in 1 Corinthians 5 and 10 and Colossians 2, Paul "attributes to them baptism and the eucharist or spiritual feeding on Christ, but to us the pass-over and circumcision, so that all things are equal on both sides". Z VI/I: 172: 1-4. See also Z XIII: 349: 37-351: 27.

19.   Z IV: 499: 1-502: 5.

20.   In his valuable study of the place of the covenant in Zwingli's theology, Cottrell argues strongly for the development of the covenant in the context of the eucharist. J. W. Cottrell, **Covenant and Baptism in the Theology of Huldreich Zwingli,** Princeton Theological Seminary, 1971.

21. Certain points in **Letter to the Princes of Germany** are dealt with under **Exposition of the Faith.**

22. Z VI/II: 803: 7-15, 22, 28-29; Z VI/III: 271: 10-13 (**Latin Works** II: 117). Contrast the earlier expression of Zwingli about the word in "Eo enim veluti vehiculo spiritus tuus trahitur; nam ipsum ociosum ad te non revertitur." Z II: 606: 28-29. " . . . ut spiritum sanctum recipere non sit baptismi opus, sed baptismus sit opus recepti spiritus sancti." Z VI/III: 267: 10-11. The way in which an emphasis on outward things challenges the freedom of the Spirit is evident in the comment on Luke 4:1. "Quod putas mentes esse quas divinus spiritus (virtus dei omnibus praesens et omnia penetrans) illustret ac penetret, quae corporalem spiritus speciem nullam cident? patris vocem externam non audiunt? Spiritus ubi vult spirat et operatur in corde credentium, non res externae." S VI/I 569: 6-10. I discuss the relation of the Spirit to the outward means (word and sacraments) in my forthcoming book **The Theology of Huldrych Zwingli** to be published by Oxford University Press in 1985. The present chapter will be a part of that work.

23. Z VI/III: 165: 1-166: 7, 172: 9-174: 2. Compare the exposition of Isaiah 6:7 in Z XIV: 174: 4-19. Zwingli turns the word sacramentarian against his opponents.

24. Z VI/III: 270: 18-21.

25. Z VI/III: 265: 19-270: 17, 277: 6-12.

26. Z VI/II: 805: 23-29; **Latin Works** 469-470. For salvation as bound to a place, see S VI/I: 386: 18-20.

27. Z VI/II: 200: 6-201: 18, 202: 26-203: 9. Compare Z VI/III: 166: 3-168: 12 and Z VI/III 253: 8-258: 20. " . . . externals can do nothing more than proclaim and represent . . . Nevertheless Christ himself does not disdain to call the bread his body, which to quote Augustine's words, is only the sign of his body." Z VI/III: 166: 3-9; **Latin Works** II: 190.

28. Z VI/II: 805: 6-7.

29. Z VI/III: 168: 4-12.

30. Z XIII: 51: 29-36.

31. S VI/I: 205: 6-10; 499: 3-14. "Adhibet aliquando deus externa quaedam, ut caro nostra tranquilletur, quemadmodum in coena externum sacramentum sensibus exhibet divina sapientia." S VI/I: 356: 1-3.

32. S VI/I: 609: 5-11, 729: 24-28.

33. Z VI/III: 112: 20-24; **Latin Works** II: 156.

34. S IV 45: 26-30, 46: 7-11, 32-34. Compare the words on baptism in **Questions concerning the Sacrament of Baptism:** "Sacramentum dat, non rem

ecclesia; sed rem significat. Solus enim Christus baptizat spiritu sancto et igni, quem Ioannes post se venturum dicebat, eum tamen ipse iam baptizaret. Est ergo baptismus externa ceremonia, quae tamen rem, non praestat. Et nemo dicit baptismus tantum esse ceremoniam, quae nihil significet: sic enim non esset ceremonia. Sed magnum est discrimen inter significare et praestare." S III: 576: 43-577: 2. The sacraments may be said to represent (darstellen) but not present (darreichen), a distinction made for baptism by Usteri and for the eucharist by Blanke. J. M. Usteri, **Darstellung der Tauflehre Zwinglis**, page 269, and Fritz Blanke, "Antwort", **Theologische Blätter**, 11 (1932): 18. Niesel expresses this in a negative and extreme way when he says, "Die Sakramente sind nicht Werkzeuge Gottes, sondern Werkzeuge des Glaubens." Wilhelm Niesel "Zwinglis 'spätere' Sakramentsanschauung", **Theologische Blätter**, 11 (1928): 15.

35. S IV: 56: 18-31. Compare S IV 46: 11-16.

36. Z IV: 856: 16-19. Jud also used it. The analogy of the ring was probably drawn from the beginning of Hoen's letter, which Zwingli published in 1525. Z IV: 512: 10-15.

37. S IV: 56: 32-46; LCC XXIV: 263. This use of the word symbol can be compared with the use of pledge (pignus) in S IV: 57: 27-29.

38. Z VI/III: 278: 19-282: 7; **Latin Works** II: 122-124. "Sic in coena Christi corpus tanto praesentius est fidei contemplatione menti . . . " Z VI/III: 281: 24-25. Zwingli refers to Psalm 104: 15 as he did in the letter to Thomas Wyttenbach. Z VIII: 85: 16-18.

39. S IV 56: 48-57: 11.

40. S IV 57: 12-58: 5.

41. Z VI/III: 261: 6-11, 269: 34-270: 15 (**Latin Works** II: 116-117), 262: 2-7 (**Latin Works** II: 111), 265: 5-9 (**Latin Works** II: 113). (The German translation renders suadent as gliebend. Z VI/III: 270, note 4.) Compare S IV: 55: 9-23 which makes it clear that the sacraments give historical faith, but that only to believers do they testify that Christ did not only die but died for us.

42. Z II: 143: 16-22; III: 411: 16-18; IV: 217: 14-19; VIII: 85: 37-86: 21; XIII: 177: 13-20; S VI/I: 356: 1-4,373: 27-32, 555: 3-14, 567: 4-7; VI/II: 58: 35-37. Compare Z IV: 228: 2-5.

43. S IV: 58: 6-15.

44. I conclude by noting that I shall deal separately with baptism and the eucharist in my forthcoming, **The Theology of Huldrych Zwingli**.

LET ZWINGLI BE ZWINGLI

Robert Walton

Huldrych Zwingli was the father of the reformed reformation in German Switzerland but his reformation was only a limited success. It won the urban cantons of Bern, Basel, and Schaffhausen, as well as the city of St. Gall, but not the territories of the abbey of St. Gall for the Reformation. The Reformation had a mixed success in the cantons of Glarus and Appenzell. It failed for the most part in territories jointly administered by the Confederacy, because Zwingli's new understanding of the Gospel did not gain acceptance in the crucial inner Swiss cantons of Schwyz, Zug, Uri, and Unterwalden and the urban canton of Lucerne. Indeed, the attempt to convert these cantons led to a disastrous war, the Second Kappel War, in which Zwingli lost his life in October, 1531. Military defeat and the internal divisions among the protestant cantons put an end to the further spread of the Reformation in German Switzerland.

At the same time, the outcome of the Second Kappel War freed protestant Bern to continue its westward expansion at the expense of the Duke of Savoy. By 1536 Bern had conquered Canton Vaud which brought the Bernese army to the borders of the territories of the city of Geneva. Bern's advance permitted Geneva to assert her independence against both her bishop and her Savoyard overlord. Protected by an alliance with Bern and Freiburg, Geneva expelled her bishop, accepted Protestantism and withdrew from the orbit of the Duke of Savoy's power. After some initial hesitation, the city also offered the French exile, John Calvin, a permanent home. Though relations between Geneva under Calvin's influence and Zwinglian Bern were not cordial, the Bernese were in the last analysis prepared to accept Geneva's deviations from its ecclesiastical norms. These norms left no place at all for a Genevan or better said, Calvinist style "consistory" which Zwingli's successor at Zurich, Heinrich Bullinger, viewed as a new form of papalism. Bern's reluctant defense of Geneva's reformed church saved the city from reconquest by

Savoy and made possible one of the great ironies in the history of reformed protestanism. By the time the 16th century had begun to wane, Geneva first under Calvin and then under Beza had begun to eclipse Zurich as a center of reformed thought and as the model of reformed piety and polity. Geneva was soon enough overshadowed by the Calvinist Rhineland-Palatinate and its internationally famous university, Heidelberg, as well as by the remarkable Dutch universities. However, today it is generally assumed that in the 16th century Calvin's Geneva was the place from which reformed Protestantism emerged and that Calvin was the true father of international reformed Protestantism. This was simply not the case. The essays in this volume will all certainly serve to clarify this point and there could be no more fitting time to do it than on the occasion of the five hundredth anniversary of Huldrych Zwingli's birth.

This essay is concerned with the problem of why so little attention has been paid to Zwingli and assumes that the neglect remains, despite the Renaissance in Zwingli Studies which has occurred in the last forty years at the University of Zurich. It also seeks to address the question of who Zwingli really was, in order to assess what role his family background played in the development of his theology.

To begin with a few general remarks are necessary. Failure is usually the best way to guarantee ones obscurity. Zwingli died fighting in the second line on the battlefield of Kappel. His body was captured, drawn, and quartered, and then burned to ashes by his Catholic enemies. The cause of this disaster was in part due to the internal and foreign policies which Zwingli advocated. However well justified it was from a theological, humanitarian, and even patriotic point of view, his campaign against the key figures within the Canton who were involved in the system of selling mercenary soldiers to foreign employers wrecked the command structure of Zurich's peasant militia. Many of the peasant soldiers were so sceptical of the officers who had replaced the traditional military leadership in the Canton that, when the Catholic cantons marched on Zurich, they did not appear for service, as Zurich's militia mustered for war. [1] Zwingli's foreign policy failed to judge accurately Bern's actual willingness to support her Zurich allies in the event of war. Bern had other interests in the west which made her uninterested in a war in the east which, if successful, only served to strengthen Zurich. [2] At least Zwingli had seen that the embargo on the sale of food supplies to the Catholic cantons of the original confederacy was a dangerous half-way measure. He had favored an all out war. However, he did not understand the economic realities which left the Catholic cantons no choice but to continue the system of mercenary service. Without it, there would not have been sufficient surplus capital to finance the food imports necessary to keep the inhabitants of the forest cantons from starving. [3] Zwingli's flawed judgments were a direct cause of his own death and of a lost war which ended the expansion of reformed protestantism in German Switzerland. This in itself should have been enough to guarantee Zwingli's obscurity but thanks to the permanent success of Zwingli's own labors in Canton Zurich and the cool judgment and diplomacy of his twenty-seven year old successor, Heinrich Bullinger, Zwingli was not forgotten. For quite different reasons he was very thoroughly misunderstood and misrepresented by subsequent generations of theologians and historians.

Two groups of scholars have, perhaps of necessity, made it very difficult for modern men to understand Zwingli. The reason for the distortions which still plague us today go back to the Reformation itself. The first of the two groups are the Lutherans whose ancient prejudice is derived from Martin Luther himself. Luther's dislike of Zwingli's theology, especially his interpretation of the Lord's Supper, had long lasting results and helped to form not only the Lutheran view of the Swiss Reformer but also the Roman Catholic view of Zwingli. [4] The vast Lutheran literature on this subject cannot be dealt with in this paper but a few examples can be given. The second group which has done probably far more to influence at least American thinking about Zwingli, are the modern Mennonite historians who will not be dealt with in this paper.

The fact is, German Switzerland's proximity to Germany has tended to make it very difficult for many German scholars to understand Zwingli's significance or to believe that he could have developed independently of Luther. Seen from a German perspective, it is quite legitimate to ask: How could a man from such a little country, the country of Heidi and chocolate bars, be anything but a derivative, pale, and a none too perfect shadow of the Great Reformer?

In his most recent work, **Geschichte der Christenheit,** vol. II the noted German scholar, Kurt Aland, remarked that Luther is so great a figure and so dominates the Reformation that it is easy to allow the other reformers to slip into the background. [5] This understanding dominates Aland's general discussion of Zwingli both in the second volume of his church history and in his earlier work **Die Reformatoren** and demonstrates how hard it is for Zwingli to be Zwingli, even in the careful world of modern academic scholarship. Like the majority of German scholars before him, Aland views Zwingli as a man much influenced by Luther and dismisses his claims that he became a reformer independently of Luther as statements dictated by caution and the tactical situation at Zurich. Aland is also convinced that, even in comparison with Calvin, Zwingli is a second rank figure. It was, Aland asserts, Calvin who harnessed the strength latent in the Swiss reformed tradition, so that it could spread throughout Europe.

Though Aland is convinced that Zwingli was dependent upon Luther, he admits that Zwingli maintained a certain independence. [6] Aland's comment that most of the recent literature on Zwingli, which he does not identify as the literature of the Zwingli Renaissance, has been written by Swiss scholars, indeed German Swiss researchers awakens the suspicion that Zwingli's importance was local and indeed confined to German Switzerland. [7] In making this carefully qualified observation, Aland does not address the question of who would, after all, be most likely to seek to alter a false or misleading interpretation of Zwingli but the German Swiss themselves. More important for our topic is the date which Aland assigns for the beginning of the Swiss Reformation. He places it in the Spring of 1522, when the Fast Ordinance was violated by some of Zwingli's followers. [8] Aland's reason for giving this date is certainly important for his own account of the Zwinglian Reformation but it also sheds light upon a very remarkable phenomenon in reformation historiography. Many German scholars take a negative view of the humanist movement. A good reformer is one who either was never deeply involved with humanism or a man who was able to free himself from such influences. Even more than Melanchthon, Zwingli was deeply involved with and influenced by the humanist movement. This fact lowers Zwingli's value and importance in the eyes of any scholar who shares the wide-spread prejudice against humanism. Aland certainly shares this hostility to humanism and like so many scholars before him is eager to stress how little humanism influenced Luther's thought and development.

When speaking of Luther and Zwingli's relationship to the humanist movement, Aland gives the impression that the issue at stake is purity. Luther remained pure, because he was not besmirched by any close contact with humanism, while it remained for Zwingli, who had tarnished his purity by involving himself with the movement to free himself from its influence. Zwingli was never able to do this completely but at least enough for him to class Zwingli as a Reformer. [9] The fact that it took Zwingli so long to purge himself of humanism is a major reason for Aland to place the date for the beginning of the Reformation at Zurich in the Spring of 1522. The Reformation could begin only after Zwingli had cleansed himself of the worst of the Humanist taint. Aland is certainly not alone in his limited judgment of humanism as a source of impurity. This view is, as has already been said, common enough among German scholars and is shared by some Swiss scholars such as Alfred Rich and Gottfried Locher. [10]

There were also other taints of impurity in the development of Zwingli's doctrine caused in part by the influence of humanism. For Aland the Platonist influence so obvious in Zwingli's doctrine of God was certainly a product of humanism. It produced a different conception of how sanctification was possible. In the Zwinglian view sanctification was not something which men thought was worth striving for but rather a state which could be achieved not through human effort but by means of the action of the Holy Spirit. To Aland, Zwingli's conception of the overwhelming power of the work of the Holy Spirit represented a basic weakening of Luther's interpretation of sanctification; Zwingli's less satisfactory doctrine was the result of the lasting influence of his humanist flirtation. It led Zwingli to see the Holy Spirit at work among the heathen before the coming of Christ and also caused him to underrate the radical consequences of original sin. [11] Zwingli's Platonic doctine of God, also made it logical for Zwingli to stress the importance of predestination and God's foreknowledge. Zwingli's emphasis upon predestination completed the deemphasis of the role of the sacraments as means of grace which was already latent in Zwingli's theology. Aland also notes another influence which caused Zwingli to adulterate the original purity of Luther's teaching on the Lord's Supper which he asserts Zwingli had in fact originally accepted. Zwingli took Carlstadt's doctrine of the eucharist seriously and was guilty of other errors. [12] As Aland sees it, Zwingli confused the realms of church and state to create a unified community which totally violated the distinctions between church state developed by Luther in his doctrine of the two kingdoms. [13]

Zwingli deviated from the norms of purity in one other very specific way. Unlike Luther, he became a priest in the "conventional" way. To become a monk, Luther had to rebel against his family which means to Aland that Luther was far more of a "Catholic" than Zwingli could ever be. To strengthen his argument, Aland cites Zwingli's liasons with women at Glarus and Einsiedeln to conclude that it was much easier for Zwingli to give up Catholicism than it was for Luther. [14] That fact that in making this comparison between Zwingli and Luther's Catholicism Aland misses a very basic aspect of the history of late medieval clerical mores is less important, though amusing, than is Aland's heavy emphasis upon the fact of Luther's moral superiority.

In all fairness, it should be added that some Swiss historians have complained that Zwingli was already idolized by his own Swiss contemporaries who were so enthusiastic about him that they did not give a clear and accurate picture of his strengths and weaknesses, as well as his achievements. However, for the most part, the literature of the Zwinglian Reformation avoided the worst pitfalls of hero worship. The Lutheran literature has not. This is due in great part, as Fritz Ringer has observed, to the influence of German Idealism and Romanticism upon the "notion of individuality" which has "engendered an unusually insistent emphasis upon great 'historic' individuals; a tendency to treat cultures, states, and epochs as personalized wholes, . . . ". [15]

Enough has been said to indicate that, when seen from the perspective of modern Lutheran scholarship, it is very difficult for Zwingli to be Zwingli. The prodigious production of works written to celebrate the five hundredth anniversary of Luther's birth will not make this task any easier. No one can expect a similar flood of literature from Switzerland which will balance this flood of Luther literature.

It is essential to take a brief look at the foundations which Luther laid for the development of German interpretations of Zwingli and his significance. Thirteen years after Zwingli's death Luther penned the **Kurzes Bekenntnis vom heiligen Sakrament**, (1544) his last attack upon Zwingli and his theology, which prompted Zwingli's successor, Heinrich Bullinger, to frame the **Wahrhaftes Bekenntnis der Diener der Kirche zu Zürich** in 1545. [16] The attack capped a rising crescendo of vehement criticism which had begun with Luther's **Sendschreiben an den Markgrafen von Brandenburg** in 1532 and continued in his **Sendschriften an die zu Frankfurt a. Main 1533** which Butzer had answered. [17] The years after 1536 had seen attempts on the part of Bucer, Capito and Melanchthon to restore peace between Luther and the Swiss Reformer. These efforts did not persuade the Swiss to accept a compromise such as the Wittenburg Agreement of 1536, which opened the way for the eventual Lutheranization of Strasbourg. [18] By 1538 Bullinger and Luther had begun to correspond with each other and there were grounds for the hope that in time some basis for an agreement could be found. The publication of the **Kurzes Bekenntnis** ended all such hopes. Luther claimed that Bullinger's publication of Zwingli's **Exposition** in 1536 had given him cause to respond to Zwingli's last work. As the Zurichers saw the matter, Luther's outburst was one of a series of violations of the agreement made at Marburg that both sides would end their polemic over the question of the Lord's Supper. [19] In their answer to Luther's **Sendbrief**, they had suggested that Luther had gone beyond the norm of Christian modesty in his attack upon the Zwinglian doctrine of the Lord's Supper.

There was little evidence of humility in Luther's final blast against Zwingli's doctrine of the sacrament. Luther lumped all his opponents together. He began by identifying Zwingli with Caspar Schwenckfeld. "Ist mir auch eben so viel, wenn er Schwenckfeld oder seine verfluchte Rotte der Schwermer, Zwingler und dergleichen mich loben oder schelten, als wenn mich Juden, Tuercken, Papst oder gleich alle Teuffel schoelten oder lobeten." [20] Zwingli belonged to the same band of "rabble" to which Schwenckfeld adhered and this element could rightly be identified with Jews, Turks, Catholics and clearly all other "undesirables". These introductory remarks set the tone for the remainder of the treatise and introduced Luther's version of the Marburg Colloquy.

At Marburg, Luther asserted, he, Zwingli, and Oecolampadius had agreed upon fourteen out of fifteen articles. The fifteenth article concerned the Lord's Supper and no agreement had been reached on it, though both sides had agreed to put an end to their polemics over the issue: "also das wir sonst solten gute Freunde sein, damit das scharffe schreiben gegenander rugen moechte." [21] The following sentence is of particular importance, because it reveals Luther's attitude toward Zwingli, whom he always deliberately called "Zwingel", and explains both what Luther had expected would happen and why he was now so angry at "Zwingel" and his "band". The Saxon had assumed that since they had given in on the other matters at issue, that Zwingli and Oecolampadius would soon enough give way to Luther's opinion on the question of the Lord's Supper: " . . . Und ich zimliche hoffnung hatte, weil der Zwingel und die seinen so viel guter Artickel nachgaben. Es solte mit der Zeit der einige Artickel sich auch finden." [22] In other words, the Swiss would eventually conform to Luther's teachings on all questions of doctrine. For reasons Luther found difficult to understand, they did not give in and accept his teachings.

Luther found the deaths of Zwingli and Oecolampadius to be troublesome. "Zwingel" was killed in battle by his Catholic opponents and Oecolampadius was not able to survive the shock of this event. Luther confessed that for two nights he was so sad about these deaths that he himself almost died. [23] However, he went on to make it clear that it was not just the manner of their death which so affected him. Luther had hoped that they would come to their senses in the question of the Lord's Supper. The fact that they did not caused him to worry about their souls, because they died lost in error and sin: "Denn ich guter hoffnung war irer besserunge, und doch fur ire Seele mich auffs hoehest bekuemmern muste, weil sie noch im irthum verteufft also in sunden untergeengen." [24] Though Luther certainly was not alone in thinking that those who did not share his views and perished had jeopardized their immortal souls, it is clear enough that his remarks show little charity to the dead dissidents. It is no small wonder that Bullinger expressed his amazement that such a respected man would speak so crudely and viciously of Zwingli and Oecolampadius. [25]

Luther then turned to consider Zwingli's last work, the **Exposition**, dedicated to the King of France, whose publication, he asserted, was a violation of the Marburg agreement that both sides would refrain from attacking each other. But Luther found worse than that in the "little book". He concluded that it was clearly Zwingli's own handiwork, because of the "wild" and "awful" way it was written and because it summed up the views Zwingli had expressed in his previous works. [26] Knowing full well that Bullinger had been its editor, Luther took occasion to complain both about the nasty way Zwingli had behaved towards his opponents at Marburg and to wonder again about the state of Zwingli's soul. He was, he said, also equally concerned about the way Zwingli's followers had made a saint and martyr out of Zwingli and could not help exclaiming: "My God! The man a saint and martyr!" [27]

To Luther Zwingli's views not only demonstrated that he was an enemy of the sacrament of the Lord's Supper but also that he was a heathen. Zwingli had dared to tell the King of France that in the next life a number of elect heathen would be joined with Christ and the other saints. Among others the elect heathen included, to Luther's horror, Hercules, Theseus, Socrates, Scipio, and his ancestors, as well as Numa, King of Rome. Ignoring the fact that Zwingli had said that election was possible only through God's grace, Luther continued with his criticism of Zwingli's paganism, especially because it had gone so far as to list King Numa of Rome among the elect. Everyone knew, Luther said, that, thanks to a revelation of the devil, he was the founder of idolatry at Rome. [28] Zwingli's paganism was clear for all to see. Even more horrible for Luther was the fact that Zwingli's journeyman honor and praise his "little book". [29] Luther assured his readers that he did not want to give up his hope for Zwingli's followers and write against Zwingli's "little book", but he had to recognize that all of his warnings and the "Christian love and loyalty" which he had shown at Marburg were for naught. [30] His unwillingness to be identified with the Schwärmer was clear for all to see.

Shifting from his attack on Zwingli's "little book" to a rejection of statements made in general, Luther refuted the charge that he and his followers ate Christ's flesh. Not even the Catholics, he added, made such charge against him and his followers. Indeed, Luther noted, he and his supporters have remained true to the fifteen hundred year old catholic tradition which was not invented by the pope as the "Schwermer" assert. Luther also explained how eating the body and drinking the blood meant taking the whole body and blood of Jesus and took the opportunity to reiterate his view that the words "take, eat, this is my body" (1 Cor. 11:24) should be taken literally. [31]

After once again calling his opponents liars, Luther returned to the story of the Marburg Colloquy to muse over the fact that he and his fellows showed abundant Christian love in going to Marburg, but the "Schwermer" attacked them as "sinful" creatures "without love". In this attack the "Schwermer" sought to show that they alone were "saints" which was an interpretation not shared by Luther. [32] It was a matter of deep regret to Luther that his exceptional love and modesty were of no use. "Was hat aber uns nu solche uberfluessige liebe und demut geholfen?" [33]

Luther's sacrifice had been in vain so he applied the advice given in 2 John 10 and Titus 3:10 not to have anything to do with those who do not share your teaching. Paul, Luther added, urged that the ostracism of such people begin only after the heretic had been warned a time or two. [34] Luther believed that he was unfairly criticized by Zwingli, Oecolampadius, and "Stenckfeld's" followers for being unreasonable and dividing the church over the article concerning the Lord's Supper which the others did not see as so important. This of course, meant to him that they saw the mote in his eye but not the beam in their own. [35]

Of course, for Luther the "beam" in their eye was enormous; they did not take Christ's words, "This is my body" seriously and instead preferred to give these words another interpretation which was blasphemy. The blasphemers were not merely "bread-eaters" (Brotfresser) and "drunkards" (Weinseuffer), they were also consumers and murderers of souls (Seelfresser und Seelmorder). [36] They had a blasphemous heart, in every way given over to the devil, and lying mouths. [37] With such elements Luther wanted to have nothing to do and he spoke the truth against them which could not be refuted by Zwingli or anyone else, in order to free the followers of the "Schwermer" whoever they might be from Carlstadt, Zwingli, Oecolampadius and Schwenckfeld, and their followers. [38] Luther made it clear that he knew God was on his side, for in the end, it was not his writings against the "Schwermer" which prevailed but rather God's vengeance upon them which was much more terrible. [39] Luther's assertion made it clear that Luther saw Zwingli's death in battle and Oecolampadius' subsequent death in November, 1531 as a vindication of his doctrine of the Lord's Supper and a repudiation of the Zwinglian doctrine. Luther clearly believed that God aided him by punishing his theological opponents.

This polemical introduction was followed by a more specific discussion of the errors which each of Luther's opponents had made. [40] For Luther the problem was that they were not inspired by the Holy Ghost in interpreting the text, "This is my body" but rather by seven other spirits which caused each interpretation to differ radically from that of the other. Luther called these seven spirits sarcastically "holy spirits" and was able to identify all seven holy spirits in the interpretation of his opponents. After considering Carlstadt, he turned to Zwingli, whose work was even more awful, for Zwingli understood the phrase, "This is my body" as "This means my body". After answering several other erroneous spirits, Luther busied himself with an attack on two of the major arguments advanced by Zwingli against the assertion that Christ was physically present in the supper.

The first argument of Zwingli concerned the importance of John 6:63 wherein the Evangelist asserts: "It is the Spirit that makes alive; the flesh profits nothing." Secondly, Zwingli argued that Christ ascended to heaven and sits at the right hand of God the Father which means that he could not be present in the sacrament. [41] Luther was proud to say that Zwingli did not use John 6:63 in the **Exposition**, for he was convinced that he had frightened Zwingli off of this verse with his earlier arguments. As far as Luther was concerned, the second assertion made by Zwingli simply contradicted Christ's own institution of the Lord's Supper. Luther argued for a literal interpretation of the Savior's words. The Lord's Supper was established in this manner, Luther argued, before Christ ascended into heaven.

Rather than pursue this argument further, Luther followed a new tack and accused Zwingli and his friends of having changed their argument since Marburg. At Marburg they had argued that Christ was not physically but rather spiritually present and that therefore one could not speak of mere bread and wine. Their additional claim that only the elect can participate in the sacrament spiritually contradicted, Luther observed, 1 Cor. 11:27f. in which, Luther claimed, Paul says the worthy and the unworthy receive the body and blood of Christ. [42] Luther also alluded to a conversation at Marburg on the question of the physical presence during which Zwingli argued very "inconsistently" and then apologized to Luther for not understanding him correctly. The Zwinglians had understood that Luther made the same argument already advanced by the papists which claimed Christ was physically and locally present like straw in a sack. Zwingli realized finally that this was false. Luther then said that Zwingli and his fellows knew full well that neither the Lutherans nor the Catholics maintained this position. [43] They believed with the "Christian Church" that Christ was physically present but not like straw in a sack: " . . . Er ist gewislich da, nicht wie stro im sack. Aber doch leiblich und warhafftig da . . . " [44]

As he had said before, Luther asserted that he left Marburg with great hope that they would in time come over to "us". [45] But the **Exposition** showed that in fact Zwingli had gotten worse, which Luther believed was the work of the devil. It should be clear, Luther said, he could have nothing to do with such people and Luther provided a list of epithets to designate the blaspheming "Schwermer". He at least could be sure, he said, that at the Last Judgment he could in good conscience say to Christ the Lord that he had warned the "Schwermer" of their error and folly which had to be on their own consciences. [46]

However, Luther explained, he did not give the final warning to Zwingli. It was given by the terrible judgment of God ("das Schreckliche urteil Gottes") when Zwingli was killed on the battlefield with five thousand of his men. Luther felt that the fact that some saw Zwingli's death as a sign of grace and had made a saint out of him was shocking. Like the Jews who had suffered for fifteen hundred years, Zwingli was punished and died as his "little book" shows in much sin and blasphemy: " . . . in grossen und vielen sunden und Gottes lesterung . . . " [47]

Luther could not leave alone the question of Zwingli being viewed as a saint because of his sufferings, for as he made clear he believed that Zwingli was punished to protect the rest of the world from damnation. It must be clear, Luther said, that only those who are without guilt before their suffering can become saints through suffering. Thus, Luther argued, sainthood could not be attributed to Zwingli, because he had blasphemed the sacrament and had also perished by the sword which was the just punishment for his having taken up the sword. [48] Like the Jews, Zwingli deserved his punishment because he perverted and falsified the sacrament. All "heretics", Luther explained, cite and use the scripture and the devil's martyrs deserve a more fiery hell than do the genuine martyrs deserve heaven. [49]

Luther felt that all the warnings issued to these "Schwermer" did no good but the fact that he had written against them enabled him to rank his warning along with those of God. In the last analysis it was really for Luther a matter of little concern to distinguish between "Stenckfeld", "Zwingel", and the others; they all deserved to be treated according to the norms of Matthew 18:17, to be viewed as publicans and sinners with whom no one should associate. [50] Luther was content to lump them together, because they did not believe that it was Christ's natural body in the Lord's Supper which all, even Judas, ate. [51]

After a brief aside on Schwenckfeld, Luther turned his attention to the argument that Christ had ascended into heaven. Luther employed Romans 4:21 and Psalm 51:6 to argue that God was able to do what he had said he could do, because he was God. This meant to Luther that Christ was physically present and that those who consulted their reason in the question of the real presence set themselves up to judge God. Such people were of course public liars. What Luther was really saying was that those who questioned his own interpretation of the Bible were liars. The crux of the argument appeared a few sentences later when he asserted that those who denied a real presence in the Lord's Supper actually were guilty of denying that Christ was truly God and truly man, because they separated the human from the divine nature in Christ. Such a view also led to a denial of the unity of the Trinity and was in effect a double heresy. [52] Having proved to his satisfaction the charge of heresy against the "Schwermer", Luther heaped fresh abuse upon them.

Then he explained to his readers that all heretics started by denying one article of faith and ended up by denying them all. The "Schwermer" were for him merely a part of a long tradition of heresy and their spiritual interpretation no better than the fig leaves used by Adam and Eve to cover their nakedness after they had eaten the forbidden fruit. [53] To those who wished to argue that surely God would be merciful to men who disagreed over the interpretation of one article of the faith, Luther could only answer that the biblical precedents indicated that the contrary was true. God showed no love or mercy to those who blaspheme and deny his Word. [54]

One final point required elaboration. It involved the elevation of the host which Luther had attacked in his early diatribes against the Catholic mass. Many, Luther noted, assumed that his call for the abolition of the practice of elevating the host meant that he had abandoned belief in the real presence. Luther hastened to explain that this was not the case. He had attacked the elevation of the host to criticize the Catholic view that the mass was a sacrifice and to make it clear that it was a gift or promise and sign from God. In fact, Luther went on, he had kept the elevation of the host in the service for the benefit of the weak during the early phases of the Reformation. To this he added that the elevation was an old custom first used by Moses to give thanks for the good things of the Land which God had given them and then taken over by the Christians. The host was elevated to show the body which was given for them. [55]

Luther took the occasion to say that he was willing to compromise when it did not involve sin, but only external matters. In these, churches can differ. Spirit, faith, Word, and sacrament were however another matter. He closed with the classic definition of the Kingdom of God found in Romans 14:17 that the Kingdom of God was not eating and drinking but rather righteousness, peace and joy in the Holy Spirit. This citation enabled him to appeal for the peace and mutual edification which only Christ, the Father, and the Holy Spirit can bring. [56] The question how he could combine this appeal with the diatribe against his and God's enemies in the body of the text was not answered by this conclusion.

As far as Lutheranism is concerned, Luther's own attitudes, as well as the historiographical presuppositions of modern Luther scholars in Germany make it virtually impossible for Zwingli ever to be Zwingli. Not even the positive and sometimes liberating perspective provided by scholars in the G. D. R. is really of any great help in this matter. In the G. D. R. Luther, as well as Zwingli, suffer from being caught in a dialectical process which makes them a part of the early modern middle-class revolution which eventually smashed the feudal order. [57] At least in the German realm, Zwingli seems doomed to be cursed as a humanist, linked to Luther as a lesser disciple, and damned as an associate of people like Carlstadt.

Heinrich Bornkamm explains the fact that the Calvinist conception of an autonomous congregation found virtually no acceptance in Germany, because, as Luther himself observes, the trained reserves of manpower necessary to make these congregations function were lacking. In addition, he observes that the kind of government with which Luther dealt was totally different from that of the city republics of Switzerland or of the German imperial cities. The republics and imperial cities had magistracies which Bornkamm claims were elected every few years. This fact made it possible for Zwingli and Calvin to develop an independent reputation. There were no territorial rulers in the cities ready to absorb the church into the structure of their territories. [58]

In describing the function of magistracies in the Swiss city republics and the German imperial cities Bornkamm ignores the fact which Peyer has stressed in his **Verfassungsgeschichte der alten Schweiz**, there was no "democratic" tradition in the Swiss city republics or in the rural cantons. The urban society of a city like Zurich, which still was in theory an imperial city, was oligarchical. As Peyer has observed, all the constitutions of the "old" Confederacy, regardless of whether the canton was rural or urban, were oligarchical but were referred to as "democratic". The few "meliores" governed the many. Where there were regional assemblies (Landsgemeinden), they never elected their own candidates for office, but merely confirmed the choice of the meliores as to who should serve the canton. In a city like Zurich the two governing Councils co-opted their own members. [59] Indirectly, Brady's work on Strasbourg adds additional confirmation to Peyer's evidence. Brady asserts that it is an error to separate the early modern city state and its society from the hierarchical social order of the territory surrounding it. According to Brady, the city state was a natural part of the same territorial and social order. [60] Such arguments of course reduce the difference between Luther's supposedly rural Saxon world and Zwingli's urban environment.

As far as Zwingli is concerned, what are the consequences of such a reduction? The consequences are that it is, perhaps for the first time, really possible to begin to let Zwingli be Zwingli. Kobelt's important work on the meaning of the Swiss Confederacy for Zwingli demonstrates that Zwingli felt the Confederacy was his "Fatherland" (Vaterland). Technically, a "Fatherland" provides its citizens both with a common history and with the necessary protection for them to make their way in the world. Zwingli's home (Heimat), however, was not the Confederacy; it was the Duchy of Toggenburg, where he had been born and spent his youth. Zwingli's Heimat was subordinated to and received its proper definition from the Confederacy of which it was only indirectly a part, as an associated member ("ein zugewandtes Glied"). [61] The Toggenburg's membership in the Confederacy was secured by a Landrecht which bound it to Glarus and Schwyz and through them to the Swiss Confederacy and its general assembly, the Tagsatzung, at which no direct representative of the Duchy ever appeared. [62]

Zwingli's father was a rural chief magistrate in the Duchy of the Toggenburg. Like his father before him, he served as the Ammann for the village of Wildhaus and the territory around it which formed part of the district of Wildenburg in the upper Toggenburg. The Ammann, or local chief magistrate, was chosen for office by the village assembly. The candidates, however, were chosen only from a small group of wealthier farmers who had the time to be involved in the problems of local government. Unlike the Landsgemeinden of the rural cantons or the city councils of the Confederacy's urban cantons, the village governing class was not strictly a self co-opting oligarchy, though the village society was clearly hierarchical. [63] It is certainly justified and sensible to call the village ruling class a "village patriciate", for they were referred to in the records of the period as meliores, seniores or the elteste, just as the urban oligarchs were. [64] At this juncture, it is worth saying that the guild oligarchy in Zurich developed for much the same reason. Wealthier peasants were chosen to be village magistrates in the rural areas of the Confederacy. They were well to do enough to take the time necessary to manage the affairs of government.

As Peyer has shown, these tasks were not small, for the village magistracies acting in the name of their local assemblies dealt with many questions reserved for the town councils in the urban cantons which did not permit the villages under their control to enjoy the same freedom exercised by the village in the rural cantons. [65] Along with his local responsibilities, Zwingli's father was responsible for representing the interests of the village and the territory around it before administrators of the Abbey of St. Gall and also before the rulers of Glarus and Schwyz. [66] This was no easy task. There can be no doubt that Zwingli's lifelong interest in politics and his pride in being a Swiss Confederate was derived in part from his family's involvement in local government. Though only a third son, he grew up in the milieu of the local rural governing class. It is of interest to note that the first Latin book Zwingli purchased when he entered Heinrich Wölflin's Latin school at Bern was Cicero's **De Officiis. [67]**

Zwingli and his successor, Bullinger, came from the "patrician" peasant class. Though the Bullingers were far wealthier than the Zwinglis, if for no other reason than that their landed wealth was centered in the rich agricultural land of the Aargau, both men came from families which played a leading role in local government and the church. Even an urban canton like Zurich relied upon the rural village patriciate to provide the assistant district bailiffs (Untervögte) who served under the bailiffs (Vögte) appointed from the urban patriciate to govern a rural district. If the rural establishment became dissatisfied, it was impossible to administer the rural areas, because the smooth functioning of government in both urban and rural cantons depended upon an alliance between the wealthier local peasantry and the regional establishment. [68]

It is also necessary to observe that in late medieval Switzerland and Southwest Germany the church was the only institution which offered the children of the peasant "patriciate" the chance for social mobility. [69] Zwingli's education and early years as people's priest in Glarus demonstrate this clearly enough. Bullinger's father was a rural dean who lived in concubinage. [70] At least in German Switzerland the leaders of the Reformation tended to come from this class of cleric, the dissidents were all too often their illegitimate children. Their world, and this is especially true of Zwingli and Bullinger, was the world of the local oligarchical government. Their theology was as much a theology which reflected a system of government based upon an alliance between urban or territorial oligarchs and a local farmer patriciate as it was an urban theology.

In Zwingli's case, an awareness of this fact helps to explain his relationship to humanism, the nascent Täufer movement at Zurich, and above all to the Zurich government. It also sets him apart from Luther. Much more than has been generally realized both men came from typical segments of the late medieval world but one came from a rural governing class and the other did not.

NOTES

1. Martin Haas, **Huldrych Zwingli und Seine Zeit, Leben und Werk des Zürcher Reformators,** 2. Auflage (Zürich, 1976), 279-283.

2. Ibid., 232ff., 241-243, 264-266, 270, 278; Potter, 350ff., 366, 385-387, 402, 407-408.

3. Ibid., 269, 270-272, 241, 247-248; Potter, 30, 367, 369, 401, 403.

4. Oskar Farner's, **Das Zwinglibild Luthers** (Tübingen, 1932), gives a brief summary of Luther's view of Zwingli. See also the standard works: Kurt Guggisberg, **Das Zwinglibild des Protestantismus im Wandel der Zeit** (Leipzig, 1934), and Fritz Büsser, **Das Katholische Zwinglibild von der Reformation bis zur Gegenwart** (Zurich, 1968).

5. "Zwar ist es verständlich, wenn angesichts der Riesengestalt Luthers die Männer neben ihm im allgemeinen Bewusstsein zurücktreten". This quote is taken from part 4, entitled "Die kleinen Reformatoren". Kurt Aland, **Geschichte der Christenheit von der Reformation bis in die Gegenwart,** 2 vols. (Gütersloh, 1982), II, 25. Hereafter referred to as KAKG with the appropriate volume and page number.

6. "Zwingli had sicher auch gespürt, sass seine eigene Frömmigkeit trotz aller Anregungen, die sie von Luther empfangen hat, trotz aller Abhängigkeit von Luther und seiner Theologie, einen besonderen Charakter besitzt und sich von Luthers Position im ganzen wie in den Einzelheiten unterscheidet." KAKG II, 148.

7. Sieht man sich die moderne wissenschaftliche Literatur über Zwingli an, so findet man hier fast ausnahmslos Schweizer Autoren; von hier aus könnte man den Eindruck gewinnen, sass Zwingli lediglich eine lokale Bedeutung für die Schweiz besitze." Kurt Aland, **Die Reformatoren Luther – Melanchton – Zwingli – Calvin** (Gütersloh, 1976), 72.

8. Kurt Aland, **Die Reformatoren,** 73.

9. Kurt Aland, ibid., 78-79, 80-82 (especially 82); cf. KAKG II, 148, 150, 105.

10. Arthur Rich, **Die Anfänge der Theologie Zwinglis,** (Zürich, 1949), 93-95 (Rich asserts here that Luther was not the main influence in Zwingli's development); 96ff. (Here Rich begins to consider the basic change in Zwingli's theology and identifies the first anti-Erasmian remarks), 104ff., 119ff. (Here Rich describes

the way in which Zwingli broke with Erasmus.). See Locher, 42-54, 115-122. Cf. Wilhelm Neusner, **Die Reformatorische Wende bei Zwingli** (Neukirchen-Vluyn, 1977), 125ff., 139ff., 142ff., 149-153.

11. KAKG II, 150-151, 105-106, "Hier wirken die Kräfte des Platonismus, hier zeigt sich der Einfluss des Humanismus auf Zwingli . . . dass die Grundgedanken Luthers hier unter dem Einfluss humanistischer Elemente abgewandelt, man möchte kritisch sagen, erweicht worden sind." KAKG II, 150; cf. Kurt Aland, **Die Reformatoren**, 76-81.

12. KAKG II, 150-153, 105-106, Kurt Aland, **Die Reformatoren**, 78, 82.

13. KAKG II, 151-152.

14. Kurt Aland, **Die Reformatoren**, 77-78.

15. Kurt Guggisberg, **Das Zwinglibild**, 10-12, 16, 18-21, 23; Fritz Ringer, **The Decline of the German Mandarins. The German Academic Community 1890-1933** (Cambridge, Mass., 1969), 102; cf. Richard Marius, **Luther: A Biography** (Philadelphia and New York, 1974), 11-12, 246-248; Thomas A. Brady, Jr. **Ruling Class, Regime and Reformation in Strasbourg 1520-1555** (Leyden, 1975), ii, 6-7, 11-12.

16. WA 54: 119-154 (**Kurzes Bekenntnis vom heiligen Sakrament**); **Heinrich Bullinger Werke**, Abteilung 1, Bibliographie, Bd. I, herausgegeben von Fritz Büsser, bearbeitet von Joachim Staedtke (Zurich, 1972), Nr. 161. Hereafter abbreviated as HBWB with the appropriate volume, item number and page number.

17. WA 30: 541-571.

18. Robert C. Walton, "Heinrich Bullinger and Martin Luther", in **Martin Luther Leben – Werk – Wirkung**, herausgegeben von Günter Vogler (Berlin, 1983), 409.

19. HBWB I, 161, 25a. The introduction to **Kurzes Bekenntnis** in the Weimar edition asserts that the agreement not to attack each other had been kept. This is not true. WA 54: 119. Köhler makes the same mistake. Walther Köhler, **Zwingli und Luther**. The Weimar edition also claims that the relationship worsened after 1538 and this too is not entirely accurate, as Bullinger's letter reveals. WA 54: 119. Bizer's account of the events leading up to the publication of the **Kurzes Bekenntnis**, i.e., the Genesis Commentary, the letter to Froschauer, etc., is good but his remark that Luther's remarks were, " . . . die zwar derb und hart ist, die aber wenigstens den Vorzug der Deutlichkeit hat" is a remarkable understatement. His summary of Bullinger's response is also useful. Ernst Bizer, **Studien zur Geschichte des Abendmahlstreits im 16. Jahrhundert** (Darmstadt, 1962), 229-231, 232, 233ff.

20. WA 54: 141: 13-16.

21. WA 54: 142: 20-21.

22. WA 54: 142: 23-25.

23. WA 54: 142: 25-30.

24. WA 54: 142: 30-143: 2.

25. HBWB, I, 161, 3a.

26. WA 54: 143: 6-7.

27. WA 54: 143: 10-14.

28. WA 54: 143: 18-144: 6; cf. Rudolf Pfister, **Die Seligkeit Erwählter Heiden Bei Zwingli** (Zollikon-Zürich, 1952), 10-12.

29. WA 54: 144: 9-10.

30. WA 54: 144: 11-15.

31. WA 54: 144: 30-31, 144: 33-145: 6, 145: 16-30.

32. WA 54: 146: 10-17.

33. WA 54: 146: 18-19.

34. WA 54: 146: 27-33.

35. WA 54: 147: 1-10.

36. WA 54: 147: 20-29, 32-33.

37. WA 54: 147: 33-34.

38. WA 54: 148: 1-5.

39. WA 54: 148: 11-16.

40. Cf. WA 54: 148: 29-151: 31.

41. WA 54: 152: 1-11; cf. S IV 2: 51-53.

42. WA 54: 153: 1-9. What Paul does say is that the unworthy who take part in the supper "profane" the body and blood of the Lord and do so to their own judgment and condemnation.

43. WA 54: 153: 10-23.

44. WA 54: 153: 27-28.

45. WA 54: 154: 1.

46. WA 54: 154: 3-16.

47. WA 54: 154: 17-28.

48. WA 54: 155: 1-8.

49. WA 54: 155: 11-17.

50. WA 54: 155: 18-29.

51. WA 54: 156: 1-3.

52. WA 54: 157: 7-158: 13.

53. WA 54: 160: 30-161: 14.

54. WA 54: 161: 30-162: 30.

55. WA 54: 162: 31-163: 27.

56. WA 54: 165: 31-167: 9.

57. For an explanation of how this involvement works see Thomas Nipperdey, "Die Reformation als Problem der marxistischen Geschichtswissenschaft", 207, 210-216, 217, 219, 220-223; cf. Adolf Laube und Günter Vogler (Leiter), Gerhard Brendler, Gerhard Heitz, Herbert Langer, Hannelore Lehmann, Ingrid Mittenzwei, **Deutsche Geschichte**, 3 vols. (Berlin, 1983), III, 12-14, 26-30, 31ff., 62-64, 79-82; Chapter 2 is entitled "Reformation und Bauernkrieg - die frühbürgerliche Revolution (1517-1525/26)", 96, 99-101, especially 101; 126 ("Anfänge der Reformation in der Schweiz"). The authors of volume three, like Aland date the beginning of the Reformation in Zurich in 1522. Laube und Vogler, et al., **Deutsche Geschichte** III, 126, 128. The **Deutsche Geschichte** sees Zwingli's and Thomas Müntzer's Reformation as creating the basis for the "left wing" of the early modern middle-class Revolution: "Beide schufen Ansätze für einen "linken Flügel" der frühbürgerlichen Revolution." Laube und Vogler, **Deutsche Geschichte**, III, 128, 129. See also Gerhard Brendler, **Martin Luther - Theologie und Revolution** (Berlin, 1983), 440-444. "Martin Luthers historische Leistung besteht darin, dass er mit den 95 Thesen die Reformation und damit die frühbürgerliche Revolution auslöst: . . . ", Brendler, **Martin Luther,** 444. Brendler gives a very clear picture of the reasons for the disagreement between Zwingli and Luther. Brendler, **Martin Luther,** 372-376.

58. Heinrich Bornkamm, "Das Ringen der Motive in den Anfängen der Reformatorischen Kirchenverfassung" in **Das Jahrhundert der Reformation** (Göttingen, 1961), 218.

59. Hans Conrad Peyer, **Verfassungsgeschichte der alten Schweiz** (Zurich, 1978), 48-51; cf. Robert C. Walton, "The Institutionalization of the Reformation at Zürich", Zwingliana, Nr. 2, Bd. XIII, heft 8, 1972, 502-503 and R. C. Walton, "Heinrich Bullinger und Martin Luther" in **Martin Luther - Leben - Werk - Wirkung** (Berlin, 1983), 408.

60. Thomas Brady, **Ruling Class, Regime and Reformation at Strasbourg 1520-1555**, vol. XXII, **Studies in Medieval and Reformation Thought** (Leyden, 1978), 22, 44-45, 93-94.

61. Edward Jacob Kobelt, **Die Bedeutung der Eidgenossenschaft für Huldrych Zwingli** (Zurich, 1970), 5-8; Martin Haas, **Huldrych Zwingli und Seine Zeit, Leben und Werk des Zürcher Reformators**, Zweite Auflage (Zürich, 1976), 17.

62. Hans Conrad Peyer, 36ff., 39ff., 43-45, 48-55; Haas, **Huldrych Zwingli**, 16.

63. Haas, **Huldrych Zwingli**, 12; Hans Conrad Peyer, 48-51.

64. Karl Siegfried Bader, **Dorfgenossenschaft und Dorfgemeinde**, 2 Bde. (Weimar/Thur., 1962), II, 279-280, 281ff. The term "dörfliche Patriziat" is taken from Bader. Bader II, 284. Bader has also drawn attention to the terms "maiores", "meliores", "seniores", "potiores" to designate the patriciate. He warns that the terms "seniores" and "elteste" do not necessarily refer to the village elders. But Bader continues, such terms do refer to the "Ehrbarkeit" in the village. Bader II, 285-287. He confirms that the "Schultheissen", "Ammann", "Dorfbürgermeister" or "Heimburgen" were generally drawn from the "bäuerlichen Oberschicht", ("peasant upper class"), Bader II, 288-289. He also speaks of the role of the children of this social group in the church. Bader, 289-290. His observation that the village aristocracy's influence extended well beyond the confines of the village is well worth noting. Bader II, 290-291.

65. Hans Conrad Peyer, 51.

66. Haas, **Huldrych Zwingli**, 12, 17.

67. Haas, 21.

68. Martin Haas, "Täufertum und Revolution", in **Festgabe Leonhard von Muralt** (Zürich, 1970), 291-295.

69. Bader II, 289-290.

70. Robert C. Walton, "Heinrich Bullinger 1504-1575", **Shapers of Religious Traditions in Germany, Switzerland and Poland 1560-1600**, edited by Jill Raitt, 69-70; Fritz Blanke, **Der junge Bullinger** (Zürich, 1942), 5-11.

THE CONTRIBUTORS

Fritz Büsser is Professor of Church History and Director of the Institute for Swiss Reformation History at the University of Zürich, Switzerland.

Dorothy Clark is a Church Historian from Edinburgh, Scotland, United Kingdom.

Edward J. Furcha is Associate Professor of Church History, Faculty of Religious Studies, McGill University, Montreal, Quebec, Canada.

Ulrich Gäbler is Professor of Church History at the Vrije Universiteit, Amsterdam and Dean of the Theological Faculty.

Timothy George is Assistant Professor of Church History and Historical Theology at the Southern Baptist Theological Seminary, Louisville, Kentucky.

Gerald Hobbs is Professor of Church History at the Vancouver School of Theology, Vancouver, BC, Canada.

Gottfried W. Locher is Professor Emeritus of Dogmatics and the History of Doctrine at the University of Berne, Switzerland.

H. Wayne Pipkin is Professor of Church History at the Baptist Theological Seminary, Rüschlikon/Zürich, Switzerland.

James M. Stayer is Professor of History, Queen's University, Kingston ON, Canada.

Peter Stephens is Tutor in Church History at The Queen's College, Birmingham, England.

Robert C. Walton is Professor of Modern Church History and Director of the Seminary Library for Modern Church History and History of Doctrine, Westfälische Wilhelms-Universität, Münster im Westfalen, Federal Republic of Germany.